Top to Tail

The 360° Guide to Picking Your Perfect Pet

Top to Tail

The 360° Guide to Picking Your Perfect Pet

by
David Alderton

photographs
Marc Henrie

D&C
David and Charles

A DAVID & CHARLES BOOK

David & Charles is an F+W Publications Inc. company
4700 East Galbraith Road, Cincinnati, OH 45236

First published in the UK in 2006

A catalogue record for this book is available from the
British Library.

ISBN-13: 978-0-7153-2589-6 paperback

ISBN-10: 0-7153-2589-2 paperback

Printed in China for David & Charles, Brunel House,
Newton Abbot, Devon, UK

Visit our website at www.davidandcharles.co.uk

David & Charles books are available from all good bookshops;
alternatively you can contact our Orderline on 0870 9908222
or write to us at FREEPOST EX2 110, D&C Direct, Newton Abbot,
TQ12 4ZZ (no stamp required UK only); US customers call
800-289-0963 and Canadian customers call 800-840-5220.

This book was conceived, designed,
and produced by

Ivy Press Limited
The Old Candlemakers, West Street,
Lewes, East Sussex BN7 2NZ, U.K.

Creative Director: Peter Bridgewater
Publisher: Jason Hook
Editorial Director: Caroline Earle
Senior Editor: Hazel Songhurst
Editor: Sophie Collins
Art Director: Kevin Knight, Sarah Howerd
Design: Jane Lanaway
Model Researcher: Fiona Henrie

Contents

Introduction 6
Picking a Pet **8**
The Origins of Today's Breeds **10**
Anatomy of the Dog **11**
Categories of Breeds **12**
Using the Pet Specs **14**

Pet Specs 16
Herding **18**
Hound **46**
Non-sporting **72**

Sporting **100**
Terrier **136**
Toy **174**
Working **212**

Resources 252
Index 254
Acknowledgements 256

Introduction

One need only look at a line-up like the one below to see the extraordinary diversity of dog breeds. Dogs are universally possessed of boundless character and sharp intelligence, but every breed and every individual dog has its own unique appearance and character. Since they come in all manner of shapes and sizes, with an array of different temperaments, part of the enduring appeal of dogs is that every owner feels there is a particular breed for them.

This book is a 360°, top-to-tail guide to picking your favourite pet, and a celebration of dog breeds and their diversity. It portrays more than 150 of the world's most popular breeds in unparalleled detail, allowing you to admire at leisure or browse with a view to investing in your perfect pet.

You can quickly discover the types of breed that suit you, because they are arranged in recognized groups such as terriers or toys. Every main entry is accompanied by a series of four photographs, showing the dog from every angle, so that you can effectively wander around your chosen breed and examine its physical features as if it were standing in front of you. All the dogs portrayed here are leading examples of their type, with virtually all having gained champion status in the show ring. So if you wish to determine the features that define particular breeds for show purposes, this book will be an invaluable resource. Studying the photographs and the annotation that makes up the 'Tech Spec' will afford you a clear insight into what judges are looking for, as well as showing pet lovers what constitutes the ideal features for their chosen breed.

Every entry is accompanied by the essential information you require if you are looking for a pet. A silhouette graphic shows instantly how large a puppy will grow. The possible colour combinations for each breed are listed alongside grooming and exercise requirements. Key symbols reveal the needs of each breed, so that quick comparisons can easily be made.

Once you have narrowed down your search, you can study the detailed individual descriptions and learn more about the ancestry of a breed that interests you. It is only over the last 100 years or so that dogs have started to leave their working ancestries behind, with the majority now being kept as household companions. It is therefore important to be aware of the background of a particular breed, because this will still have a significant bearing on its temperament today, and on its behaviour as your pet.

Whether you want to browse through the wonderful world of dog breeds, pick a selection of breeds that you wish to consider as part of your family, or study the details of your chosen dog, *Top to Tail* will provide the complete view.

Dogs have an extraordinary range of personalities. Whether you are looking for a lively runner to accompany you on long walks in the country, or a grumpy but lovable partner to share your home, there is sure to be a breed in the identity parade to suit your requirements.

Picking a Pet

Picking a purebred dog is a decision that needs to be considered very carefully, and it must never be rushed. You will be selecting a companion who, with luck, will be part of your daily life for well over a decade, so you need to be certain that you are making the right choice.

Never be tempted to select a dog purely on the basis of its looks, even if appearance is a good starting point for your deliberations. Delve into the ancestry of a breed that appeals to you, and you will gain the best insight into its personality. This is the ideal way to begin studying many vital considerations, such as how much exercise your new pet will need, and how easily your puppy can be trained. In this way, you can be sure of finding a pet to suit your lifestyle.

There are a number of key factors about your home life that will affect your choice. You must have enough time to care for your dog's needs on a daily basis. If you live in a small flat with no access to a garden and you're out at work all day, then you might need to think about a type of pet that is less demanding than a dog. Dogs must have enough space to exercise and they are highly social by nature, so they will not settle well if they are left alone for long periods, and in some cases they may even become destructive.

The size of a breed is, of course, a vital factor. Large dogs have correspondingly bigger appetites and also tend to have shorter lifespans. The grooming needs of the different breeds should also be a consideration. Smooth-coated dogs require relatively little grooming, whereas those with profuse coats will need daily combing and brushing to prevent their fur becoming matted, as well as possibly regular visits to a dog groomer. Assess how much time you will have to devote to your pet before you make your choice.

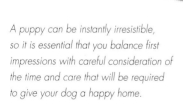

A puppy can be instantly irresistible, so it is essential that you balance first impressions with careful consideration of the time and care that will be required to give your dog a happy home.

The extremes in size in the dog world are illustrated here by a Great Dane towering over a Papillon. Keeping large dogs can be very demanding. Their dietary requirements are expensive, they need a much more spacious environment than their smaller relatives and they are usually more demanding in terms of their care.

The cost of keeping a dog will impact on the family budget. You can minimize the cost by choosing a smaller dog and taking out a health insurance policy for your pet. Picking a short-haired dog will reduce the need to pay for professional grooming services.

Some breeds of dog make much better family pets than others, because they are instinctively friendly by nature. Children who have not had a dog as a pet before need to be taught how to play with their new companion, and never to tease the dog with food or toys.

Once they are properly trained, dogs need to be allowed to run off the leash. Running and playing with your pet is one of the joys of keeping a dog, but do remember that certain breeds will need much more exercise than others.

The Origins of Today's Breeds

Although domestic dogs vary significantly in appearance, they are all descended from the Grey Wolf (*Canis lupus*), which was once among the most widely distributed of all mammals, being found throughout most of the northern hemisphere. The great diversity in form that exists in domestic dogs today was anticipated in wolf populations, which showed a marked variance in size and colour depending on their area of origin.

Almost certainly, there were several ancestral lines of the domestic dog, with domestication occurring in various separate localities at different times. This process began at least 12,000 years ago, and the likelihood is that it may have started much earlier. Sight hounds (dogs that hunt by sight rather than scent) were developed in the vicinity of Egypt and northern Africa, with the Greyhound of today bearing a distinct resemblance to the ancestral form depicted on artifacts dating back thousands of years. Sight hounds probably represent the earliest lineage of the domestic dog, as well as the fastest. They have long legs, relatively narrow heads and broad chests that allow for a good lung capacity.

The large mastiff breeds probably originated in Asia, and were then taken westward along the Old Silk Road into Europe. Meanwhile, the far north was home to the sled breeds, whose descendants (such as the Alaskan Malamute) are still kept for working purposes in the region today. One of the characteristics of these and other so-called spitz breeds from the Arctic area is the shape of the tail, which curls forwards over the back. These dogs have pricked ears and powerful bodies, and a coat that provides them with good insulation against the cold.

Small companion dogs developed at a much later stage, but were certainly quite well-established by the Roman era, some 2,000 years ago. They may well have been the result of selective breeding, with the smallest individuals from litters being mated together, leading to a progressive reduction in the size of their offspring over successive generations.

Up until quite recently, there would not have been such well-defined breeds as there are today. These have only come into existence over the past century or so, as the result of a growing interest in competitive dog showing.

For show purposes, the ideal appearance of each breed is specified by a breed standard. This outlines all the desirable physical features that judges will be looking for, as well as highlighting perceived faults, with dogs in each class being assessed against the standard rather than against each other. Prior to breeding for show, there would have been what can be called 'proto-breeds'. These were dogs sharing a common ancestry and clearly resembling each other in appearance, having been bred to carry out specific tasks. By refining their distinctive characteristics through careful adherence to the breed standards, the breeds of today have been developed.

Top to Tail allows you to assess breed standards as if you were stepping into a show ring, by providing a photographic parade of champion dogs that have been named 'best of breed'.

The ancestry of dog breeds can be traced from the natural magnificence of the Grey Wolf (far right), through the domestication of the dog, to purebred examples such as the Basenji (right).

Anatomy of the Dog

Selective breeding has refined the appearance of modern dogs, with each part of the dog being assessed according to the breed standard. The diagram below illustrates the correct terminology for each part of the dog's anatomy.

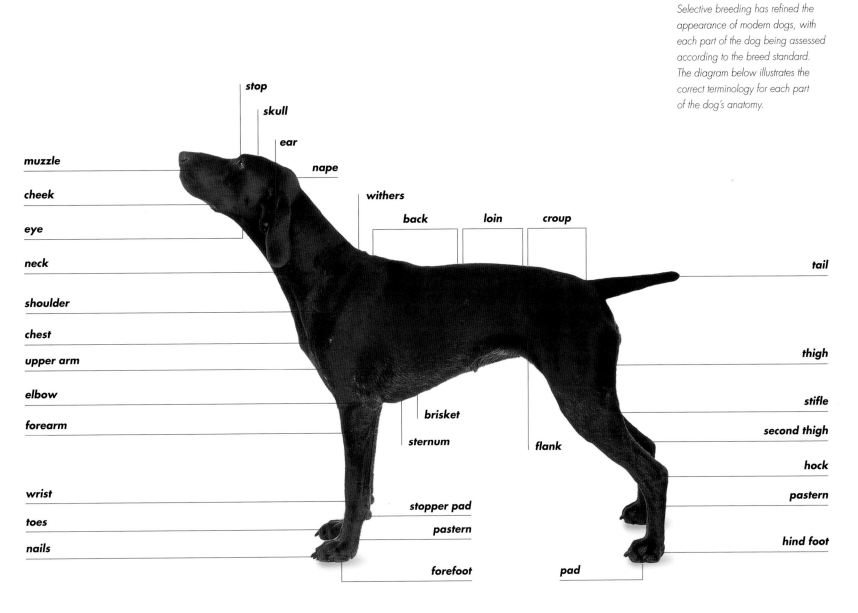

stop

skull

ear

muzzle

nape

cheek

withers

eye

back   loin   croup

neck

tail

shoulder

chest

thigh

upper arm

elbow

stifle

forearm

brisket

second thigh

sternum   flank

hock

wrist

stopper pad

pastern

toes

pastern

nails

hind foot

forefoot   pad

Categories of Breeds

The way in which breeds are categorized is not standardized throughout the world, and there are some obvious differences in the groupings of the various registration bodies. The Kennel Club in Britain and the American Kennel Club (AKC) have seven divisions, while the European FCI (Fédération Cynologique Internationale) has ten divisions. Fundamentally, these groupings are based on the original purpose for which the breed was developed, even if its role has changed significantly since its early days. Anomalies in the listings are most likely to arise in the case of breeds that were created for varying tasks, as with dogs that were developed as farm breeds. They may have been used for herding purposes, as guard dogs, and also as hunting companions.

There are now approximately 400 different breeds of dog in the world today. The word 'breed' is used to describe a population of dogs that, when paired together, will produce puppies of corresponding appearance. In a few instances, there may only be a very marginal difference between breeds, as shown by the case of the Norwich and Norfolk Terriers, where the division is based essentially on a variance in their ear carriage. Norwich Terriers have pricked ears, while the ears of Norfolk Terriers hang down the sides of the head.

About half of the breeds in the world today are well-known in show circles. Many of the others are localized, and may not be known outside their country of origin, where they may still be kept as working dogs. They will be of recognizable appearance or 'type', but there might not always be a specific show standard drawn up for that particular breed.

While some breeds are rare, and even on the verge of extinction in certain cases, there are still new breeds being created today. The tendency over recent years has been to cross existing breeds and so develop dogs of attractive appearance that will make good companions – although this is often frowned on by purists. The best-known variant of this type developed to date is the Labradoodle – a cross between the Labrador Retriever and the Poodle. Although such dogs have not yet obtained international recognition in show circles, they are highly sought-after as pets.

The book is divided into the seven divisions of the American Kennel Club in the order shown here: Herding, Hound, Non-sporting, Sporting, Terrier, Toy, and Working. A full description of the main breeds is given in each section, followed by an overview of six further breeds within the division.

Herding

These dogs have been developed primarily to work with livestock, and so form a close bond with their owners. Herding breeds are characterized by their natural intelligence and their ability to learn quickly. They are energetic by nature, and will rapidly become bored, frequently proving to be destructive around the home unless they can be given plenty of exercise.

Hound

Members of this group represent the oldest category of dogs, having been bred as hunting companions. Based on existing archeological evidence, it seems that their appearance has changed little in some cases over the course of thousands of years. The Hound group is usually subdivided into sight hounds, which are the natural sprinters of the dog world, and the slower scent hounds, which often hunt in packs.

Non-sporting

This AKC division effectively represents a miscellaneous group, corresponding to the Utility division adopted by the Kennel Club in Britain. It therefore comprises a diverse group of dogs, which were originally created for a number of different tasks, and do not fit conveniently into any of the other groupings. Unsurprisingly, this is therefore the most varied division.

Many pets in the Hound group are descended from working scent hounds, like the hunting dogs in this 1830 painting by Benjamin Marshall. It is of course essential that dogs with this sort of ancestry are given regular exercise.

Working

Many members of this group were originally bred as guard dogs, and so are not necessarily friendly by nature. They are generally large and powerful dogs, and must be firmly trained. There are some, however, whose strength has been used for more gentle purposes, such as pulling carts.

Sporting

Although these breeds are often described today as gun dogs, their origins in many cases predate the development of shooting as a leisure sport. They are used to locate, flush and then retrieve game after it has been shot. These dogs are easily trained and work well alongside people, and so have become popular as pets. However, it is essential that they have plenty of exercise.

Terrier

Members of this group are relatively small, rather independently minded dogs. The group was largely developed in Britain, where such dogs were often sent underground to flush out foxes and other creatures, which could then be pursued by hounds. Terriers were also popular on farms for their rodent-killing abilities, while their boldness led to a period when certain breeds were used for dog-fighting.

Toy

A group characterized by their small size, toy dogs were created primarily as companions. Many of today's most popular breeds were originally bred as the pets of wealthy ladies around the royal courts of Europe. Some, like the Italian Greyhound, are effectively scaled-down versions of larger breeds, whereas others are quite distinct in appearance. They are affectionate, friendly dogs.

Using the Pet Specs

All the various components on the Pet Spec pages have been carefully designed both to facilitate easy access to the relevant information and to assist in easily comparing the needs of different breeds. The photographs taken from four different angles give a much clearer indication of the overall appearance of the dog than the standard profile seen in most dog books, as features such as the width and depth of the chest and the breadth of the body are clearly apparent. This is not just useful in terms of a show guide, but will also serve as an ideal reference point when assessing whether or not a particular individual of any breed is under- or overweight.

In all cases, the symbols in the 'Overview' section refer to a young, fit adult dog. It is important to bear in mind that as dogs grow older, so their dietary and exercise needs are likely to decrease. Neutering will also have an impact, particularly on feeding requirements. Less food is required after surgery of this type, to guard against weight gain. The 'Child friendliness' rating is based on children who live with the dog. A house pet is often likely to be less inclined to play with other children visiting the home, and may bark at them initially, viewing them as strangers. This can cause problems, and you should always be cautious when allowing your pet to mix with your children's friends, particularly if they are nervous of dogs or not used to playing with them.

There are a number of hereditary and congenital health problems that may occasionally afflict different breeds. Some, such as hip dysplasia, are much more common among some breeds than others. Many conditions will be apparent at birth or can be picked up by an early veterinary check, so there is no need to be unduly worried by this information. This is especially the case if you obtain a puppy bred from stock that has been screened as far as possible for such illnesses.

The Pet Spec will provide you with a very good starting point both in choosing your new dog and in ensuring that its care, diet and exercise are appropriate. However, if you have any concerns at all about your pet, you should always seek the expert advice of a vet.

Recognition *This confirms how widely the breed in question is recognized for show purposes. In some cases, where there is more than one official registry in a particular part of the world, this is no guarantee that all bodies will recognize the breed or classify it in the same group.*

Colour *The acceptable range of colours associated with a particular breed is highlighted here, along with mention of specific markings that may be required. A colour reference for the solid, bicolour and tricolour shades is shown below.*

Symbols *In each case, a rating of 1–3 is given, with 1 meaning least and 3 the most. A breed with 1 brush symbol, 1 bone, 2 children, and 2 running dogs needs minimal grooming, has a small appetite, is reasonably child-friendly and has average exercise requirements.*

Solid colours

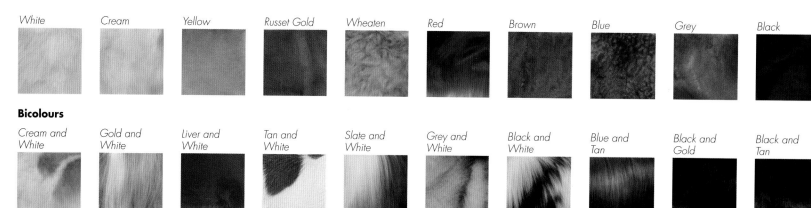

White | Cream | Yellow | Russet Gold | Wheaten | Red | Brown | Blue | Grey | Black

Bicolours

Cream and White | Gold and White | Liver and White | Tan and White | Slate and White | Grey and White | Black and White | Blue and Tan | Black and Gold | Black and Tan

Group *The breed entries are divided into seven distinct groups, relating to their original function and their show categorization. These are Herding, Hound, Non-sporting, Sporting, Terrier, Toy and Working.*

Features *The vital statistics of each breed show the proportions of head, eyes, ears, chest, tail and bite, which collectively contribute to its 'type' or appearance. Also listed are height, measured to the highest part of the shoulder, and ideal weight.*

Images and annotation *The photos show the same dog, in a show stance, from four different angles, allowing you to take a virtual tour of each breed's features The letters relate to the Features text, and are consistent across all entries, enabling instant comparisons to be made.*

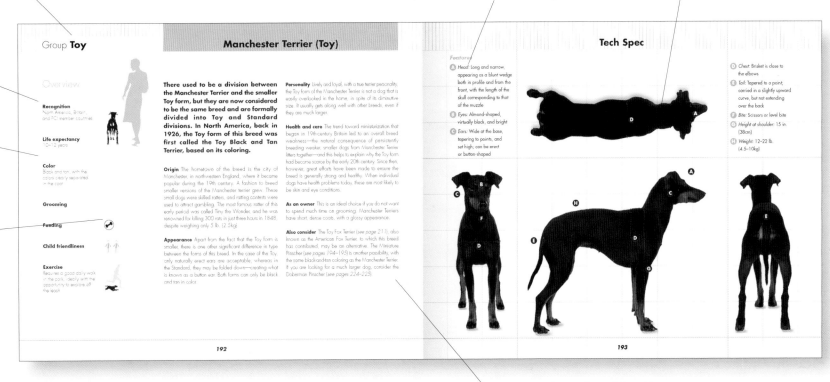

Group **Toy**

Overview

Recognition
North America, Britain, and FCI member countries.

Life expectancy
10–12 years

Color
Black and tan, with the colors clearly separated in the coat.

Grooming

Feeding

Child friendliness

Exercise
Requires a good daily walk in the park, ideally with the opportunity to explore off the leash.

Manchester Terrier (Toy)

There used to be a division between the Manchester Terrier and the smaller Toy form, but they are now considered to be the same breed and are formally divided into Toy and Standard divisions. In North America, back in 1926, the Toy form of this breed was first called the Toy Black and Tan Terrier, based on its coloring.

Origin The hometown of the breed is the city of Manchester, in northwestern England, where it became popular during the 19th century. A fashion to breed smaller versions of the Manchester terrier grew. These small dogs were skilled ratters, and ratting contests were used to attract gambling. The most famous ratter of this early period was called Tiny the Wonder, and he was renowned for killing 300 rats in just three hours in 1848, despite weighing only 5 lb. (2.5kg).

Appearance Apart from the fact that the Toy form is smaller, there is one other significant difference in type between the forms of this breed. In the case of the Toy, only naturally erect ears are acceptable; whereas in the Standard, they may be folded down—creating what is known as a button ear. Both forms can only be black and tan in color.

Personality Lively and loyal, with a true terrier personality, the Toy form of the Manchester Terrier is not a dog that is easily overlooked in the home, in spite of its diminutive size. It usually gets along well with other breeds, even if they are much larger.

Health and care The trend toward miniaturization that began in 19th-century Britain led to an overall breed weakness—the natural consequence of persistently breeding weaker, smaller dogs from Manchester Terrier litters together—and this helps to explain why the Toy form had become scarce by the early 20th century. Since then, however, great efforts have been made to ensure the breed is generally strong and healthy. When individual dogs have health problems today, these are most likely to be skin and eye conditions.

As an owner This is an ideal choice if you do not want to spend much time on grooming. Manchester Terriers have short, dense coats, with a glossy appearance.

Also consider The Toy Fox Terrier (see page 211), also known as the American Fox Terrier, to which this breed has contributed, may be an alternative. The Miniature Pinscher (see pages 194–195) is another possibility, with the same black-and-tan coloring as the Manchester Terrier. If you are looking for a much larger dog, consider the Doberman Pinscher (see pages 224–225).

Tech Spec

Features

Ⓐ *Head:* Long and narrow, appearing as a blunt wedge both in profile and from the front, with the length of the skull corresponding to that of the muzzle

Ⓑ *Eyes:* Almond-shaped, virtually black, and bright

Ⓒ *Ears:* Wide at the base, tapering to points, and set high; can be erect or button-shaped

Ⓓ *Chest:* Brisket is close to the elbows

Ⓔ *Tail:* Tapered to a point; carried in a slightly upward curve, but not extending over the back

Ⓕ *Bite:* Scissors or level bite

Ⓖ *Height at shoulder:* 15 in. (38cm)

Ⓗ *Weight:* 12–22 lb. (4.5–10kg)

192

193

Images and annotation

Text entry *The entry for each breed features an introduction, and then concise descriptions of origin, appearance, personality, health and care, owner requirements, and finally a feature suggesting similar breeds that might appeal.*

Other variants

Liver Spotted

Blue Roan

Brindle

Tricoloured

Salt and Pepper

Pet Specs

Australian Cattle Dog

Overview

Recognition
North America, Britain and FCI member countries

Life expectancy
14–20 years

Colour
Blue, sometimes with mottling and speckled red

Grooming

Feeding

Child friendliness

Exercise
This is a very energetic breed and needs a great deal of exercise

This tough working breed is still kept for herding cattle on ranches in Australia, but in recent years it has also built up an international reputation in the show ring. The Australian Cattle Dog's extremely high energy levels make it unsuitable for living in a city unless you can provide it with plenty of regular exercise off the leash.

Origin Herding dogs brought from Britain and elsewhere did not adapt well to the harsh climate of Australia. Stockmen tried crossing various breeds with the native dingo, and these ultimately gave rise to the Australian Cattle Dog. Its distinctive colouring can be traced back to two blue merle (a marbled effect created when separate hair colours mix together) Smooth Collies brought from Scotland in 1840, which made a major contribution to its development. The breed finally became firmly established in the late 19th century. Puppies are sometimes white at birth and gain their colour as they grow – this characteristic reflects early Dalmatian input to the breed.

Appearance Stocky, with a powerful head and upright ears, the Australian Cattle Dog often has a blue mottled coat. The colouring of individual dogs varies widely, allowing them to be distinguished from one another easily at a distance. Its conformation is strong, and it has both the stamina to go long distances and the ability to run at speed when necessary. Its strong, rounded feet are protected by thick, tough pads.

Personality These dogs are energetic and, like most intelligent working dogs, need to be kept busy. They are also alert, watchful and suspicious of outsiders, although they make a strong bond with their owners.

Health and care The Australian Cattle Dog has no common weaknesses and is notably long-lived – a member of the breed is the oldest dog on record, surviving for 29 years and working for 16 of them. Their care is straightforward: they need little grooming and they are self-sufficient. However, they tend to put on weight if they do not get enough exercise.

As an owner When kept as a pet, this dog needs to be carefully socialized, both with people and other dogs, and must be trained to curb its powerful herding instinct, especially around livestock.

Also consider The Stumpy-tailed Cattle Dog, also called the Smithfield Heeler, is closely related to the Australian Cattle Dog, but has a short tail or no tail at all. However, it is found mainly in its native Australia. Popular and more widely known herding breeds include Corgis (*see pages 30–31 and 40–41*) and the Swedish Vallhund (*see page 45*).

Tech Spec

Features

A *Head:* Broad, with a definite stop; muscular cheeks; powerful, medium-length muzzle

B *Eyes:* Medium-sized and oval; dark brown in colour

C *Ears:* Relatively small, widely spaced and pricked in appearance

D *Chest:* Muscular and deep

E *Tail:* Set moderately low, curving slightly at rest; must not extend vertically above the base of the tail

F *Bite:* Scissors bite

G *Height at shoulder:* Dogs 45.5–51cm (18–20 in); bitches 43–48cm (17–19 in)

H *Weight:* 16–20.5kg (35–45 lb)

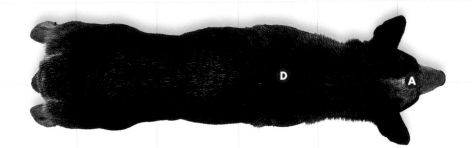

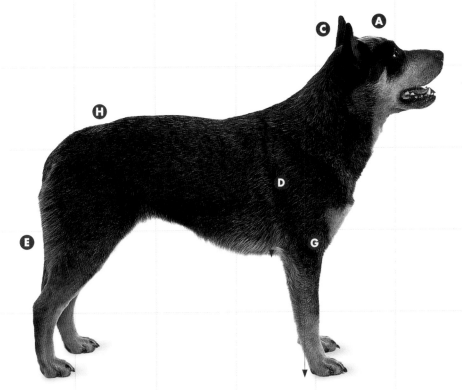

Australian Shepherd

Overview

Recognition
North America, Britain and FCI member countries

Life expectancy
11–13 years

Colour
Black, red, blue or red merle, with or without white markings and/or tan points

Grooming

Feeding

Child friendliness

Exercise
Regular long walks required

In spite of its name, this breed's origins lie in the Basque region of the Pyrenees, between France and Spain, while its later development took place primarily in California. It has grown significantly in popularity over recent years, and it won the prestigious Best-in-Show award at the Crufts Dog Show in Britain for the first time in 2006. It is a versatile breed, with a keen natural intelligence and acute powers of observation.

Origin The origins of the Australian Shepherd, often simply called the Aussie, are complex. Basque shepherds emigrated to Australia, taking their dogs with them, and it was here that the breed gained its name. Subsequently there was a second wave of emigration towards the end of the 19th century, this time from Australia to North America, and once again the dogs moved with their owners and the breed was further developed, particularly in California. Today these dogs still work on American ranches, but they are also trained to work with disabled people, for search-and-rescue work, and as sniffer dogs to detect illegal drugs.

Appearance The Australian Shepherd has the typical attributes of most sheepdogs. It has a slightly tapering muzzle and ears set high on the head, forming a rose ear and giving the dog an alert look. The eyes can be blue as well as brown, and the coat may be solid red, liver or

black, or blue or red merle. It is common for merles to darken with age. White and tan markings are also allowed. The coat is of medium length, and male dogs have a more pronounced mane than bitches.

Personality Friendly, tolerant and quiet, the Australian Shepherd has a responsive nature. As a worker, it is an effective herder of both sheep and cattle; as a pet, it has a steady temperament, but with plenty of energy for play. It is usually good with children.

Health and care This breed is well-equipped to work under a variety of conditions, with a double-layered, weather-resistant coat. Its grooming needs increase during the spring, when much of the undercoat is shed. Jaw conformation is important in the breed standard and a scissors or level bite is required. Any deviation from this will disqualify an Australian Shepherd as a showdog. A heavily pink-spotted nose is also a fault.

As an owner The colouration of this breed is highly individual. It is common for merles to darken with age, and any pink spotting on the nose should reduce in extent. Indeed, if more than a quarter of this area remains pink, judges will regard this as a serious fault. Active by nature, this breed will happily exercise in all weathers.

Also consider If the standard Australian Shepherd is too large for you, a miniature form exists. Originally known as the Miniature Australian Shepherd, it was renamed as the North American Shepherd, but today is widely known as the Mini Aussie. It typically stands about 38cm (15 in) tall. The Shetland Sheepdog (*see pages 42–43*), which has a luxuriant coat and is widely popular as a pet, may be another possibility.

Tech Spec

Features

A *Head:* Flat to slightly domed top; muzzle about the same length as the rear part of the skull

B *Eyes:* almond-shaped; brown, amber, blue, or any combination of these colours

C *Ears:* Set high; triangular and medium-sized

D *Chest:* Deep but not broad, reaching to the elbows

E *Tail:* Straight, sometimes naturally bobbed

F *Bite:* Scissors or level bite

G *Height at shoulder:* Dogs 51–58.5cm (20–23 in); bitches 45.5–53cm (18–21 in)

H *Weight:* 16–32kg (35–70 lb)

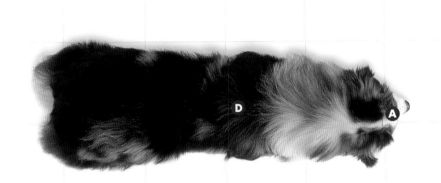

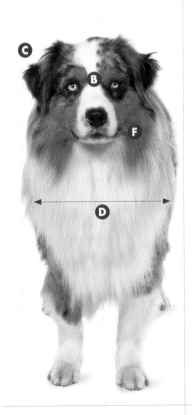

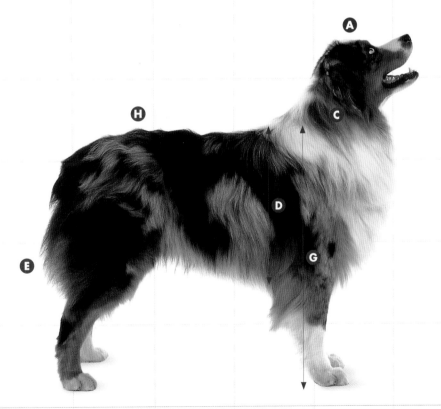

Bearded Collie

Overview

Recognition
North America, Britain and
FCI member countries

Life expectancy
11–13 years

Colour
Puppies are brown, fawn,
blue or black at birth,
sometimes with white
markings; most lighten
with age

Grooming

Feeding

Child friendliness

Exercise
This breed needs long
daily walks

The Beardie's long flowing coat creates an elegant impression. This old Scottish breed is so widespread today that it is hard to believe that it had declined so far in popularity that it almost vanished in the 1940s. Since then it has undergone a significant revival. The dog in the photograph is a direct descendant of the 1989 Crufts Best-in-Show winner.

Origin The origins of the Bearded Collie are disputed. The breed may be descended either from the now-extinct Old Welsh Grey Sheepdog or alternatively from Polish Lowland Sheepdogs, which were known in Scotland as early as the 16th century. Bearded Collies worked as drovers' dogs, overseeing the movement of stock, especially cattle, on the Scottish hills. Mrs Willison, owner of the Bothkennar Kennels, almost singlehandedly saved the breed from extinction in Britain when she obtained a breeding pair in 1944, and breeding of the Bearded Collie began in North America in the late 1960s.

Appearance The profuse coat of this collie is of medium length, hanging down the sides of its long lean body. For show purposes, the coat must lie naturally and should not be parted. The outer coat is flat and harsh, but the undercoat is softer and gives the dog good insulation. The eyes are large and expressive, and the tail is carried in a curve and is thickly covered with hair. The coat often lightens as the dog reaches maturity, black puppies turning to a shaded slate colour, and brown puppies becoming a shaded dark sand-to-chocolate colour.

Personality Lively, even boisterous, and self-confident, the Bearded Collie makes a loyal and affectionate pet. Active by nature, and with considerable stamina, it thrives on plenty of outdoor exercise and will be an untiring companion on hilly walks.

Health and care In spite of the limited gene pool from which it was re-created in the 1940s, the breed has proved extremely sound. Like all herding dogs, the Bearded Collie needs plenty of activity and opportunities to exercise every day if it is not to become bored and destructive around the home. It needs extensive grooming, too. A wet, muddy coat is best left to dry and then brushed out. The coat must never be trimmed in show dogs.

As an owner You must be prepared to spend plenty of time training your Bearded Collie puppy. The breed's natural exuberance, while charming, needs to be tempered with responsiveness.

Also consider If you would be interested in a larger breed, the Old English Sheepdog (see pages 38–39) has a similar temperament, while the Briard (see page 44) is an even bigger dog, with a similar profile. A smaller alternative would be the Bearded Collie's relation, the Polish Lowland Sheepdog (see page 45).

Tech Spec

Features

A *Head:* Broad, flat skull with a moderate stop; strong muzzle with a square-shaped nose

B *Eyes:* Widely spaced, large and affectionate

C *Ears:* Medium-length, hanging down the sides of the head and covered in hair

D *Chest:* Deep, extending at least to the level of the elbows

E *Tail:* Set and carried low-set, never above the vertical; can reach the hocks

F *Bite:* Scissors bite

G *Height at shoulder:* Dogs 45.5–56cm (21–22 in); bitches 51–53cm (20–21 in)

H *Weight:* 18–27kg (40–60 lb)

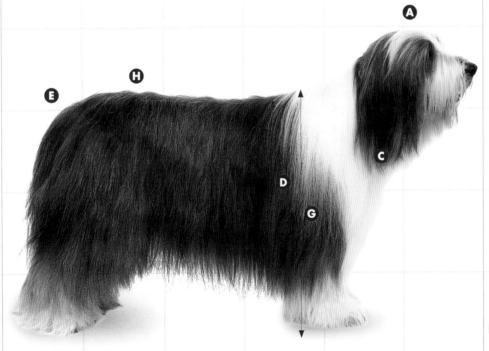

Overview

Recognition
North America, Britain and
FCI member countries

Life expectancy
10–12 years

Colour
Shades of fawn to
mahogany, combined
with black; a silver and
black combination exists
but is rare

Grooming

Feeding

Child friendliness

Exercise
A good daily walk
is essential

The Tervuren, or Belgian Shepherd Dog, is one of four closely related breeds; another, the Groenendael, from which the Tervuren may have arisen, is known in North America as a Belgian Sheepdog (*see page 44*). The Tervuren is classified as a separate breed under its own name however, as are the Belgian Laekenois and the short-coated Belgian Malinois.

Origin The Tervuren and the Groenendael are certainly closely related, with matings of the latter breed sometimes producing Tervuren puppies in their litters, as 'throwbacks', having been mated together in the past. These Belgian shepherd dogs are probably no more than regional variants – the Tervuren is named after the Belgian town where it was first created by a breeder called Corbeel. The breed was known in North America by 1918, but the first litter was not born here until 1954.

Appearance The main distinction between the Tervuren and the Groenendael is in their colour: the latter is solid black, but the former is a combination of black and fawn, with the lighter hairs of the coat tipped in black. The only solid black area is the facial mask. The nails are also black. There is a noticeable difference between the sexes as they mature, with the black tipping to the hair becoming more prominent in the males.

Personality The Tervuren is a hard-working breed that learns quickly: it is successful both in the show ring and in agility competitions. It is also used as a guide dog and as a sniffer dog by the police.

Health and care Epilepsy is a hereditary problem recognized in the Tervuren, although not in the Groenendael. An EEG examination can help to diagnose the problem in a young dog. Grooming is straightforward, in spite of the long dense coat.

As an owner The Tervuren is renowned as a guard dog, and it is unlikely to back down if challenged by an intruder. The breed is independent and has a strong will by nature, and puppies must be trained well from an early age. Few breeds display greater loyalty to people they know well, and choosing one of these dogs will guarantee you an affectionate companion.

Also consider The Belgian Shepherd Dog (*see page 44*) may be a possibility if you like the Tervuren's appearance but would prefer a pure black dog, while the Belgian Malinois is another similar breed, but with a short coat. You may also want to consider a German Shepherd Dog (*see pages 34–35*), which is a larger, stockier breed.

Tech Spec

Features

A *Head:* Skull and muzzle correspond in length, with the muzzle being reasonably broad

B *Eyes:* Slightly almond-shaped, medium-sized and dark brown

C *Ears:* Set high and erect, with the height the same as the width at the base

D *Chest:* Deep and intermediate in width; black or black and grey in colour

E *Tail:* Kept low at rest; may be raised to the level of the back when moving

F *Bite:* Scissors or level bite

G *Height at shoulder:* Dogs 61–66cm (24–26 in) preferred, but 58.5–67.5cm (23–26½ in) acceptable; bitches 56–61cm (22–24 in) preferred, but 53–62cm (21–24½ in) acceptable

H *Weight:* 25–29.5kg (55–65 lb)

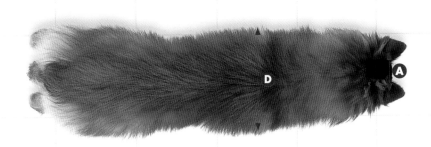

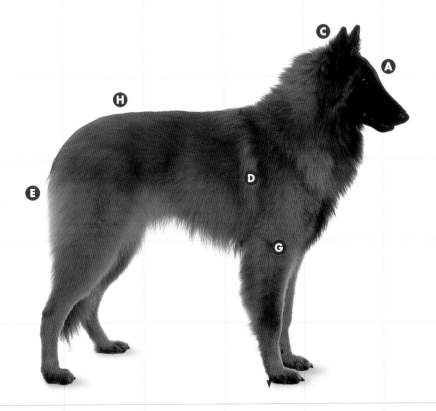

Border Collie

Overview

Recognition
North America, Britain and FCI member countries

Life expectancy
11–13 years

Colour
No restrictions, although most often found in black and white; can be tricoloured

Grooming

Feeding

Child friendliness

Exercise
Requires a good period of exercise daily

Widely considered to be the most talented and intelligent of all the sheepdog breeds, the Border Collie excels both at sheepdog trials and in agility and fly ball competitions. However, if you like the idea of a Border Collie as a pet, it is essential that you have enough time to dedicate to this demanding breed.

Origin Sheepdogs have been bred in Britain since Roman times. The Border Collie was named after the area on the border between Scotland and England, where it was first bred. Rather than taking part in dog shows, these dogs traditionally competed in sheepdog trials, the first of which took place in Wales in 1873. Old Hemp, born in the 1890s, was the most famous Border Collie of all time. He was undefeated in all the events in which he participated. Border Collies were first seen in North America in the 1880s.

Appearance In the past, its working ability was considered to be the only relevant attribute of a Border Collie, but since being recognized for show purposes – it was acknowledged by the British Kennel Club in 1976 – judging standards have been drawn up for the breed. Both rough- and smooth-coated forms are acceptable for show. The sheepdog's gait is still regarded as more significant than its colouration and markings.

Personality Capable of developing an intuitive relationship with its owner when working, this breed is highly responsive and intelligent and learns quickly. It also has great reserves of stamina and is affectionate with its owner and the people immediately around it.

Health and care These collies are susceptible to a hereditary eye condition known as progressive retinal atrophy (PRA), which ultimately causes blindness. Symptoms only emerge when dogs are between 3 and 5 years old. Check with the breeder that their stock has been screened for this problem.

As an owner Assess whether you can dedicate enough time to a Border Collie. This breed can become both neurotic and destructive when bored, and it needs to be given plenty to think about, as well as exercise on a daily basis. These dogs retain strong working instincts, and they must be adequately trained and kept on a leash in the presence of sheep. If you are looking for a canine partner for agility competitions, the Border Collie will be an excellent choice.

Also consider The Australian Shepherd (*see pages 20–21*) is a possibility if you are looking for a slightly larger breed. Other options include British collie breeds, including the Smooth and Rough Collies (*see pages 32–33*). However, the Border Collie has a specific look and personality, and no other breed is quite like it.

Tech Spec

Features

A *Head:* Flat, with moderate width to the skull; the muzzle length matches that of the skull

B *Eyes:* Oval, medium-sized and well-spaced

C *Ears:* Medium-sized, well-spaced, and may or may not be held erect or semi-erect

D *Chest:* Deep, relatively broad, reaching as far as the elbow

E *Tail:* Set low; carried low when concentrating during work

F *Bite:* Scissors bite

G *Height at shoulder:* Dogs 48–56cm (19–22 in); bitches 45.5–53cm (18–21 in)

H *Weight:* 13.5–20kg (30–44 lb)

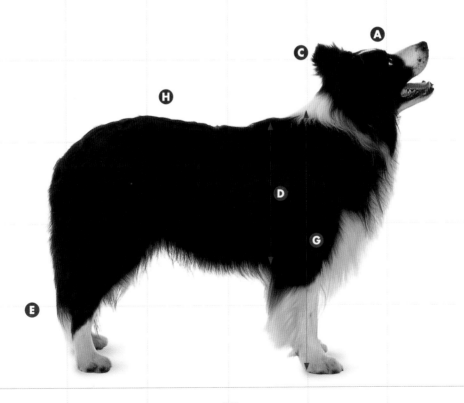

Bouvier des Flandres

Overview

Recognition
North America, Britain and FCI member countries

Life expectancy
11–13 years

Colour
Can vary from fawn to black, although white, chocolate and parti-coloured are not recognized for show purposes

Grooming

Feeding

Child friendliness

Exercise
A good daily walk will be essential

The word *bouvier* literally means 'bovine herder', and refers to the Bouvier's original function as a cattle dog in its native Belgium. The imposing Bouvier des Flandres is almost the last surviving type of Belgian herding dog, although the future of the breed is now secure because it has become popular internationally.

Origin The ancestry of the Bouvier des Flandres probably involved a range of different breeds, including the Beauceron (*see page 250*). Its tousled appearance may reflect some Schnauzer heritage. Several local Bouvier breeds existed in Belgium before World War I, but the level of destruction in this part of Europe led to the extinction of three distinct strains. The tireless efforts of an Army veterinarian, Captain Barbry, ensured the Bouvier's survival through this period.

Appearance Powerfully built, with a distinctive beard of longer hair hanging down on each side of its muzzle, the Bouvier des Flandres has a rough-textured, weather-resistant double coat, which is shorter on the skull and the upper back. The undercoat, which provides good insulation, becomes noticeably thicker in winter. The tail is set high on the back. Occasionally puppies are born altogether without tails.

Personality Fearless and trustworthy, the breed served as a messenger and ambulance dog in World War I. Bold by nature, the Bouvier des Flandres makes an excellent guard dog and is also trained as a guide dog for the blind.

Health and care The coat needs little care. In show dogs slight trimming is permitted to keep it to a length of about 6.5cm (2½ in), taking care not to compromise the breed's hardy appearance. The Bouvier des Flandres does not suffer from any particular hereditary weaknesses. It is not unusual for puppies to be born without dew claws.

As an owner The Bouvier des Flandres is a physically strong and determined breed, which must be adequately trained to ensure that you are in control at all times. The Bouvier is comparatively easy to train, and it is usually both good-natured and intelligent. Male puppies will grow slightly larger than bitches, but the size difference between them is not pronounced.

Also consider The only other surviving member of this group of dogs, known as the Bouvier des Ardennes, was the result of crossbreeding between the Bouvier des Flandres and the Belgian Malinois (*see page 24*). This breed is now rare and would prove exceedingly hard to acquire. Other possibilities, and ones that are much more easily available, would be the Briard (*see page 44*), whose coat is significantly longer, or the Schnauzer (*see pages 248–249*).

Tech Spec

Features

A *Head:* Large head with skull longer than the muzzle, which is broad and slightly tapered

B *Eyes:* Oval and dark brown, with an alert expression

C *Ears:* Set high; give an impression of alertness

D *Chest:* Broad, with the brisket reaching the elbow

E *Tail:* Set high and carried upright; some puppies are born tail-less

F *Bite:* Scissors bite

G *Height at shoulder:* Dogs 62–70cm (24½–27½ in); bitches 60–67.5cm (23½–26½ in)

H *Weight:* (27–40kg) (60–88 lb)

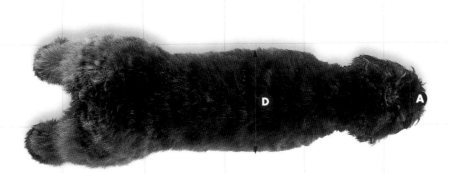

Cardigan Welsh Corgi

Overview

Recognition
North America, Britain and
FCI member countries

Life expectancy
11–13 years

Colour
Sable, brindle and red;
blue merle or black dogs
also exist, both of which
may have tan and/or
brindle points

Grooming

Feeding

Child friendliness

Exercise
Must have a reasonably
long daily walk

The ancestors of this breed have been kept in Wales for over 1,000 years. The breed is named after the old Welsh county where it was created, distinguishing it from its better-known relative, the Pembroke Corgi. These dogs are now carefully maintained as separate breeds, but in the past they were often bred together.

Origin The ancestry of these short-legged dogs is a mystery, although it has been suggested that they may be related to the Swedish Vallhund, which is similar in appearance – although how the ancestral stock reached Wales from Scandinavia remains unclear. The breed's short legs make them effective as cattle drovers – they can encourage a reluctant cow to keep moving by nipping at its heels, with little risk of being kicked.

Appearance The breed is larger than its tail-less Pembroke relative. It is known in Welsh as *Ci Llathaid*, literally 'yard long', as an indication of its length from the top of its nose to the tip of its tail. The Cardigan breed is therefore longer than its tail-less Pembroke relative. The Cardigan's huge ears are another point of distinction between the breeds: they are upright in both, but the Cardigan's are both larger and more rounded than those of the Pembroke.

Personality Tough and hardy, these corgis have a much more dominant personality that their size might suggest. They are also surprisingly energetic and active by nature. They certainly should not be considered as lap dogs.

Health and care In common with a number of other herding breeds, Cardigan Welsh Corgis can suffer from the hereditary eye condition known as progressive retinal atrophy (PRA), which ultimately leads to blindness. Check with the breeder that their stock has no predisposition to this problem. The dense undercoat is shed in spring, when your dog will need a good deal of grooming.

As an owner These small working farm dogs may retain an instinctive desire to nip, originally an active part of their role, and this must be curbed as much as possible from puppyhood. This tendency makes them unsuited to a home with young children. Plenty of exercise is important to prevent these corgis from becoming bored at home.

Also consider The Pembroke Welsh Corgi (*see pages 40–41*), and the Swedish Vallhund (*see page 45*) are both possible alternatives. A modern re-creation of a traditional English breed is the Lancashire Heeler, which has characteristic black and tan colouring. Should you want a larger breed, consider the Australian Cattle Dog (*see pages 18–19*).

Tech Spec

Features

A *Head:* Flat top to skull between the ears, with flat cheeks; muzzle is shorter than the skull

B *Eyes:* Medium to large, evident corners, and widely spaced

C *Ears:* Large and prominent, with rounded tips

D *Chest:* Evident breastbone; medium-width with deep brisket

E *Tail:* Set and carried low, never above the back

F *Bite:* Scissors bite

G *Height at shoulder:* 26.5–31.5cm (10½–12½ in)

H *Weight:* 11.5–15.5kg (25–34 lb)

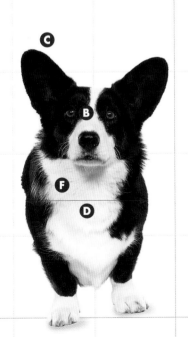

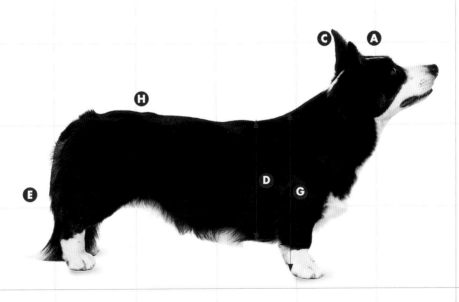

Collie

Overview

Recognition
North America, Britain and
FCI member countries

Life expectancy
12–14 years

Colour
White, blue merle, tricolour
or sable and white

Grooming

Feeding

Child friendliness

Exercise
Needs regular opportunities
to explore off the leash

There are two distinct coat types to choose from in this breed – the longer-haired Rough-Coated form and the Smooth-Coated. They are sometimes classed separately, although essentially the only difference between them is the length of their coats. Both types of Collie are popular as family pets.

Origin The Rough Collie is the older form. Its ancestors were probably brought to Britain by the Romans as working sheepdogs more than 2,000 years ago. It was the introduction of Borzoi blood to the Collie lineage that ultimately changed the breed's appearance, giving it a more elegant outline and longer legs. These Collies were a particular favourite of Britain's Queen Victoria, which raised their public profile in the later 19th century. The breed's popularity was also boosted by the numerous *Lassie* films, in which a Rough Collie starred, which began showing in 1943.

Appearance The Rough Collie has a long, straight, harsh-textured outer coat, with a pronounced frill of fur extending between the forelegs. The coat is generally less profuse during the summer. The body profile is much clearer in the case of the Smooth Collie, because of its relatively sleek coat. Blue merle colouring is common, the mixture of black and white hairs in the coat creating a greyish-blue impression.

Personality Responsive and affectionate, a Collie will gain an almost instinctive understanding of what its owner requires over a period of time. The breed is also active and energetic, thanks to its working ancestry.

Health and care Merle Collies should not be allowed to mate together, because the genetic mix in such a case means that on average one in four of a resulting litter will be born blind, with small, nonfunctioning eyes. Puppies of this breed are also at particular risk of having umbilical hernias at birth. In addition, Collies are prone to various eye conditions. The best known of these is Collie eye anomaly. Your vet can detect the condition by examination of the eyes although the problem will not necessarily impact severely on your pet's sight.

As an owner Significant grooming time must be spent on a Rough Collie, particularly in spring when the more profuse winter coat is shed. These dogs are easy to train, but be careful if you are in rural areas around sheep – although Collies are not often used for working purposes today, they still retain strong herding instincts.

Also consider The Shetland Sheepdog (*see pages 42–43*) is a smaller breed that looks like a scaled-down form of the Rough Collie. Other possibilities that may appeal are members of the Belgian Shepherd group such as the short-coated Malinois or the Tervuren (*see pages 24–25*), although they have a less elegant profile and are bred in a different range of colours.

Tech Spec

Features

A *Head:* Lean and wedge-shaped, with a blunt-ended muzzle, tapering evenly from the ears to the nose

B *Eyes:* Obliquely positioned, almond-shaped and medium-sized

C *Ears:* In proportion to the size of the head; carried three-quarters erect when dog is alert

D *Chest:* Deep, reaching to the elbows

E *Tail:* Medium-length and carried low; raised, but never over the back when the dog is excited

F *Bite:* Scissors bite

G *Height at shoulder:* Dogs 61–66cm (24–26 in); bitches 56–61cm (22–24 in)

H *Weight:* Dogs 27–32kg (60–70 lb); bitches 22.5–29.5kg (50–65 lb)

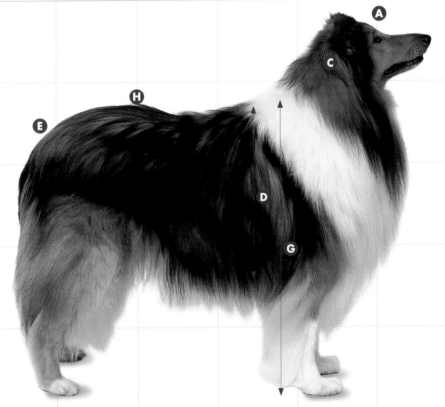

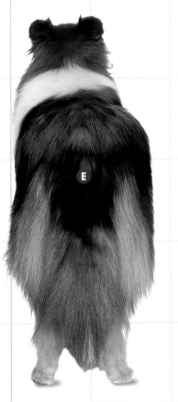

German Shepherd Dog

Overview

Recognition
North America, Britain and FCI member countries

Life expectancy
10–12 years

Colour
All colours, the richer, darker shades preferred; white dogs are disqualified for show purposes

Grooming

Feeding

Child friendliness

Exercise
Needs regular opportunities to run

By far the most popular of the herding breeds worldwide, the German Shepherd Dog is also known as the Alsatian, a name that came about as a result of anti-German sentiment over World Wars I and II. The breed has a huge following, influenced both by its character and its commanding appearance.

Origin The German Shepherd was developed using a number of localized herding dogs in the region that is now Germany. These earlier breeds tended to have straighter backs than the modern German Shepherd, and taller, squarer profiles. The German Shepherd in its familiar form is the result of a concentrated breeding programme started in the 1890s by a single breeder, Captain Max von Stephanitz. Long-coated German Shepherds gradually became scarcer, and an early wirehaired form has now died out completely.

Appearance The German Shepherd Dog is an imposing breed and is often described as having a wolflike appearance. The graceful downward curve of its top line should be continuous when seen in profile, extending from the pointed ear tips down to the end of the tail. Its gait is also characteristic – an easy trotting movement that covers a considerable amount of ground with every strike.

Personality Slightly reserved but confident, the German Shepherd has proved to be a loyal and highly intelligent breed that is receptive to complex training. It is often employed in dangerous situations, such as in the security field or with the police, thanks to its dependable and responsive nature.

Health and care The major problem affecting this breed is hip dysplasia. In recent years, breeders have sought to overcome this weakness, introducing a screening process for breeding stock. Beware of hobbyist breeders who may not follow the strict criteria applied by the professionals, and who offer noticeably less expensive puppies to unsuspecting purchasers.

As an owner Do not contemplate acquiring a German Shepherd without having the dedication to devote sufficient time to training. Few breeds are more responsive; conversely, an inadequately trained German Shepherd is likely to be a liability to its owner and those around it. Regular grooming of the double-layered, dense coat is essential, particularly during the twice-yearly moult. Be alert to any prolonged digestive upsets in this breed – they can be indicative of pancreatic problems.

Also consider The Tervuren (see pages 24–25), which is closest in colouring as well as appearance, may be a possibility and the Belgian Shepherd Dog (see page 44), with its distinctive black coat, is another one. Both breeds are slightly lighter in build than the German Shepherd. There is a white form of the German Shepherd, which has been recently developed into a separate breed.

Tech Spec

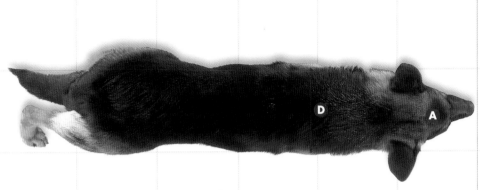

Features

A *Head:* Skull extends into the long wedge-shaped muzzle with no stop

B *Eyes:* Almond-shaped, set slightly obliquely

C *Ears:* Erect, moderately pointed and balanced in size on the skull

D *Chest:* Deep

E *Tail:* Never curled forwards beyond a vertical point; carried in a sabrelike position at rest

F *Bite:* Scissors bite

G *Height at shoulder:* Dogs 61–66cm (24–26 in); bitches 56–61cm (22–24 in)

H *Weight:* 34–43kg (75–95 lb)

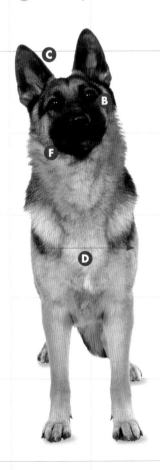

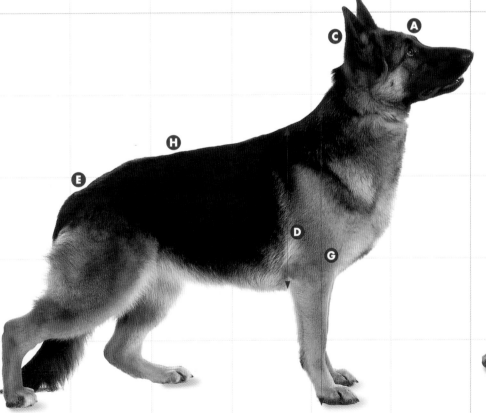

Norwegian Buhund

Overview

Recognition
North America, Britain and FCI member countries

Life expectancy
11–13 years

Colour
Ranges from cream and wheaten shades through red to black

Grooming

Feeding

Child friendliness

Exercise
A good daily walk is essential

The Buhund has been bred in Norway for over 1,000 years, but it was not until the late 1940s that this breed was brought to Britain and only since the 1970s has it built up a strong international following. Apart from its appearances in the show ring, and as an increasingly popular pet, the Buhund has also been used in Australia as a working sheepdog.

Origin Descended from the ancient Iceland Dog, in its home country the Buhund was kept largely for herding sheep. Its unusual name derives from the addition of the Norwegian word *bu*, the name that was given to the temporary shelters built by shepherds in their summer, to *hund*, which means 'dog'. During the winter, the breed also acted as a sled dog and as a companion on hunting expeditions.

Appearance The Norwegian Buhund still closely resembles its Icelandic relative. Its curved tail is set high on the back, and it has the raised ears typical of a spitz breed. However, unlike most spitz dogs, the muzzle is short and compact. It is protected against the elements by a dense undercoat for insulation, and a short, rough-textured topcoat. Colours range from black, red and cream to wheaten. The eyes are dark brown.

Personality The Norwegian Buhund has an intelligent, adaptable nature and is a good guard dog, alert to the presence of strangers. Energetic and lively, this breed needs plenty of exercise.

Health and care The grooming requirements of this breed are modest in general, although heavier in spring, when the dogs moult. They have a tendency to hip dysplasia, so ensure that any puppy you are considering has been bred from stock that has been properly screened for this condition.

As an owner Norwegian Buhunds can be trained easily. However, they have a tendency to develop into one-person dogs, so, if possible, involve everyone in the family in your pet's care. The breed's working instincts are strong, so train your dog carefully, and be especially cautious if it is around livestock.

Also consider Other similar northern breeds include the Icelandic Sheepdog, which is similar to the Buhund in appearance. The Japanese Shiba Inu (*see pages 90–91*) represents a slightly smaller option, and the various Elkhounds, two of which originate from Norway (*see pages 64–65*) and one from Sweden, are further possibilities, although they are bred in a more limited range of colours.

Tech Spec

Features

A *Head:* Broad and wedge-shaped, with the muzzle tapering slightly along its length

B *Eyes:* Dark and almond-shaped

C *Ears:* Large and rounded at the tips; located well back on the skull and held erect

D *Chest:* Deep, contributing to the breed's strength

E *Tail:* Set high and bushy; curled forward over the back and down the side of the body

F *Bite:* Scissors bite

G *Height at shoulder:* 43–45.5cm (17–18 in)

H *Weight:* 24–26kg (53–58 lb)

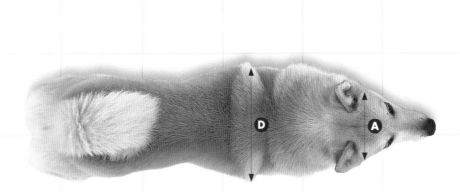

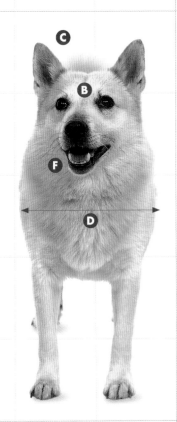

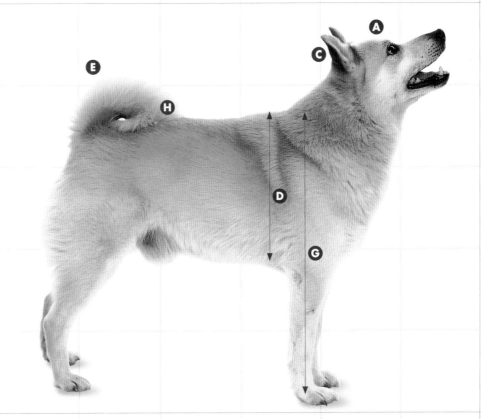

Old English Sheepdog

Overview

Recognition
North America, Britain and
FCI member countries

Life expectancy
10–12 years

Colour
Grey, grizzled, blue merle
or blue, with or without
white markings

Grooming

Feeding

Child friendliness

Exercise
Needs an energetic
daily run

The Old English Sheepdog is inaccurately named: it was created barely 200 years ago and was bred at least in part from dogs imported into England. Nor was it ever a true sheepdog; it worked instead as a drover's dog, driving both cattle and sheep to market. Its attractive personality and characteristic ambling gait have made it a fashionable pet in recent years.

Origin The breed was developed in the southwest of England, and it is descended from Bearded Collies crossed with larger breeds, possibly including the Russian Ovtcharka, which originates in the Ukraine and is a much bigger dog, standing up to 91cm (3 ft) tall at the shoulder. Its profile is similar to that of the modern Old English Sheepdog. The new breed resulting from the crosses was known as the Bobtail for a time, because of its naturally short tail length (some are born completely tail-less), while docking of the tail was commonplace.

Appearance A profuse covering of hair is a feature of this breed. The coat has a hard texture but tends to fluff out, which gives the dog a decidedly shaggy appearance. It should not curl or lie flat. The ears fall flat against the sides of the head, echoing the fall of the coat. The skull should be square in shape. This breed moves with little apparent effort, ambling when it walks, and with an elastic movement when trotting or running at full pace.

Personality As good-natured as its appearance and bearlike movements suggest, the Old English Sheepdog is a friendly, playful, and intelligent breed. Because of its size and natural energy, this dog needs plenty of space if it is to thrive happily.

Health and care The Old English Sheepdog is protected by the insulating properties of its coat and is not much affected by either heat or cold. Hereditary problems are rarely encountered in this breed, although they may occasionally suffer from cataracts on the eyes, a disorder that is commonly an inherited weakness.

As an owner You will be rewarded with an amiable companion if you opt for one of these dogs. Its coat needs regular care to keep it looking its best. If dogs are unlikely to be shown, it can be clipped back, but this does radically alter its appearance. The Old English Sheepdog is a good guard dog with a deep, distinctive bark.

Also consider The Bearded Collie (*see pages 22–23*) is smaller, but equally cheerful and lively, while the Bergamasco Sheepdog, an Italian breed with an unusual corded coat – which some people believe may have made a contribution to the development of the Old English Sheepdog – is now seen more frequently outside its homeland and may be another possibility. Both share some characteristics with the Old English Sheepdog.

Tech Spec

Features

A *Head:* Large and relatively square, with well-developed supraorbital ridges over the eyes

B *Eyes:* Brown, blue, or a combination of these colours; hidden by hair

C *Ears:* Medium-sized; lie against the sides of the head

D *Chest:* Relatively broad with a deep brisket

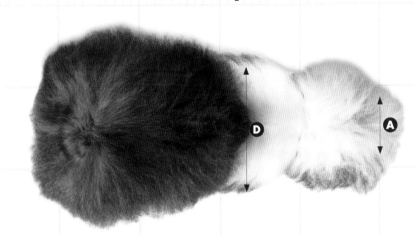

E *Tail:* May be naturally bob-tailed in appearance

F *Bite:* Scissors or level bite

G *Height at shoulder:* Dogs 56cm (22 in) or more; bitches 53cm (21 in) or more

H *Weight:* 27–29.5kg (60–65 lb)

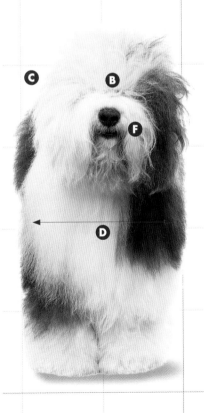

Pembroke Welsh Corgi

Overview

Recognition
North America, Britain and
FCI member countries

Life expectancy
11–13 years

Colour
Sable, fawn, red and
black-and-tan, with or
without white areas

Grooming

Feeding

Child friendliness

Exercise
A good daily walk
will be essential

The Pembroke Corgi has a more fox-like appearance than its Cardigan relative, thanks to its smaller ears. The name 'Corgi' is thought to be derived from the Celtic words for 'watch' and 'dog', giving us an idea of the breed's ancient origins. There are records of these dogs existing as far back as the 10th century.

Origin This breed is closely associated with the old southern Welsh county of Pembrokeshire. When the Pembroke and Cardigan Corgis were recognized as individual breeds in 1934, the Pembroke was by far the more numerous and had a more uniform appearance. It remains more popular than its northern rival, possibly because it is the favoured breed of Queen Elizabeth II, who has kept Pembroke Welsh Corgis since 1933. The breed was recognized in North America in 1936.

Appearance Unlike the Cardigan, the Pembroke Welsh Corgi is usually tail-less, as stipulated in the show standard, and is often slightly less long in the back. It is also shorter in height and lighter in weight. The colour range is more restricted than that of the Cardigan, with no blue merle form, and it is rarer for it to have white markings. It is normal for the short legs to turn slightly inward.

Personality The two breeds share their personality traits, and the Pembroke Welsh Corgi is just as inclined to nip. This is instinctive rather than aggressive behaviour, and the breed is lively by nature.

Health and care The Pembroke Welsh Corgi has a hereditary predisposition to a weakness of the intervertebral discs in the neck. In consequence, it is recommended that these dogs are exercised on a leash with a harness that fits around the body, so there is no pressure on the vulnerable neck area if the dog pulls. The Pembroke Welsh Corgi also has a tendency to suffer from epilepsy.

As an owner Your corgi may sometimes nip your ankles in impatience when anticipating a walk or a meal, or if he feels that he is being ignored. Corgis can also be quarrelsome with each other and with other breeds, and you need to bear this in mind when exercising your pet. Corgis also suffer from more birthing difficulties than many other breeds.

Also consider The Cardigan form of this breed (see pages 30–31) is one option, as well as another short-legged herding dog, the Swedish Vallhund (see page 45). The Australian Cattle Dog is another choice (see pages 18–19), a breed which is still widely kept as a working dog in its homeland, as well as becoming known internationally as a show breed.

Tech Spec

Features

A *Head:* Skull wide and flat between the ears, with slightly tapered muzzle

B *Eyes:* Oval, obliquely set and medium-sized

C *Ears:* Medium-sized, erect and tapered slightly to rounded points

D *Chest:* Deep

E *Tail:* Short

F *Bite:* Scissors or level bite

G *Height at shoulder:* 25.5–30.5cm (10–12 in)

H *Weight:* Dogs 12.25–13.5kg (27–30 lb); bitches 11.5–12.5kg (25–28 lb)

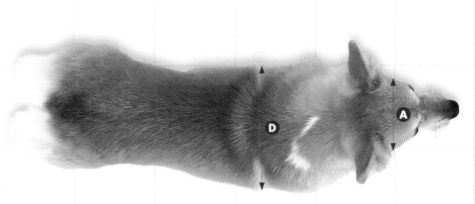

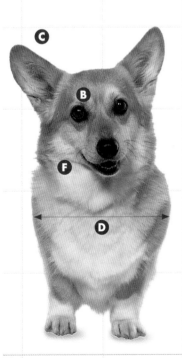

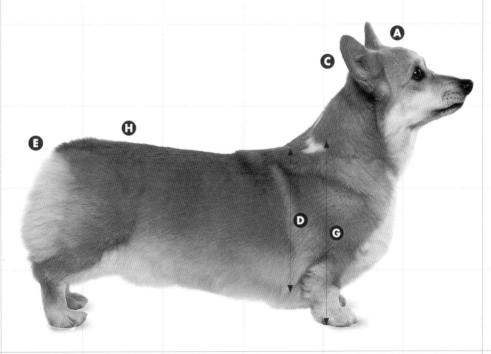

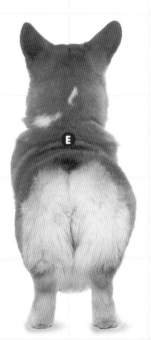

41

Overview

Recognition
North America, Britain and
FCI member countries

Life expectancy
11–14 years

Colour
Sable, blue merle, or black
with white and/or tan
markings

Grooming

Feeding

Child friendliness

Exercise
Moderate daily walks
are necessary

The Shetland Sheepdog, affectionately known as the Sheltie, has left its working past behind and emerged as the most popular of all the collie breeds worldwide, both in the show ring and as a companion. This breed gets along with children, and it is an excellent choice for obedience or junior handling competitions.

Origin These sheepdogs originate from the Shetland Islands, off Scotland's northwest coast. It seems likely that they evolved there over the course of centuries, but how or when the original stock reached the islands was never recorded. It is likely that they are descended from the same ancestral line as the Rough Collie, which developed on the Scottish mainland. In common with other native breeds from these islands, such as the Shetland Pony, these sheepdogs are relatively small in size.

Appearance The hair on the face is short, and the head is framed by a ruff behind the ears, which is at its most profuse during the winter. Sable colouring can vary from a golden shade to mahogany, and the breed standard specifies that any white on the coat must take up less than 50 per cent of its total area. Some Shelties may have an unusual blue and white iris (the coloured area around the pupil), which is known as a 'wall eye'.

Personality The Sheltie has a loyal, affectionate and friendly nature towards people it knows well, but it is also an alert guard dog and does not accept strangers readily. Few breeds are as quick to learn.

Health and care This breed is prone to hip dysplasia, arising from a congenital malformation of the hip joints. Shelties are also susceptible to a number of eye problems, including progressive retinal atrophy (PRA), signs of which emerge at between three and five years of age. The vision of affected dogs is better when light levels are low. Check with your breeder about the incidence of these problems in their stock.

As an owner Thorough, regular grooming is essential to maintain this dog's attractive appearance and prevent its coat from becoming matted. This is an agile breed and can jump well, which means that your garden must be adequately fenced. If you want a dog with which to enter agility competitions, the Sheltie is an excellent choice.

Also consider The Collie, in either its Rough- or Smooth-Coated forms (see pages 32–33), is slightly larger in size but the breed closest to the Sheltie in appearance. The Bearded Collie (see pages 22–23) or the smaller Polish Lowland Sheepdog (see page 45) may also appeal.

Tech Spec

Features

A *Head:* Blunt, wedge-shaped and tapered from ears to nose; skull and muzzle are of even length

B *Eyes:* Medium-sized and set obliquely, with dark, almond-shaped rims

C *Ears:* Raised three-quarters erect when alert; folded lengthways at rest

D *Chest:* Deep, with brisket reaching to the point of the elbows

E *Tail:* Hangs straight down or slightly curved at rest; raised when dog is alert, but never curved over the back

F *Bite:* Scissors bite

G *Height at shoulder:* 33–40.5cm (13–16 in)

H *Weight:* 6.5–7kg (14–16 lb)

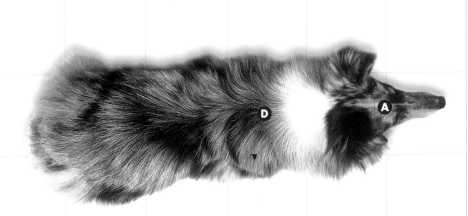

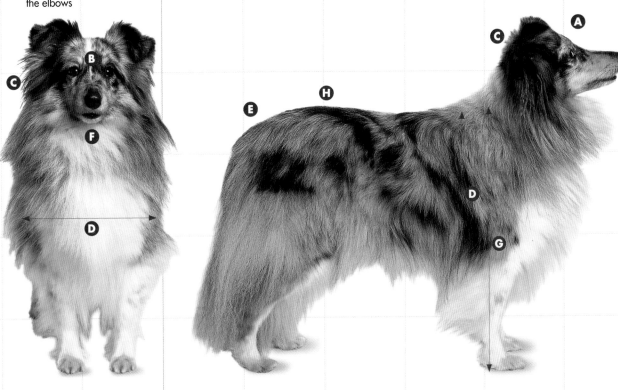

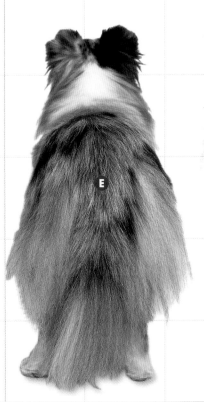

Pet Spec
Belgian Shepherd Dog

This alert and intelligent breed is known as the Groenendael in its homeland, bearing the name of the chateau close to Brussels where it was first bred. Responsive by nature, the Groenendael was created in the late 19th century, and its versatile nature has allowed it to be used for a range of jobs – in its original role as a working sheepdog, as a police dog and working with customs officers, and as a guard dog.

Appearance In profile this resembles a slimmer version of the German Shepherd Dog. It has erect, triangular ears. All Groenendaels are black, although a small amount of white hair on the front of the chest or between the toes is permitted. The coat is relatively long, especially around the neck and on the chest.

Breed care and health Regular grooming is important to maintain the condition of the coat. If the dog gets dirty, it is easier to let mud dry and then brush it out than to try to wash it out of the thick fur.

As an owner This is a loyal breed that does not take readily to strangers. Good training and early socialization are crucial to ensure that it does not become nervous of people.

Also consider Of the Belgian Shepherd Dog breeds, the Tervuren (see pages 24–25) is bred in a wider range of colours. The other options are the shorter-coated Malinois and the curly-coated Laekenois. All four breeds are of a similar size, and the bitches are generally smaller than dogs.

Height 56–66cm (22–26 in)
Weight 27.5–28.5kg (61–63 lb)
Exercise An opportunity to run off the leash every day is important

Pet Spec
Briard

Dogs with a similar appearance to the Briard have existed in France for over 1,300 years, although it is uncertain if they were first bred in the province of Brie, after which the breed is named. Initially they worked as flock guardians, helping to protect the sheep against attacks by wolves, but the breed gradually evolved into a herding dog. The Briard served during World War 1, carrying out a range of tasks at the front.

Appearance Long-coated and solid in appearance, the Briard has broad, high-set ears. It also has unusual double dew claws on its hind legs. Colours range from tawny shades through to grey and black. More than one colour may be present in some cases, and there may be occasional white hairs evident, as well as a small white spot, up to 2.5cm (1 in) in diameter, on the chest.

Breed care and health Grooming is very important to maintain the Briard's appearance. The double dew claws on the hind feet must not be removed in the case of show dogs, but the nails here must be trimmed so they do not grow around into the pads.

As an owner This breed is responsive to training and also needs plenty of exercise. The Briard covers ground quickly, with a trotting gait. These dogs are territorial and are likely to be reserved in the company of strangers.

Also consider The Picardy Shepherd (also known as the Berger de Picard) is slightly smaller, with a less profuse coat. The Bearded Collie (see pages 22–23) has a similar, flowing coat to the Briard, but with longer, more pendulous ears. If you are looking for a short-coated breed with similar stamina, the Australian Cattle Dog (see pages 18–19) may prove to be a good choice.

Height 58.5–68.5cm (23–27 in)
Weight 34kg (75 lb)
Exercise The Briard is an active dog and needs plenty of daily exercise

Pet Spec
Canaan Dog

This breed is related to pariah dogs, which live in a state of semidomestication around human settlements. The ancestors of today's Canaan Dog were redomesticated from the mid-1930s, and the breed is now represented worldwide. The ancestry of most of today's Canaan Dogs can be traced back to the Shaar Hagai Kennels in Jerusalem.

Appearance Although it originates in the Middle East, the Canaan Dog is clearly of spitz descent, with pricked ears and a brushlike tail, which curves forwards over its back. The coat of these dogs is relatively short, however, and they are bred in a range of colours from cream to shades of red to black. They have a compact appearance, with straight front legs and strong feet.

Breed care and health As befits a breed that has only recently been developed from free-ranging ancestors, the Canaan Dog is generally fit and healthy, in spite of the fact that it has been bred from a small gene pool. Its grooming needs are minimal.

As an owner This breed is loyal but prone to wandering. It is not a good choice for urban living, settling better in rural areas where there is plenty of space. Training can sometimes present difficulties because of its independent streak.

Also consider The only other pariah dog at all known at present is the New Guinea Singing Dog. There are a number of spitz-type dogs of similar appearance to choose from, with the Russian breeds known as Siberian Laikas being the most similar in looks to the Canaan Dog. They also have a similar, energetic temperament.

Height 48–61cm (19–24 in)
Weight 16–25kg (35–55 lb)
Exercise Once trained, plenty of opportunity to run off the leash is essential

Pet Spec
Polish Lowland Sheepdog

This breed has become popular internationally over recent years. In Poland it was a working sheepdog, and it dates back over 400 years. It was bred in the area of Nizinny, and is known as the Polski Owczarek Nizinny in its native country. These sheepdogs nearly died out in the late 1940s, but a handful of breeders ensured their survival.

Appearance A shaggy-coated dog, with a rectangular profile, the hair of this sheepdog trails down over the face, obscuring the ears, which lie flat at the sides of the head. Puppies are frequently born without tails, and it has been traditional to dock those that had tails soon after birth. Although the dogs exist in a wide range of colours, black or grey, often combined with white, are the most typical and the most widely found.

Breed care and health A hardy breed, the Polish Lowland Sheepdog needs to be groomed regularly to maintain its coat in good condition. The feet should also be checked and burrs and grass seeds combed out.

As an owner This is an intelligent and responsive breed, which can be trained easily and settles well in the home as a pet. It should not be allowed to come into direct contact with sheep, as its herding instinct remains strong.

Also consider This breed exists in three different sizes, although only the middle-sized one is well-known outside Poland. The Bearded Collie (see pages 22–23) and the somewhat larger Old English Sheepdog (see pages 38–39) are alternative choices to consider.

Pet Spec
Hungarian Puli

The Hungarian Puli (pronounced 'Poo-lee') is a Hungarian sheepdog, with a highly distinctive corded coat. This gave excellent protection against the harsh winter weather, and it was sheared off when the sheep were sheared, regrowing in time for the following winter. The breed is believed to be descended from dogs of Tibetan origin.

Appearance The corded coat has tended to become longer in show stock, now frequently extending right down to the ground. There has also been a move in North America to show Hungarian Pulik (the plural form) with their coats in a woolly, rather than natural corded, style. Black is the colour most commonly associated with this breed, but a number of other solid colours are recognized, including grey, while mixed colours used to be common in Hungary.

Breed care and health Unusually, the Puli's colour fades in the sun. The coat is naturally corded, so if you opt for a woolly style, considerable grooming will be needed to maintain it.

As an owner It is normal for a Puli puppy to have a tufted coat. The outer and inner layers of the coat gradually become entwined, forming clumps at first, before growing out to make the distinctive cords. These dogs are intelligent and responsive to training.

Also consider The larger Komondor (see page 251) is the only other breed with a similar coat. A smaller variant of the Hungarian Puli, called the Pumi, has resulted from crosses between this breed and Pomeranians.

Pet Spec
Swedish Vallhund

This breed is a native of Sweden, bred to herd cattle by darting into the herd and nipping at their feet if they were reluctant to move. The word 'vallhund' simply means farm dog, reflecting the fact that these dogs also acted as watchdogs and hunted rodents. In its homeland, the breed is known as the Vasgotaspets, named after the Vastergotland area of southwest Sweden where it originated.

Appearance Short legs and a relatively long body characterize the Swedish Vallhund. It has broad, erect ears that contribute to its alert appearance. Its coat is harsh and is of medium length. Sable patterning is a feature of this breed – the mask on the face is clearly defined and the shoulders are lighter in colour.

Breed care and health Robust by nature, the Swedish Vallhund is an easy breed to care for, with minimal grooming needs. It shows no susceptibility to the back problems that affect some other long-backed breeds.

As an owner Although the Vallhund is small, it is a lively, active companion rather than a lap dog. It is also likely to be an alert watchdog in the home. On the downside, its heritage means that it has a natural tendency to nip.

Also consider The Welsh Corgi breeds (see pages 30–31 and 40–41) are close relatives of the Swedish Vallhund, although slightly smaller in size. Both dogs were bred originally to perform identical tasks, and so are similar in nature, too. Another possible choice is the Lancashire Heeler, created from crosses between Corgis and Manchester Terriers. The original stock of the Heeler died out, but the dog was carefully re-created in the 1960s.

Height 45.5–51cm (18–20 in)
Weight 13.5–16kg (30–35 lb)
Exercise A breed with plenty of stamina that requires good walks

Height 35.5–48cm (14–19 in)
Weight 9–18kg (20–40 lb)
Exercise A good daily walk is essential for this naturally active breed

Height 30.5–35.5cm (12–14 in)
Weight 11–15kg (24–33 lb)
Exercise A lengthy daily walk will be essential for these active dogs

Afghan Hound

Recognition
North America, Britain and
FCI member countries

Life expectancy
10–12 years

Colour
No restrictions on colour,
although white areas are
not encouraged

Grooming

Feeding

Child friendliness

Exercise
Needs the opportunity of
a daily run

The appearance of the Afghan Hound today has altered considerably from the examples of the breed first seen outside its homeland in the early 19th century. A very elegant hound, it needs a considerable amount of time spent on grooming. Otherwise its magnificent flowing coat will rapidly become matted.

Origin Named after its home area, centred on modern-day Afghanistan, this sure-footed sight hound has been bred in this region for centuries, hunting game ranging from hares to antelope and deer. With little natural cover in the barren landscape, pace and stamina were both essential attributes for these hounds. The Afghan was first brought to Britain in the late 19th century, but it initially aroused little interest, and it was not until the 1920s that the breed started to build up an international following.

Appearance The early Afghan Hounds varied noticeably from one another in appearance, depending on their area of origin Those that founded the Bell-Murray strain in the 1920s were from desert areas, and they were relatively pale in colour and small. The stockier, darker Ghazni strain consisted of individuals with longer coats that originated from more mountainous areas, although no such divisions exist in modern bloodlines.

Personality Rather aloof by nature, the Afghan is a breed that can still retain keen hunting instincts, in spite of its aristocratic appearance. These hounds are athletic by nature, possessing an independent spirit, and tend to form strong relationships with their owners.

Health and care Daily grooming is essential to maintain the thick, silky coat in top condition. The breed is prone to a variety of eye problems, ranging from cataracts to a disorder of the cornea, which covers the surface of the eye. Afghan Hounds can also suffer from transient 'blue eye' following vaccination against infectious canine hepatitis.

As an owner You need to have time to groom your dog's coat daily. An Afghan Hound must also be carefully trained, ensuring that it will not chase after small dogs when off the leash. It may even be necessary to muzzle your pet when he is off the leash if you are uncertain about whether he can resist temptation.

Also consider A Greyhound (*see pages 60–61*) would be a good alternative if you would prefer a smooth-coated sight hound of similar size that does not need as much grooming and has a less assertive temperament. A Borzoi (*see pages 56–57*) is another long-coated sight hound, but differs significantly in appearance from an Afghan Hound. There are also several rare breeds of Indian hound that are believed to be quite closely related to the Afghan, but they are not found in Europe or North America.

Tech Spec

Features

A *Head:* Refined, with good length and a silky topknot

B *Eyes:* Dark and almond in shape, almost triangular

C *Ears:* Long, reaching to the nose if extended, and level with outer corners of the eyes

D *Chest:* Deep and narrow

E *Tail:* Not set very high and with a curve at the end

F *Bite:* Level bite

G *Height at shoulder:* Dogs 66–71cm (26–28 in); bitches 61–66cm (24–26 in)

H *Weight:* Dogs approximately 27kg (60 lb); bitches about 22.5kg (50 lb)

Basenji

Overview

Recognition
North America, Britain and
FCI member countries

Life expectancy
11–13 years

Colour
Black or red with white
markings; there are also
brindle and tricolour forms

Grooming

Feeding

Child friendliness

Exercise
Needs a daily opportunity
to explore off the leash

These unusual dogs originate from Central Africa, where they have been kept as hunting companions for centuries. They are a highly responsive, intelligent and loyal breed, but show a number of unusual mannerisms – the Basenji's behaviour has sometimes been described as catlike. They spend a lot of time grooming themselves, are agile climbers, and may also spend long periods simply watching from a window.

Origin A pair of Basenjis was brought to England for the first time in 1895, but died from distemper soon afterwards. Thereafter, these dogs remained almost unknown outside their African homeland until 1937, when the breed was reintroduced to Britain and then to America where, sadly, all but one of the initial Basenjis again succumbed to distemper. Gradually, however, Western bloodlines were developed. New stock was obtained from Zaire to expand the existing gene pool at the end of the 1980s.

Appearance The forehead is wrinkled – especially so in puppies – giving the Basenji a rather worried look. As befits a breed originating close to the Equator, the Basenji's coat is short and fine. These hounds have white markings on the chest, the underparts of the body and at the tip of the tail. There may also be a white blaze extending down between the eyes.

Personality Always alert, the Basenji is a breed that has evolved to work closely with people. It has a friendly nature towards those whom it knows well, but is likely to be reserved with strangers. Although it does not bark, it is quite capable of growling, and has an unusual yodelling call when excited or at play.

Health and care The first Basenjis kept outside Africa proved to be very delicate because they were encountering diseases to which they had no natural immunity, but now that the breed is well-established, it is relatively hardy. It is particularly important, though, to keep their immunizations current. The coat length has also increased somewhat to cope with colder climates. Puppies should be checked for umbilical hernias. Older dogs may be susceptible to digestive upsets, and this problem is linked to certain bloodlines. Check with your breeder about the incidence of these problems in their breeding stock.

As an owner The Basenji is a quiet pet, although its description as the 'Barkless Dog' is not strictly accurate. When on the move, this breed has an unusual trotting gait. If you are hoping to breed Basenjis, bear in mind that they only have one period of heat annually, rather than two, like most breeds.

Also consider Some of the hound breeds from the Mediterranean islands, such as the Pharaoh Hound (*see page 70*) and the Ibizan Hound (*see page 70*), which may be distant relatives of the Basenji, may be possible alternatives. A similar breed originating from Asia is the New Guinea Singing Dog, which has a long history as a hunting companion in this part of the world, but is very rare elsewhere.

Tech Spec

Features

A Head: Flat skull, tapering between the eyes, with the muzzle shorter than the skull, ending in a black nose

B Eyes: Almond-shaped, dark-brown to hazel colour, set obliquely

C Ears: Small, erect and set forwards on top of skull

D Chest: Medium-width

E Tail: Bends forwards , curled to one side

F Bite: Scissors bite

G Height at shoulder: Dogs 43cm (17 in); bitches 40.5cm (16 in)

H Weight: Dogs 10kg (22 lb); bitches 9kg (20 lb)

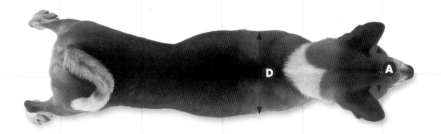

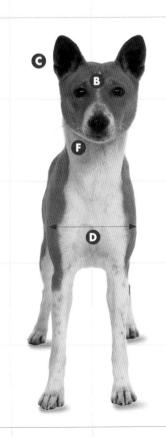

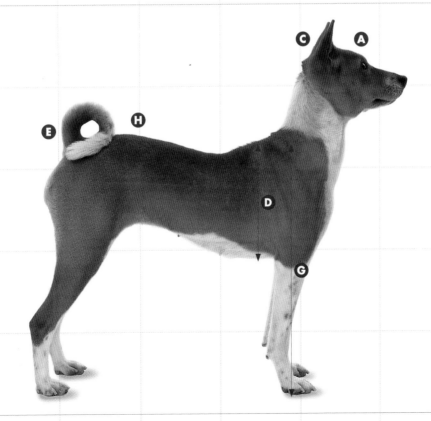

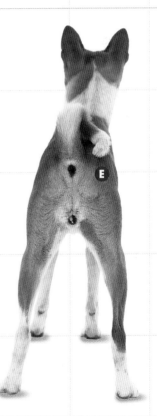

Basset Hound

Overview

Recognition
North America, Britain and
FCI member countries

Life expectancy
10–12 years

Colour
Any hound colour – often
bi- or tricoloured

Grooming

Feeding

Child friendliness

Exercise
Boredom will set in if a
Basset Hound does not
have a good daily walk

There are a number of different hounds described as 'bassets', of which the Basset Hound itself is by far the best-known example. The word comes from the French *bas*, meaning 'low', and describes their short legs. However, unlike a number of other basset types, there is not a taller form of this particular breed.

Origin The ancestors of today's Basset Hounds were brought to England from France in 1866. Crossbreeding with Bloodhounds subsequently helped to improve the Basset Hound's scenting skills, as well as resulting in a stockier build and a longer head. Basset Hounds are highly valued for hunting small game, such as rabbits, working in packs accompanied by huntsmen on foot.

Appearance A domed head and long pendulous ears are characteristic of this breed, with the skin on the legs being markedly wrinkled in appearance. Their feet are remarkably large in comparison with their legs. Bassets are bred in typical bi- or tricoloured hound patterning, with the exact markings varying, enabling individuals in a pack to be recognized easily, even from some distance away. They have long tails, which ensure that they can be seen even in deep undergrowth.

Personality A friendly, exuberant breed, the Basset Hound has a rich, baying call, frequently heard when it scents its game. As a scent hound it is not especially easy to train, but it is very affectionate by nature. A breed with a hearty appetite, these dogs may steal food if you give them the chance.

Health and care Because the Basset Hound has short hair, it requires little grooming, even when muddy – the dry mud brushes out very easily. Puppies are susceptible to a range of conditions, especially inguinal hernias, when part of the abdomen is displaced. The third vertebra in the neck is sometimes malformed at birth, causing pressure on the spinal cord, and needs surgical correction, as does a condition known as ectropion, in which the eyelids hang away from the eyes.

As an owner Be aware that these hounds will head off if they discover a scent when you are out walking. Their naturally social nature means that they will live together in relative harmony if you want more than one dog. Beware of their gluttony, because this can cause them to become obese very easily, to the stage where the underside of the body can almost be dragging along the ground. Any significant degree of overweight can cause health problems.

Also consider Other basset varieties share many of the Basset Hound's characteristics. The Basset Artesian-Normand is a smaller, more refined version of the Basset Hound and is bred in similar colours. There are wire-coated bassets, too. If you want a similarly coloured hound, but with longer legs, the Beagle (*see pages 52–53*) is an obvious option.

Tech Spec

Features

A *Head:* Large, with a well-domed skull and flat at the sides, not rounded

B *Eyes:* Slightly sunken, showing the haws, and brown in colour with a sad expression

C *Ears:* Long, set low on the head, but far back and pendulous

D *Chest:* Long, broad rib cage

E *Tail:* Curves upwards, with hair coarser on the underside

F *Bite:* Scissors or level bite

G *Height at shoulder:* 35.5cm (14 in)

H *Weight:* 22.5kg (50 lb)

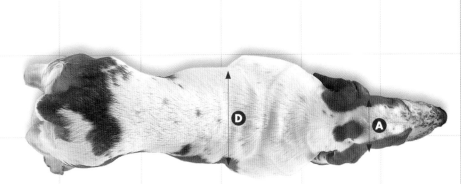

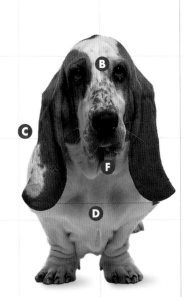

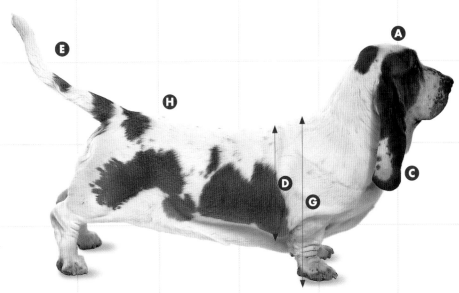

Beagle

Overview

Recognition
North America, Britain and
FCI member countries

Life expectancy
10–12 years

Colour
Any hound colour – often
bi- or tricoloured

Grooming

Feeding

Child friendliness

Exercise
Beagles must have good
periods of regular exercise

The Beagle is a very good choice for a home with older children – it is an energetic, exuberant breed with a playful side to its nature. As it has considerable stamina, it will also delight in long walks through the countryside. It usually gets on well with other dogs.

Origin Beagles were originally bred to hunt hares in packs, accompanied by hunt followers on foot, rather than mounted. Their origins are now unknown, although in the past there was a miniature strain called the Pocket Beagle, about half the size of the breed known today; Queen Elizabeth I owned a pack in the late 16th century and miniatures continued to be bred until the 1930s. Beagles first started to become popular in the United States during the 1860s. They participate in both field trials and shows.

Appearance The Beagle resembles a smaller version of the Foxhound. The breed has straight legs and particularly appealing brown eyes. Beagles occur in the same colours as the Basset Hound, with the same range of highly individual markings. The coat itself has a hard texture and is short. When working, the short tail is held up, forming a slight curve.

Personality Lively and instinctively friendly, Beagles make excellent companions, although they will often tend to disappear off on the trail of a scent rather than wait on command or return to you. In other respects, they make an ideal choice as a pet.

Health and care Be careful not to overfeed a Beagle, because this is a breed that can rapidly become seriously overweight. The dog will then suffer from associated complications ranging from diabetes to heart trouble. Some Beagle strains are susceptible to epilepsy, but fits rarely occur within the first year of life. Careful veterinary management and medication will stabilize this condition in affected dogs.

As an owner Do not be misled by the small size of these hounds – they need plenty of exercise, including the opportunity to run off the leash every day. If bored and underexercised, a Beagle is likely to be destructive around the home. They are very affectionate dogs and will form strong bonds with members of the family. Like other hounds, they will not thrive in city areas where exercise options are limited.

Also consider A Basset Hound (*see pages 50–51*) is a shorter-legged possibility, and some of the Scandinavian breeds, such as the Hamiltonstovare, offer other options. The Hamiltonstovare is a tricoloured breed, larger than the Beagle, typically standing 51–61cm (20–24) in tall and weighing up to 27kg (60 lb). Less well-known outside its homeland at present is the Dunker, another tricoloured hound, with a distinctive marbled 'saddle' on its back.

Tech Spec

Features

A *Head:* Relatively long, slightly domed, with a medium-length muzzle

B *Eyes:* Brown or hazel; well-spaced, large and appealing

C *Ears:* Set relatively low, reaching almost to the tip of the nose if extended; and broad, lying close to the head with rounded tips

D *Chest:* Deep and broad

E *Tail:* Set moderately high, but short and carried with a slight curve

F *Bite:* Scissors bite

G *Height at shoulder* (two categories): up to 33cm (13 in) and 33–38cm (13–15 in)

H *Weight:* 8–13.5kg (18–30 lb)

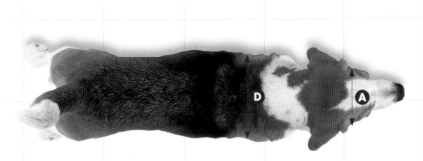

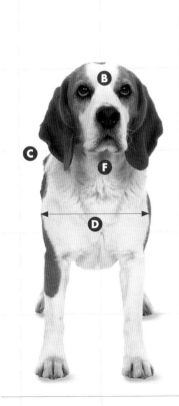

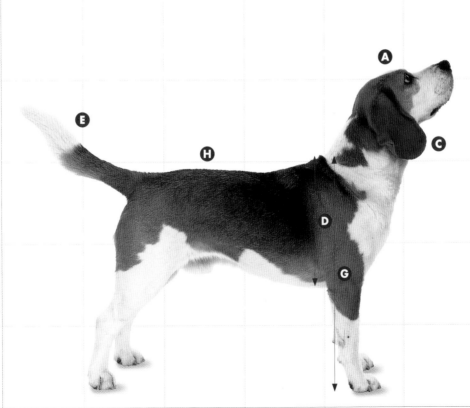

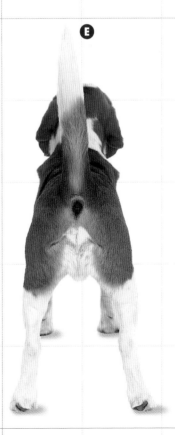

Bloodhound

Recognition
North America, Britain and
FCI member countries

Life expectancy
10–12 years

Colour
Black and tan; liver and
tan; red

Grooming

Feeding

Child friendliness

Exercise
Demanding – not a breed
that will be happy with a
stroll in the park

In spite of its reputation for tracking criminals, the Bloodhound's name simply reflects the fact that it has a long lineage. These are gentle, if determined, hounds and develop a very close rapport with their owners. You may well find yourself being dragged along, and you can compete with your pet in field trials.

Origin The Bloodhound is descended from an ancient breed known as the St Hubert Hound, which was first recorded around AD 600. The dog's remarkable tracking abilities were first used to locate injured stags, but they were subsequently put to work tracking people.

Appearance In the past, a white strain of the Bloodhound called the Talbot Hound existed, but this has become extinct. Many of today's breed are solid tan with a black area forming a 'saddle' on the back. The long pendulous ears are set low on the head, and the nose is distinctively broad.

Personality Lively and friendly, but with a determined nature, the Bloodhound is unlikely to be thrown off the scent, even if this is days old. They are not aggressive hounds at all, even when they catch up with their quarry, and they have been recorded following trails for as far as 220km (138 miles).

Health and care The skin folds on the head are occasionally problematic because they can become infected and will require treatment. Regular bathing of the affected area may subsequently be necessary. The eyelids can also be a cause for concern. This breed suffers both from ectropion, when the eyelids extend away from the eyes, and entropion, in which the eyelashes rub on the surface of the eye. Surgical correction is likely to be necessary for either of these conditions.

As an owner Be prepared for long walks on a daily basis if you choose this breed, as well as for an affectionate companion. The Bloodhound has a wonderful baying call, which it will use to indicate its presence to you, particularly in woodland. Grooming needs are minimal.

Also consider Other tracking breeds include the various Laufhunds of the Swiss Alps, with both the Bruno and St Hubert Jura Laufhunds being closest to the Bloodhound in terms of colouring. They are only slightly smaller in size, but much lighter overall, averaging 15.5–20kg (34–44 lb). The St. Hubert form has the heavier build, and more skin folds on its face suggest a closer affiliation to the Bloodhound. There are also short-legged forms of some other Laufhunds, which are known as Niederlaufhunds, averaging about 40.5cm (16 in) tall.

Tech Spec

Features

A *Head:* Long and yet relatively narrow, with a pronounced occiput and folds of loose skin

B *Eyes:* Well-sunken; hazel often preferred

C *Ears:* Very long and set low, forming folds on the sides of the head

D *Chest:* Extends down low between the forelegs, forming a keel

E *Tail:* Carried upright and curved in a scimitar fashion

F *Bite:* Scissors bite preferred, but can be level

G *Height at shoulder:* Dogs 63.5–68.5cm (25–27 in); bitches 58.5–63.5cm (23–25 in)

H *Weight:* Dogs 41–50kg (90–110 lb); bitches 36–45.5kg (80–100 lb)

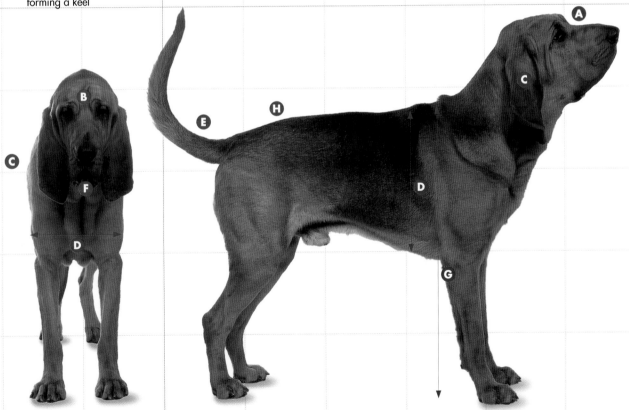

Borzoi

Recognition
North America, Britain and
FCI member countries

Life expectancy
10–12 years

Colour
No restrictions on
colouration

Grooming

Feeding

Child friendliness

Exercise
Plenty of space required for
daily running

For sheer elegance, both in motion and at rest, the Borzoi is a breed with few rivals. Its narrow head reveals that it is a sight hound, and its name derives from the Russian word *borzyi*, meaning 'swift', reflecting its remarkable pace. For many years it was known in the West as the Russian Wolfhound.

Origin It is believed that the Borzoi is descended from Greyhound-type stock that was crossed with native long-coated sheepdogs in its homeland. Traditionally these hounds were pitted against wolves, hunting them in pairs. They became popular with the Russian Royal family, and the breed's aristocratic associations almost led to its demise after the Russian Revolution of 1917. Luckily by this date Borzois were already represented elsewhere in Europe.

Appearance The Borzoi's coat is long and slightly wavy, with a silky texture. Although there are no restrictions on the colour of these hounds, they tend to be mainly white. The head is long and slender, with a domed skull. Their long hind legs help them to run with considerable grace and power.

Personality Rather aloof towards strangers, the Borzoi has a nature in keeping with its high-bred looks. It also has a reputation for considerable bravery – in the past it pursued wolves and brought them to the ground, holding them there until a huntsman could inflict a fatal blow.

Health and care Always check the mouth of a Borzoi, since it is not uncommon for the breed to be afflicted by missing teeth, which simply fail to develop in the jaws. The failing is penalized in show circles, and will therefore be important if you want to exhibit and breed from your Borzoi. This breed is one of the more responsive hounds in terms of training, and it can do well in obedience competitions. Regular grooming of the longer areas of fur on the coat is necessary.

As an owner It is only fair to choose this breed if you have adequate space near where you live to exercise it. Having evolved to hunt in couples, Borzois generally get on well together, although their size means that they will need a good deal of space in the home. It is a sensitive dog, and it will be a quiet companion, not predisposed to barking loudly even at strangers.

Also consider There are a number of local Russian breeds that bear some resemblance to the Borzoi, such as the Circassian Wolfhound – from further south, named after the mountainous region where it is found – but none is well-known in other parts of the world. Among the better-known hounds, Salukis (*see page 71*) are perhaps the most similar in type to the Borzoi, but with shorter coats. They were first bred in ancient Persia.

Tech Spec

Features

A *Head:* Long and narrow, with virtually no stop, and slightly domed above

B *Eyes:* Dark in colour, creating an intelligent impression and set obliquely

C *Ears:* Small in size, held back against the neck, but raised when the dog is alert

D *Chest:* Narrow and deep

E *Tail:* Long, set low, and carried in a curve below the level of the back

F *Bite:* Scissors or level bite

G *Height at shoulder:* Dogs 71cm (28 in) or more; bitches 66cm (26 in) or more

H *Weight:* Dogs 34–47.5kg (75–105 lb); bitches 27–43kg (60–95 lb)

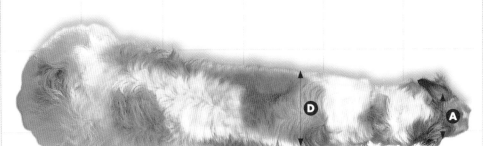

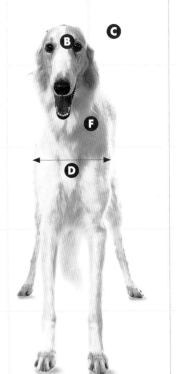

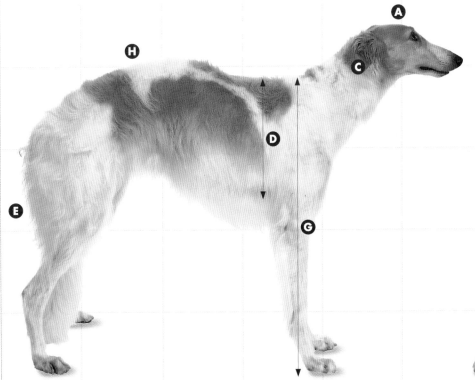

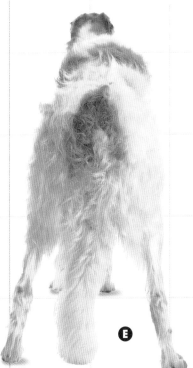

Dachshund

Overview

Recognition
North America, Britain and
FCI member countries

Life expectancy
12–13 years

Colour
Variable, but white should
be restricted to only the
chest

Grooming

Feeding

Child friendliness

Exercise
Not especially active

They may not look like traditional hounds, but these short-legged German dogs are more than a match for their game, and they have just as brave a heart for the hunt as any larger breed. Their unusual, elongated body shape led to the unflattering nickname of German Sausage Dogs. A 1903 cartoon showed a Dachshund in a bread roll – and so 'hot dog' became a fast-food description.

Origin It is probable that Dachshunds owe their origins to the French Revolution of 1789, which saw French noblemen fleeing from their homeland bringing bassets of various types with them to the region that is present-day Germany. These in turn were crossed with native German dogs, introducing the short-legged characteristic, with further crossings being responsible for the various coat types that now exist. Dachshunds were originally bred to hunt badgers in their sets underground, while miniature forms were used against rabbits.

Appearance The standard, smooth-haired Dachshund is the original form of the breed. It is believed that the longhaired variety arose as the result of crossbreeding with spaniels. It is unclear which breed introduced the wirehaired characteristic to the Dachshund bloodline, but it may have been the Wirehaired German Pinscher. Subsequently the breed was scaled down, creating the miniature varieties of each coat type that are also popular as companions today.

Personality Bold and fearless in spite of their small stature, Dachshunds are both loyal and good-natured towards people in their immediate circle, although they are not well-disposed to strangers. Dachshunds are alert watchdogs, with a more intimidating bark than their size might suggest.

Health and care Dachshunds are unfortunately rather vulnerable to intervertebral disc problems, probably because of their relatively long bodies. They must not be encouraged to venture upstairs or jump onto chairs for this reason. It is also important that they are not allowed to become overweight, as this will place extra strain on the vertebral column. Short-coated Dachshunds are susceptible to skin mites, too, which must be treated to avoid extensive hair loss.

As an owner Choose the coat type carefully, bearing in mind that a long–haired Dachshund will need more grooming than either of the other variants. The breed does not need spacious surroundings and is suitable for urban areas where there are parks nearby for exercise. Dachshunds should be exercised on a harness rather than a collar to protect against back problems.

Also consider If you like the short-legged appearance of the Dachshund, one of the basset type may be an alternative, although these dogs are generally taller overall. The Drever, a native Swedish short-legged hound with prominent white markings, which is now popular in Canada, would be another possibility.

Tech Spec

Features

A *Head:* Tapers to the tip of the nose, with the muzzle being slightly arched

B *Eyes:* Almond-shaped and of medium size, with the bridge bones above being prominent

C *Ears:* Rounded and set close to the top of the head, with the forward edges touching the cheeks

D *Chest:* Prominent breastbone with a depression on each side

E *Tail:* Carries on without greater curvature at the end of the body

F *Bite:* Scissors bite

G *Height at shoulder:* Classified on weight, not height

H *Weight:* 7–14.5kg (16–32 lb)

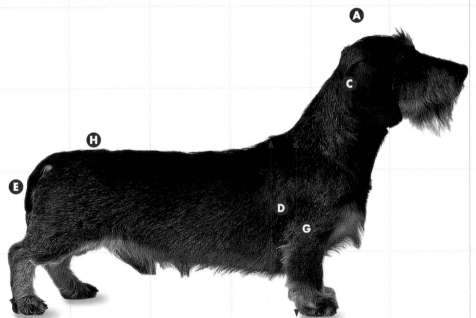

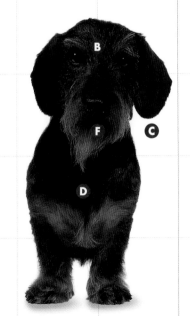

Greyhound

Overview

Recognition
North America, Britain and
FCI member countries

Life expectancy
10–12 years

Colour
Any colour or combination
acceptable

Grooming

Feeding

Child friendliness

Exercise
Sprinters by nature,
Greyhounds are not
endurance runners

The Greyhound is known for its extraordinary pace. It is the fastest breed of all the domestic dogs, and is capable of sprinting at speeds of 64kph (40 mph) over short distances. Unfortunately, many slower ex-racing greyhounds are retired from the track each year and end up in need of good homes.

Origin Hounds with an almost identical appearance to the contemporary Greyhound can be seen on the tombs and other art of ancient Egypt, dating back over 6,000 years. The breed has since been highly valued for its hunting abilities, and it is often crossed with sheepdogs to create Lurchers, which are favoured in Europe as poachers' companions and, increasingly, as pets. They possess the Greyhound's pace combined with the instinctive intelligence of a sheepdog, and they are fast, easy to train and highly responsive to their owners.

Appearance Greyhounds are smooth-coated, with narrow heads, small ears and a deep-chested appearance. The chest allows them good lung capacity, which is vital for their athletic performance. Their long tail hangs low. There are usually slight differences in type apparent between more refined show greyhounds and stock bred for racing.

Personality Gentle and friendly by nature, Greyhounds are quiet dogs, not given to barking. It is usually possible to train them easily, and they can be very affectionate. Couples get along well together, and they will often run with each other.

Health and care Ex-racing greyhounds sometimes have residual injuries, which may be behind the decision to retire them from the track. It is important not to exercise them after a meal, because they are susceptible to bloat, a condition in which the stomach twists, trapping air. Greyhounds also sometimes have difficulties in giving birth, simply because the bitches can become unusually nervous.

As an owner Be prepared to muzzle an ex-racing Greyhound when you take it off the leash in an urban park – its chasing instinct is very strong, and it will chase after and could actually kill a smaller pet. One of the surprises of owning a Greyhound is the fact that it requires only a fairly short run, often looping around in a circle rather as if it were running on a racetrack. The sleek short coat means that grooming is straightforward.

Also consider If you want a small variant, then a Whippet (see pages 68–69) is a good choice, and there are various localized greyhound breeds, including the Magyar Agar or Hungarian Greyhound, which is shorter and more stocky in appearance.

Tech Spec

Features

A *Head:* Long, narrow and relatively wide between the ears; virtually no stop

B *Eyes:* Bright, intelligent and dark in colour

C *Ears:* Small, set high and fine-textured; they are kept semi-folded, but become semi-pricked if excited

D *Chest:* Deep and relatively wide, with ribs that are well-sprung

E *Tail:* Set low, long and tapering, with a slight curve and carried low

F *Bite:* Scissors bite

G *Height at shoulder:* Dogs 71–76cm (28–30 in); bitches 68.5–71cm (27–28 in)

H *Weight:* Dogs 29.5–32kg (65–70 lb); bitches 27–29.5kg (60–65 lb)

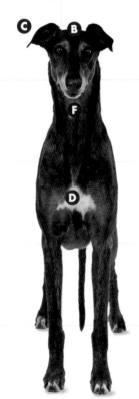

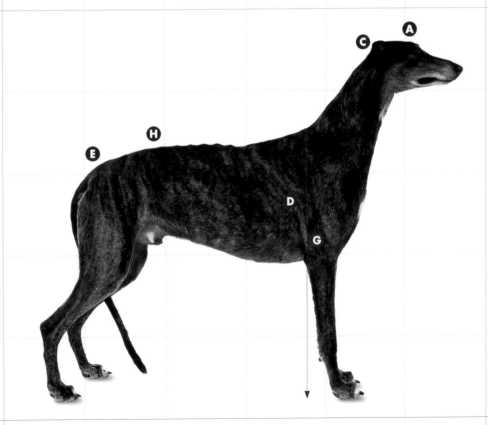

Irish Wolfhound

Overview

Recognition
North America, Britain and FCI member countries

Life expectancy
8–10 years

Colour
Colours corresponding to the Deerhound are accepted, including white, fawn, red, grey, black and brindle

Grooming

Feeding

Child friendliness

Exercise
Plenty of scope needed

The Irish Wolfhound towers over other breeds, but in personality it is a gentle giant. Sadly, it is relatively short-lived, with a life expectancy of just a decade on average – significantly less than the majority of smaller breeds.

Origin As their name suggests, these giant dogs were originally bred in their Irish homeland to hunt wolves, but when the wolf became extinct in the 1770s, the future of the hounds became increasingly uncertain Thanks to crossbreeding, with the Deerhound in particular, and an assortment of other breeds believed to include the Great Dane and the Pyrenean Mountain Dog, the Irish Wolfhound was saved from extinction. Today it is a relatively common breed.

Appearance A tall, tousle-haired dog with a long powerful head, the Irish Wolfhound has a body profile not unlike that of a Greyhound, allowing it to run very fast. Its long stride makes it appear as if it is covering the ground almost effortlessly. Its nails are strong and curved, helping the hound to maintain its balance when it is running quickly. Pale colours often predominate.

Personality This breed has an innately friendly character. The Irish Wolfhound is docile and affectionate by nature, but can also be exuberant, particularly when young. These hounds respond well to training, which is vital in view of their considerable size.

Health and care It is important to avoid overexercising puppies of this breed because it can lead to joint problems later in life. Regular, relatively short spells of exercise are much better than more occasional long marathons. The coat needs little care, and it is remarkably damp-proof in wet weather. Older individuals are susceptible to bone tumours, known as osteosarcomas. These sometimes necessitate the amputation of the affected limb, but Irish Wolfhounds often adapt surprisingly well to this handicap.

As an owner You need to have plenty of space if you want to keep one of these giant dogs. They can be clumsy, so any delicate or valuable ornaments are best kept well out of reach – their long strong tails can easily sweep things off any low surface. Irish Wolfhounds are best accommodated with access to a secure paddock, where they can run around as they wish.

Also consider The Deerhound (*see page 71*) is the Irish Wolfhound's closest relative, but is slightly smaller overall. Another possibility, which may have played a crossbreeding part in the Irish Wolfhound's revival, is the Borzoi (*see pages 56–57*).

Tech Spec

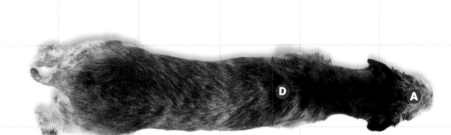

Features

A *Head:* Long and level, with a long and moderately pointed muzzle

B *Eyes:* Dark in colour

C *Ears:* Small and corresponding to those of a Greyhound in carriage

D *Chest:* Very deep and moderately broad

E *Tail:* Long, slightly curved and a medium thickness, with a good covering of hair

F *Bite:* Not specified

G *Height at shoulder:* Dogs 81–86cm (32–34 in); bitches 76cm (30 in) or more

H *Weight:* Dogs 54.5kg (120 lb); bitches 41kg (90 lb)

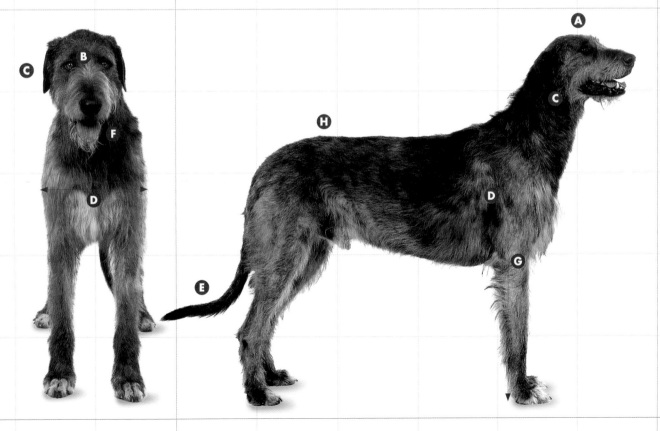

Norwegian Elkhound

Overview

Recognition
North America, Britain and
FCI member countries

Life expectancy
10–12 years

Colour
Shades of grey

Grooming

Feeding

Child friendliness

Exercise
Another breed with good
stamina

This Nordic hound is a very ancient breed, whose ancestors, based on archaeological evidence, have lived in Norway for about 7,000 years. Bred into a harsh environment, with bitterly cold winters, the Norwegian Elkhound has proved to be an adaptable dog, whose popularity has now become international.

Origin The Norwegian Elkhound is one of the oldest of all breeds and its precise origins are unknown. It may be the ancestor of all today's spitz breeds. It is believed that the way in which elkhounds and similar breeds curl their tails forwards over their backs was a trait deliberately encouraged by the early owners of such dogs, because it offered an easy means of distinguishing them from wolves at a distance – wolves keep their tails behind their bodies at all times.

Appearance The Norwegian Elkhound has upright, triangular ears and a foxlike face, in common with other spitz-type dogs. The dense coat, complete with an insulating under layer, provides excellent protection from the cold. It has a distinctive colour of a deep grey, usually darkest over the saddle area, with a lighter chest and mane of longer fur around the neck. The underparts are silvery, and the muzzle, ears and tip of the tail are black.

Personality A breed developed to work individually with people, the Norwegian Elkhound makes an intelligent companion. These dogs also possess great energy. They are loyal by nature and are good watchdogs at home.

Health and care Plenty of grooming is essential, especially in the spring when elkhounds moult much of their long, thick winter coat. The condition known as progressive retinal atrophy (PRA), which results in irreversible damage to the retina and, ultimately, blindness, is a problem in this breed. Check that breeding stock has been screened before acquiring a puppy.

As an owner Be prepared for a dog that must have plenty of exercise in the countryside, rather than sedate walks around a park. The Norwegian Elkhound also requires a good deal of grooming to look at its best. They are bold dogs – as their name suggests, they were originally bred to hunt elk (better known as moose in North America) – yet their intelligence and versatility ensure that they will learn quickly when trained.

Also consider The similar but rarer Black Elkhound – jet black in colour, with a shorter coat – is a lighter dog, typically weighing 18kg (40 lb). Other members of the spitz group, such as the German spitz breeds, afford further possibilities, particularly if you want a smaller dog.

Tech Spec

Features

A *Head:* Broad and wedge-shaped, with no folds of loose skin; the muzzle is broadest at its base and tapering

B *Eyes:* Oval, medium-sized and dark brown in colour, not protruding

C *Ears:* Set high on the head, erect, and firm but mobile

D *Chest:* Deep and relatively broad

E *Tail:* Tightly curled, set high and carried over the midline of the back

F *Bite:* Scissors bite

G *Height at shoulder:* Dogs 54.5cm (21½ in); bitches 49.5cm (19½ in)

H *Weight:* 25kg Dogs (55 lb); bitches 22kg (48 lb)

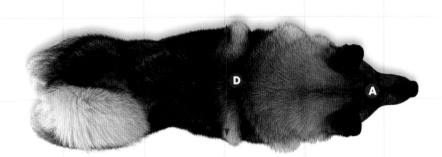

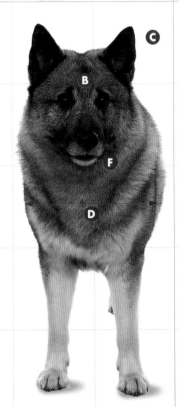

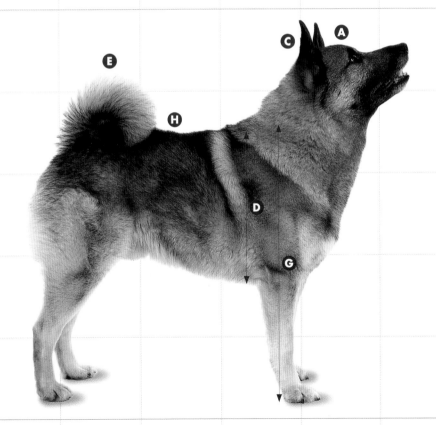

Rhodesian Ridgeback

Overview

Recognition
North America, Britain and
FCI member countries

Life expectancy
10–12 years

Colour
Wheaten-tan

Grooming

Feeding

Child friendliness

Exercise
Plenty required on a
daily basis

Most breeds of dog have been developed in the northern hemisphere, but the Rhodesian Ridgeback is an exception, having been bred originally in southern Africa, in the area that is now Zimbabwe. As its name suggests, it has a very distinctive ridge of hair running down its back.

Origin This breed was created by the early European settlers, using a combination of dogs brought from Europe crossed with an African breed they called the Hottentot Dog, named after the tribe that created it. Although the Hottentot Dog is now extinct, its most characteristic feature, the ridge of hair running down its back, lives on in the Rhodesian Ridgeback. This new breed was created to hunt lions, and it is sometimes also known as the African Lion Hound.

Appearance All Ridgebacks are a wheaten-tan colour, which varies in its depth – some dogs are darker than others. A small area of white on the chest, as well as on the toes, is permitted but not encouraged. The coat itself is very sleek and short. The ridge starts behind the shoulders and extends down to the hip bones. The whorls of fur, known as crowns, should be positioned directly opposite each other.

Personality Bold and fearless by nature, as befits a dog that was bred to hunt lions, the Rhodesian Ridgeback will display great stamina and must be given a lot of exercise.

Health and care There is a rare genetic weakness in Ridgebacks that occasionally causes the development of a cyst either in front of or behind the ridge. This is the result of a developmental abnormality, which is due to the failure of the skin to separate properly from the spinal cord during the puppy's development in its mother's womb, creating what is described as a dermoid sinus. Grooming the Rhodesian Ridgeback is straightforward – simple brushing is adequate. Not all dogs develop perfect ridges for show purposes, but non-show Ridgebacks are often good companion dogs.

As an owner Be prepared to take on a strong-willed dog that requires firm training from puppyhood to prevent behavioural problems from arising. Rhodesian Ridgebacks are fiercely protective of the family and property, and this characteristic needs to be harnessed with good, reliable responsiveness. They can also be aggressive towards other dogs unless carefully trained.

Also consider The Basenji (*see pages 48–49*), has similar colouring to the Rhodesian Ridgeback, and is also of African origin. It is smaller and in many ways an easier hound to manage.

Tech Spec

Features

A *Head:* Flat skull and broad between the ears, with a well-defined stop

B *Eyes:* Round in shape with an intelligent expression; reasonably spaced

C *Ears:* Medium-sized and set high; wide at the base and tapering to a rounded point

D *Chest:* Not especially wide but very deep

E *Tail:* Strong and tapering towards the tip, with a slight upward curve

F *Bite:* Scissors bite

G *Height at shoulder:* Dogs 63.5–68.5cm (25–27 in); bitches 61–66cm (24–26 in)

H *Weight:* 38.5kg Dogs (85 lb); bitches 32kg (70 lb)

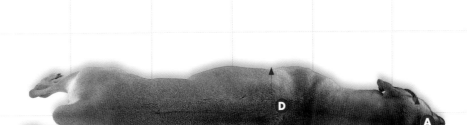

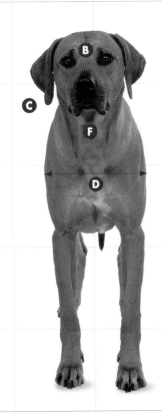

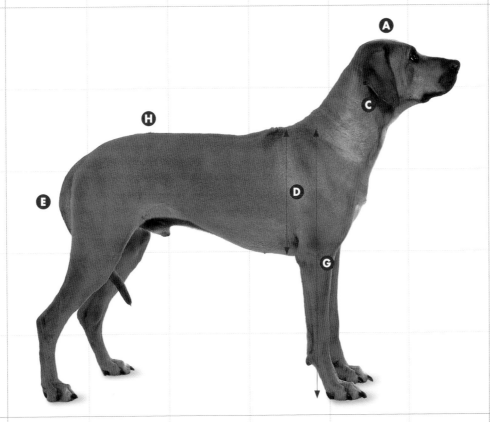

Whippet

Overview

Recognition
North America, Britain and
FCI member countries

Life expectancy
13–15 years

Colour
Any colour

Grooming

Feeding

Child friendliness

Exercise
Likes a good daily run

Often described as the poor man's racehorse, the Whippet was bred for its pace. These elegant small hounds are very fast, able to sprint at speeds of up to 56kph (35 mph) for short distances. Today, their responsiveness makes them an ideal choice for obedience competitions, while their natural athleticism means the breed often excels in more energetic activities, including fly ball and agility contests.

Origin Whippets were created in the north of England, and they obviously bear a clear resemblance to the Greyhound, which would have played a part in their ancestry. It is unclear exactly which other breeds were used to create the Whippet, but terriers – particularly Bedlingtons, which also originated in this part of the world – and some form of spaniel may have had an input.

Appearance Whippets look like a scaled-down Greyhound, with slender, deep-chested bodies and a so-called 'roach back' that curves down to the tail. Their coats are sleek, smooth and short. This helps to reinforce the well-muscled appearance of the breed, which is especially apparent over the hindquarters. The ears are small and are set well back on the head, which can be folded back slightly against the upper part of the neck. The eyes should be dark in colour, and the nose must always be black.

Personality Rather shy and sensitive, especially in unfamiliar situations, Whippets are very affectionate towards people they know well and are eager to please. They love playing games, and they make good retrievers when chasing after balls.

Health and care Whippets are low-maintenance dogs, with coats that need very little grooming to remain sleek. Nor are they greedy as far as food is concerned, so obesity does not spoil their athletic build. In male dogs, check that both testes descend into the scrotum, because Whippets can occasionally suffer from cryptorchidism, when one or both are retained within the body and have to be removed surgically.

As an owner Bear in mind that a Whippet will need space to run, ideally sometimes in open countryside, rather than just in an urban park. They may sometimes dig in the backyard at home, and you need to check that fences are both high and secure, because Whippets are also effective jumpers.

Also consider A Greyhound (see pages 60–61) may be suitable if you are looking for a larger hound of similar appearance, or, if you want a smaller dog, you might consider the diminutive Italian Greyhound (see pages 186–187). Some short-coated African sight hounds, such as the Sloughi or the Azawakh, may be other possibilities. Both are slightly taller and heavier than a Whippet.

Tech Spec

Features

A *Head:* Long and lean, broadest between the ears with little sign of a stop

B *Eyes:* Must be large, dark and of the same colour, with eyelids pigmented

C *Ears:* Small, rose ears, which are folded back along the neck when dog is resting

D *Chest:* Deep, reaching almost down to the elbow, with well-sprung ribs behind

E *Tail:* Not carried higher than top of the back, and normally kept low with an upward curve

F *Bite:* Scissors bite

G *Height at shoulder:* Dogs 48–56cm (19–22 in); bitches 45.5–53cm (18–21 in)

H *Weight:* Approximately (12.5kg (28 lb)

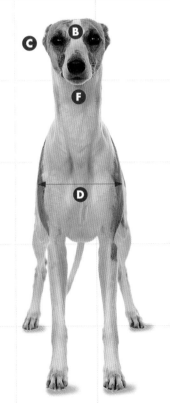

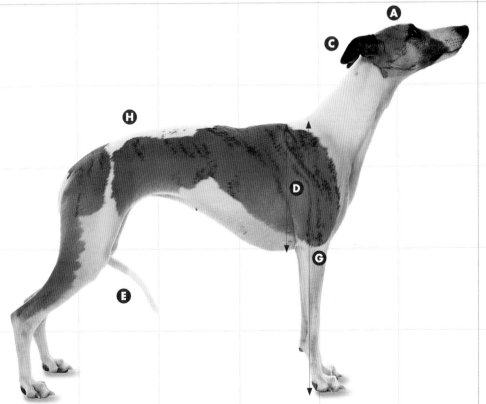

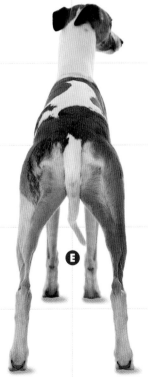

Pet Spec
Ibizan Hound

This is a breed of hound from the Mediterranean region, whose ancestors, like those of the Pharaoh Hound, probably originated from ancient Egypt. It is named after the island of Ibiza, where it has been developed to hunt rabbits and other small game by running them down at speeds equivalent to 64kph (40 mph). The Ibizan Hound is a friendly, enthusiastic breed, with a loyal nature. It was first seen in the United States in 1956.

Appearance Large erect ears are an indication that the Ibizan Hound hunts by sound as well as sight. This breed has long straight legs and powerful hindquarters. White areas are evident in its coat, distinguishing it from the Pharaoh Hound. Although most members of the breed have a smooth coat, wirehaired individuals crop up occasionally. Its glossy coat is especially noticeable in sunlight.

Breed care and health Unlike a number of hound breeds, the Ibizan can be trained easily, and it is a versatile companion that will adapt well to children. This is particularly essential, given the speed at which these hounds can run. Watch their weight, because they can be susceptible to becoming overweight. Male dogs are slightly larger in size.

As an owner Grooming is relatively simple, because its sleek coat is easy to keep in immaculate condition with the use of a hound glove, which helps to maintain its glossy appearance. The Ibizan Hound is a friendly and playful breed.

Also consider If you prefer a hound of roughly the same size, but with more white in its coat, then the Pharoah Hound (*see page 71*) will be ideal. The rare Sicilian Greyhound, also known as the Cirneco dell'Etna, is a smaller possibility, standing barely 51cm (20 in) tall and weighing 11.75kg (26 lb). All these breeds probably share a common ancestor and have since evolved in isolation on these different Mediterranean islands.

Height 59.75–69.75cm (23½–27½ in)
Weight 20.5–22.5kg (45–50 lb)
Exercise Must have a good daily run every day, for at least 30 minutes

Pet Spec
Otterhound

The Otterhound is a British breed with an ancestry extending back almost 1,000 years. It faced extinction when the hunting of otters was banned in the 20th century, but it has undergone something of a revival in numbers over recent years. Otterhounds were introduced to North America in about 1900. They are now featuring increasingly in obedience and agility competitions.

Appearance An unmistakeably tousled appearance is characteristic of the Otterhound. Its distinctive coat may measure up to 15cm (6 in) long over the back and has a water-repellent, oily quality. As further confirmation of its close ties with water, this breed also has webbed toes. They are powerful dogs, with a muscular physique and straight, strong forelegs.

Breed care and health It is normal for these hounds to display a shuffling gait – an economy of movement that helps them to cover miles without tiring noticeably. The only genetic problem associated with the breed is a rare blood-clotting disorder.

As an owner Remember that the Otterhound still has a close affiliation with water, and it will plunge readily into rivers and other stretches of water when out for a walk. Although they are strong swimmers, be careful that they do not run into problems as a result.

Also consider The Otterhound resembles a number of the rough-coated French hounds, such as the Griffon Vendéen group, which may have contributed to its development in the past. The Grand variety of the Griffon is closest to the Otterhound in size, although developed to hunt deer and wolves rather than otters. Another similar French hound is the Griffon Nivernais.

Height 58.5–68.5cm (23–27 in)
Weight 29.5–54.5kg (65–120 lb)
Exercise Not for the sedentary, this is a hound that needs plenty of exercise

Pet Spec
Petit Basset Griffon Vendéen

This is the smallest of the four Griffon Vendéen breeds, all of which originated centuries ago in the Vendée district of western France. This particular variety, often known simply as PBGV, was originally bred to hunt rabbits in packs. The breed has come to prominence outside France over recent years, and it is now the best-known member of this particular family.

Appearance Rough-coated, with long ears set low on the side of the head, below the level of the large eyes, these hounds have a straight back and a tapering tail that is often held upright. The forelegs are relatively straight, compared with those of most bassets. White areas are often prominent in the coat, helping these bassets to be seen in the field.

Breed care and health This is a breed that can be shown with the minimum of grooming – in spite of the presence of a short thick undercoat, its coat needs little attention. Bowing of the legs is a serious flaw. These bassets usually have a sound skeletal structure in spite of their short limbs.

As an owner PBGVs are naturally active, social dogs, bred to hunt in packs, and are better off being kept in the home in pairs, or even trios, rather than on their own.

Also consider You could choose one of the other members of this group – their size ranges from the Grand form, measuring some 66cm (26 in) at the shoulder, to the Grand Basset form, which is approximately 25.5cm (10 in) shorter. There are a number of other similar French hound breeds, too, among them the tawny-coloured Basset Fauve de Bretagne, which has a shorter but still hard-textured coat.

Height 33–38cm (13–15 in)
Weight 14–18kg (31–40 lb)
Exercise A breed that needs a good run off the lead

Pet Spec
Pharaoh Hound

Representative of a lineage shown in images in ancient Egyptian tombs and artifacts, the ancestors of today's Pharaoh Hound are believed to have been taken from their Egyptian homeland to the Mediterranean island of Malta by Phoenician traders, where they were used to hunt rabbits. It was not until 1967 that this breed was first seen in North America.

Appearance A long, lean face with distinctive amber eyes are characteristics of this breed. The ears are broad, erect, and flexible. The short, glossy coat is tan or chestnut. There may be a small area of white on the chest, called the 'star'. Additional white markings can often be seen on the feet, too, and on the tip of the tail, and there is a narrow white blaze between the eyes.

Breed care and health Lively and alert by nature, the Pharaoh Hound is amenable to training – and, given the speed at which these hounds can run, this is essential. They are susceptible to becoming overweight. Male dogs are slightly larger in size.

As an owner The sleek coat is easy to keep in immaculate condition with the use of a hound glove. The Pharaoh Hound is a friendly and playful breed and gets on well with children.

Also consider The Ibizan Hound (*see page 70*) is roughly the same size, but with more white in its coat. The rarer Sicilian Greyhound, also known as the Cirneco dell'Etna, is a smaller possibility, standing barely 20 in (50cm) tall and weighing 26 lb (12kg). All three breeds probably share a common ancestor, and each has since evolved in isolation on a different Mediterranean island.

Pet Spec
Saluki

This elegant and athletic sight hound is named after the city of Saluk, in the Yemen, and has evolved in an inhospitable, arid landscape. It has remained almost unchanged in appearance for over 5,000 years. The Saluki remained largely unknown in the West until 1895. Originally called the Persian Greyhound, the Saluki was bred to chase gazelles, regarded as the fastest of all antelopes.

Appearance The most common form of the Saluki seen today has long hair on its ears and tail and feathering on the back of the legs, although a rarer smooth-coated form also exists. They are bred in a range of pale colours, including white and cream, as well as in combinations, such as black and tan. The coat has a silky texture. The breed's elegant appearance is emphasized by its long, narrow head.

Breed care and health The Saluki is generally a fit, healthy breed. It has powerful feet with hair between the toes, which helps to cushion the dog from injury when running at speed. Grooming is straightforward, but the longer hair, especially on the ears, must be thoroughly combed.

As an owner You need to train diligently, and avoid exercising these hounds in the vicinity of cats or much smaller dogs. They have remarkable stamina when running and must be trained to return when called.

Also consider There are other sight hounds that have evolved in the Middle East and North Africa and have similar needs, although none displays the feathering that is a feature of the Saluki. They include the Sloughi, a slightly larger, heavier breed that is probably closely related to the Saluki, and the Azawakh, bred by the Tuareg tribespeople of Mali.

Pet Spec
Deerhound

These hounds became familiar from their constant appearance in paintings by the Victorian artist Landseer. Although originally bred to run down and overpower deer in the Scottish Highlands, today the Deerhound is kept mainly as a companion breed and for show purposes.

Appearance The long, wiry coat of the Deerhound affords good protection against the wet and often cold climate of Scotland. Its head is narrow, and the small ears are covered in short fur with a surprisingly soft texture. The tail is long, and hangs down almost to the ground. Dark blue-grey is the most popular colour, but there are also reddish variants.

Breed care and health Sound conformation, with broad, muscular hindquarters, is considered vital in this athletic breed. The coat must be harsh and never woolly, especially in show dogs, although the texture may be influenced in part by the local climate.

As an owner You must have sufficient space to care adequately for what is one of the largest of all breeds. Deerhounds are affectionate dogs and need companionship. They were bred to live with people, rather than in kennels with other dogs.

Also consider Bigger still, and heavier in build, is the Irish Wolfhound (*see pages 62–63*) – the two breeds share common ancestors. The Deerhound also shares ancestry with the smooth-coated Greyhound (*see pages 60–61*), and some Lurchers are hound-collie crosses derived from Deerhound stock. They tend to be dark in colour, and display many of the characteristics of the Deerhound, including its wiry coat.

Height 21–25 in (53–63.5cm)
Weight 45–55 lb (20.5–25kg)
Exercise Allow for a good run off the leash every day, for at least 30 minutes

Height 22–28 in (56–71cm)
Weight 44–66 lb (20–30kg)
Exercise Salukis must have daily runs in countryside, away from sheep and other livestock

Height 28–32 in (71–81cm)
Weight 75–110 lb (34–50kg)
Exercise Do not overexercise young dogs, because this can lead to joint problems later

Boston Terrier

Overview

Recognition
North America, Britain and
FCI member countries

Life expectancy
9–11 years

Colour
Black, brindle or seal (black
with red highlights), with
white markings

Grooming

Feeding

Child friendliness

Exercise
Active by nature; needs
good daily walks

A solid, dependable breed, the Boston Terrier gives the impression of being a larger dog, although it has been markedly scaled down in size from its early days. It has a gentle, appealing expression, which has undoubtedly contributed to its popularity, particularly in North America, where the breed was developed.

Origin The breed's founder was a dog named Judge, bred in the English port of Liverpool, which was taken to Boston by ship in the early 1870s. He was the result of a cross between an English Bulldog and an English White Terrier. Other breeds that later contributed to the Boston Terrier's development included the Boxer and the Bull Terrier. Initially, the new breed was used in dog fights, but it entered the show ring in the 1890s. By the 1950s, it had become the most popular breed in North America.

Appearance The broad square head is free of wrinkles and is topped with prominent upright ears located at the corners of the skull. The traditional colouring is brindle and white, mirroring that of Judge, the breed's founder, although a wider range of colours is now accepted. Boston Terriers have a compact appearance with strong limbs and move in a straight, sure-footed way.

Personality In spite of its combative origin, the Boston Terrier today is not an aggressive breed in the company of other dogs, although it still creates a powerful impression. It is an intelligent, responsive breed and makes an excellent companion.

Health and care The sleek short coat of the Boston Terrier is easy to keep in good condition. The large head can cause difficulties when bitches are whelping. Puppies become trapped in the birth canal, with the result that litters have to be born by Caesarean section. Boston Terriers can develop other hereditary health problems, including cleft palates or lips, and various heart defects.

As an owner Make sure that your puppy is checked out at an early stage by a vet to ensure that it has no underlying medical problems. Think carefully before breeding from a bitch because of the risk and considerable expense attached to a caesarean birth. Try to discourage your pet from plunging into the undergrowth, because it can easily injure its thin ears or its prominent eyes here.

Also consider The French Bulldog (*see pages 82–83*) is a smaller dog with a stockier build, which, despite its name, was developed largely in North America. It has bat ears, which are upright, but not as tall as those of the Boston Terrier. French Bulldogs stand about 30.5cm (12 in) tall and have been bred in similar colours to the Boston Terrier. If you want a larger dog, the Boxer (*see pages 220–221*) may be worth considering, too.

Tech Spec

Features

A *Head:* Square in shape, with a flat top and a well-defined stop; short square muzzle

B *Eyes:* Large and round, with outer edges aligned with the cheeks

C *Ears:* Small, erect, and located close to the edge of the skull

D *Chest:* Wide and deep, with well-sprung ribs behind

E *Tail:* Short, set low and tapered, not extending above the horizontal

F *Bite:* Undershot bite

G *Height at shoulder:* 38–43cm (15–17 in)

H *Weight:* Categories extend from under 7kg (15 lb) to over 11.5kg (25 lb)

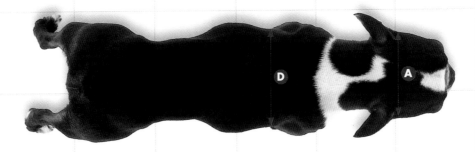

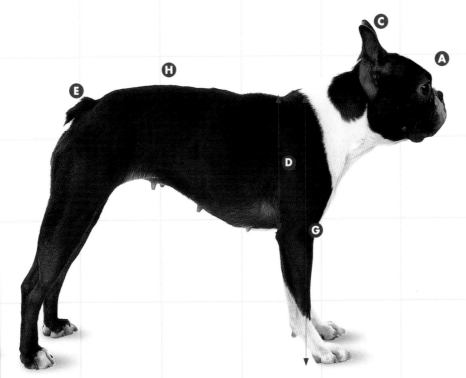

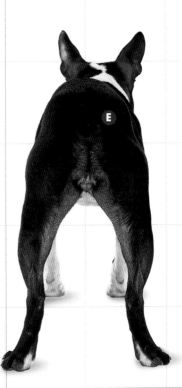

Bulldog

Overview

Recognition
North America, Britain and
FCI member countries

Life expectancy
8–10 years

Colour
Brindle, piebald, white,
red, fawn and fallow

Grooming

Feeding

Child friendliness

Exercise
Bulldogs like slow, ambling
walks, but they must be
given careful and regular
exercise

This is a breed that has changed dramatically in appearance over the course of the past century. It used to be much taller than it is today, and contemporary illustrations suggest that Bulldogs resembled Boxers much more closely 100 years ago. Today, they are popular companions, with a distinctive appearance and a characteristic rolling gait.

Origin Bulldogs were originally bred to take part in bull-baiting contests, which called for fearlessness, stamina and agility. They had to leap up onto the bull's head, and cling on with their strong jaws. When bull-baiting was banned in 1835, efforts were made to transform these dogs into companions, and the Bulldog was one of the first breeds to be recognized for show purposes. It subsequently shrank significantly in stature, and unfortunately has also become one of the weaker members of the purebred dog breeds.

Appearance A broad, massive head with an upturned nose and strong jaws are features clearly recalling the breed's past. The forehead and sides of the face are wrinkled, and the dog has dewlaps, a folded area of skin, beneath the lower jaw. The ears are small and located well back on the sides of the head. The legs are powerful, short and bowed, and the shoulders are bulky. The coat is smooth and glossy, with a fine texture, emphasizing the breed's profile.

Personality Today's Bulldog is a placid breed, with a dignified bearing. It is stoic, too, as its appearance suggests, and it is a loyal and affectionate pet. This dog does not require a great deal of space, and will get along well with others.

Health and care Because Bulldogs have a number of congenital problems, check the breeding stock carefully before acquiring a puppy and take your dog to the vet soon after bringing it home. Congenital heart and spine problems are not uncommon. Bitches frequently have difficulty giving birth and require an emergency Caesarean section, because of the size of the puppy's head.

As an owner Look out for eye irritations and also watch for any signs of infections in the folds of skin on the Bulldog's face. Breeders are working to eliminate problems as much as possible, partly by adjustments to the breed standard, but it will take time to establish problem-free stock. Avoid exercising a Bulldog in hot weather; the breed is prone to heatstroke, and this could have serious consequences if your dog has a weak heart.

Also consider The Boxer (*see pages 220–221*) may be an option. In North America, too, there are a number of other taller, powerful breeds with healthier conformation, descended from old Bulldog stock. They often have localized names – the Arkansas Giant Bulldog is just one example – but they may not be as friendly as the Bulldog, because many have a dogfighting ancestry.

Tech Spec

Features

A *Head:* Exceedingly large, with well-rounded cheeks and a short, upturned muzzle

B *Eyes:* Set low, round and moderate-sized; confined within the cheeks from the front

C *Ears:* Set high on the skull, as far from the eyes as possible; rose-eared in appearance, showing some of the inner surface

D *Chest:* Deep and broad

E *Tail:* Short, tapering and hanging low

F *Bite:* Undershot bite

G *Height at shoulder:* 30.5–35.5cm (12–14 in)

H *Weight:* Dogs 22.5kg (50 lb); bitches 18kg (40 lb)

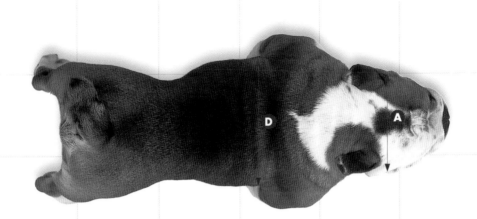

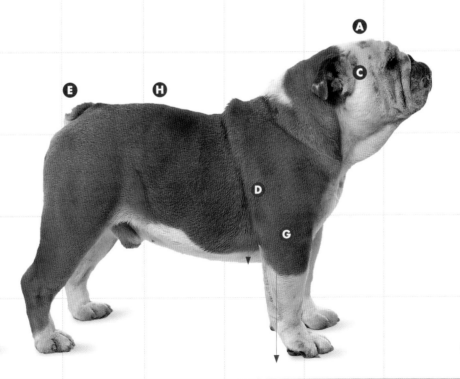

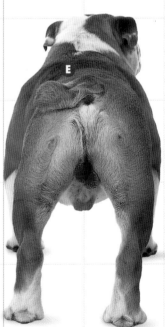

Shar-Pei

Overview

Recognition
North America, Britain and
FCI member countries

Life expectancy
10–12 years

Colour
Any solid colour apart from
albino is acceptable

Grooming

Feeding

Child friendliness

Exercise
This energetic breed needs
a good daily walk

The survival of the Shar-Pei and its widespread international popularity today are the results of the efforts of a single Hong Kong dog fancier. In the 1970s he wrote an article about the plight of this ancient Asian breed, when it had almost died out. As a result, some American enthusiasts imported stock to save the Shar-pei from extinction.

Origin This is an extremely old breed, developed in southern China from the Han Dog, which was also an ancestor of the Chow Chow (see pages 78–79). It was originally used for dogfighting, but it was no match for breeds that were obtained from Europe for this purpose in the 19th century. The Shar-pei started to fall out of fashion, and the breed suffered further under Communist rule in China, when pet dogs were perceived as symbols of Western decadence.

Appearance Puppies have deep, loose folds of skin on their bodies, which become less conspicuous – although they remain a characteristic feature – as the dog literally grows into its skin The skin itself is pliable, so it would have been difficult for a rival dog to gain a grip on the Shar-pei in a fight. The breed's name means 'sandpaper-like coat', describing its rough, bristly texture. Another highly unusual feature of the Shar-Pei is its blue tongue.

Personality A bold, fearless breed, the Shar-pei displayed aggression towards other dogs when it first became known in the West, but this undesirable characteristic has been reduced by careful breeding.

Health and care At one point the Shar-pei was regarded as the rarest breed of dog in the world, reduced to a total of fewer than 60 individuals, so today's stock is built on a small gene pool. Excessive folds of skin can lead to localized infections, particularly during periods of hot weather. Problems affecting the eyes, again because of the folds of skin around them, can also arise.

As an owner It is usual for the length of the coat to vary markedly in this breed – short-coated Shar-peis are described as having horse coats, while those with coats about 2.5cm (1 in) in length are said to have brush coats. Shar-peis need training from puppyhood, because they can easily develop a dominant nature.

Also consider The Chow Chow (see pages 78–79) has some historical links with the Shar-pei, but is different in appearance, lacking the so-called 'hippopotamus' muzzle of this breed. Since the Shar-pei became known in the West, some American breeders have tried to create a miniature form, not exceeding 40.5cm (16 in) tall. It is unlikely, however, that one of these miniature puppies will be easy to obtain yet, although their numbers are beginning to increase.

Tech Spec

Features

A *Head:* Large, with a distinctively broad muzzle; a broad skull, which is flat on top with an evident stop

B *Eyes:* Small, sunken and almond-shaped

C *Ears:* Set high, widely spaced and usually lie flat, although they can be moved

D *Chest:* Deep and broad, with the brisket reaching to the elbow

E *Tail:* Set high on the back, round at the base and tapering to a point; curled over or to the side of the back

F *Bite:* Scissors bite

G *Height at shoulder:* 45.5–51cm (18–20 in)

H *Weight:* 20.5–27kg (45–60 lb)

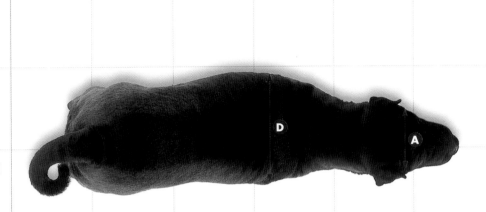

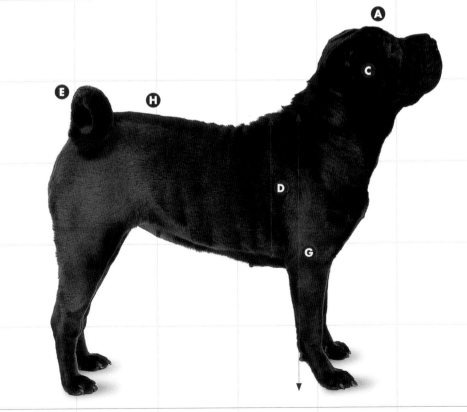

Overview

Recognition
North America, Britain and FCI member countries

Life expectancy
11–13 years

Colour
Cream, red, cinnamon, blue or black, sometimes with lighter shading on the ruff, tail and feathering

Grooming
(depending on coat type)

Feeding

Child friendliness

Exercise
This is a breed that will need a good daily walk

The unusual name of this breed is a source of controversy. It may be derived from a Chinese term for ship's cargo, reflecting how these dogs were first brought to the West in 1780, or it may come from the Cantonese word *chow***, meaning 'edible'. What is certain is that the Chow Chow was bred in China in the past for food.**

Origin Descended from the Han Dog, which was known over 2,000 years ago, the Chow Chow then seems to have split off into a separate lineage from the Shar-pei, and was kept primarily, but not exclusively, to be eaten. Young puppies were carefully reared as food on a diet of grain The breed seems to have performed a number of other utilitarian tasks, too: there are records of Chow Chows being used to pull carts and act as guard dogs. One Emperor of China kept 5,000 Chow Chows to serve as hunting companions.

Appearance The ruff of longer fur around the head of the Chow Chow has been likened to a lion's mane and is a distinctive feature of the breed. There are two recognizable coat types and the mane is seen only in the rough-coated form. The Chow Chow is a stoutly built, muscular breed, with relatively small ears and a bushy tail that curls over the back.

Personality The Chow Chow is highly intelligent and is far less instinctively playful than many breeds. It does not take readily to strangers and is aloof and reserved.

Health and care Some Chow Chows are born with tails that are significantly shorter than normal, and this precludes them from competing at shows, although they are suitable companion dogs. This breed also has a tendency to develop problems affecting the eyelids, including entropion and additional rows of eyelashes. Both these problems are likely to require surgery.

As an owner The Chow Chow is one of the hardest breeds to train successfully, displaying a strong independent streak. It needs someone with the inclination and energy to give it a lot of time. If you are not particularly enthusiastic about grooming, opt for the smooth-coated variety. Chow Chows have deep-set eyes that limit their peripheral vision, so may prove nervous if approached from the side.

Also consider The Shar-pei (*see pages 76–77*), which is related to the Chow Chow, may appeal to you. Other possibilities, particularly if you like the long-coated form of the Chow Chow, include the larger spitz breeds, such as the Samoyed (*see pages 244–245*), while the Akita, a shorter-coated option from Japan (*see pages 212–213*), has a similar presence.

Tech Spec

Features

A *Head:* Broad skull and a short but broad muzzle, with a moderate stop between them

B *Eyes:* Deep-set, widely spaced and obliquely positioned; dark brown

C *Ears:* Triangular, with slightly rounded tips; erect, but tilting slightly forwards

D *Chest:* Deep, muscular and broad

E *Tail:* Set high on the back and carried low over the back

F *Bite:* Scissors bite

G *Height at shoulder:* 45.5–56cm (18–22 in)

H *Weight:* 22.5–32kg (50–70 lb)

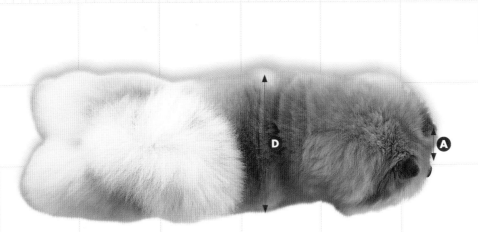

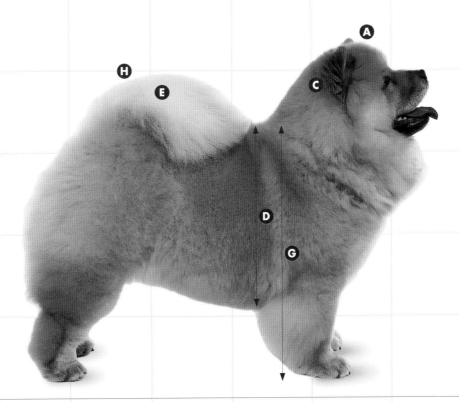

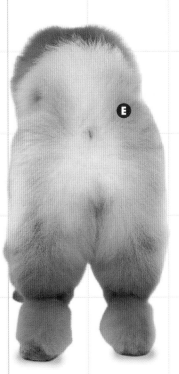

Dalmatian

Overview

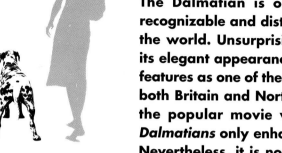

Recognition
North America, Britain and
FCI member countries

Life expectancy
12–14 years

Colour
Acceptable colourings are
white with liver spotting,
and white with black
spotting; tricoloured dogs
with both black and liver
spotting are rare and
cannot be shown

Grooming

Feeding

Child friendliness

Exercise
Plenty of daily exercise
is required

The Dalmatian is one of the most recognizable and distinctive breeds in the world. Unsurprisingly, in view of its elegant appearance, it consistently features as one of the top 30 breeds in both Britain and North America, with the popular movie versions of *101 Dalmatians* only enhancing its image. Nevertheless, it is not a breed that is suited to urban living today.

Origin The breed's precise origins are a mystery, although it is believed to be named after Dalmatia, on the coast of the Adriatic. It first became known in Britain as a carriage dog, running alongside the horse-drawn conveyances of the aristocracy, possibly as a deterrent against attacks by highwaymen. In the 19th century, American fire departments used this breed to help control the horses that pulled fire appliances through the busy city streets.

Appearance The most evident feature of the Dalmatian is its spotted coat. The spots are random and enable individual dogs to be told apart easily. In a show dog the spots should be round, can vary in size from a 5p coin up to a 10p, and should be smaller on the head, legs and tail. They must be evenly distributed and ideally should not overlap at all.

Personality Friendly, energetic and tolerant, the Dalmatian is not a shy breed, but its size and exuberance mean that it is not the best choice as a pet in a home alongside young children.

Health and care This breed may develop a number of hereditary conditions. The Dalmatian can be susceptible to the formation of stones in its urinary tract, which are both painful and potentially dangerous. Deafness is not unknown among puppies. The breed can also develop dermatitis, which may cause the dog to scratch and nibble constantly at its skin All of these conditions should be given prompt veterinary attention.

As an owner Dalmatian puppies are white at birth and only develop their spots as they mature. The breed is athletic and makes a great running or jogging companion. Be aware that puppies should not be encouraged to run too far when young.

Also consider If you feel the Dalmatian is too large for your home, but would like an alternative breed with a highly distinctive appearance, consider the Finnish Spitz (*see page 99*) – although these dogs do need a considerable amount of grooming. Another possibility is the Weimaraner (*see pages 130–131*), which has a similarly sleek appearance to that of the Dalmatian.

Tech Spec

Features

A *Head:* Fair length; no loose skin

B *Eyes:* Medium-sized, rounded, brown or blue, set deep in the skull

C *Ears:* High, tapering

D *Chest:* Deep in proportion to its width, but not barrel-shaped

E *Tail:* Long and tapered, reaching the hock

F *Bite:* Scissors bite

G *Height at shoulder:* 48–58.5cm (19–23 in)

H *Weight:* 22.5–25kg (50–55 lb)

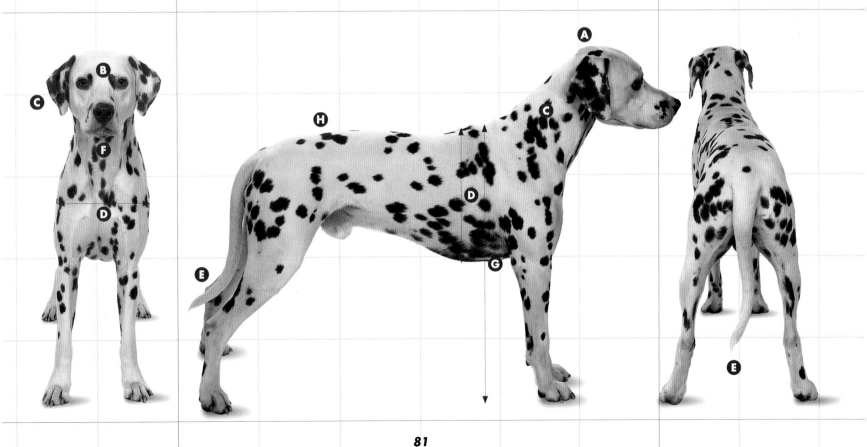

81

French Bulldog

Overview

Recognition
North America, Britain and
FCI member countries

Life expectancy
10–12 years

Colour
Most colours are
acceptable, apart from
solid black, including liver,
mouse, and black-and-tan
and black-and-white
combinations

Grooming

Feeding

Child friendliness

Exercise
A modest daily walk in
a park will suffice

These lively and popular small dogs are easily recognized by their characteristic batlike ears. In the late 19th century breeders debated whether folded ears, more like those of the Bulldog, should be preferred, but American fanciers of the breed persisted, and the distinctive upright ears are now part of the standard.

Origin In the mid-19th century, a Toy Bulldog breed was developed in the industrial towns of England. It seems likely that this dog was taken to northern France by lacemakers when they took their trade there, and it was in France that the breed was further developed by crossings with terriers that resulted in the breed's pricked ears. The French Bulldog gradually became a fashionable pet in Paris, and it soon gained an international following, notably in North America.

Appearance The top of the skull is flat and the forehead slightly rounded. The raised ears are positioned at a high point on the head. The chest is broad and, despite the dog's small size, the dog is well-muscled with straight forelegs. The tail is short and may have a slightly screwed appearance, but it is not actually curly.

Personality Active, friendly and easily trained, the French Bulldog makes an excellent companion dog. Known affectionately as a 'Frenchie', this dog makes an alert guard dog, but is not noisy or excitable by nature.

Health and care Grooming is straightforward, thanks to the breed's short, smooth coat. French Bulldogs are sometimes born with a malformation of the spinal vertebrae, which is not always immediately apparent, but which may lead to other problems. This breed occasionally develops haemophilia, an inherited disorder of the blood. It is wise to check the health of the breeding stock with your breeder before you buy a puppy.

As an owner This breed has much in its favour if you are looking for a personable pet that will be happy. It will also be equally contented living in a family with children or with a single owner. Like other breeds with large square heads, French Bulldogs sometimes have difficulty in giving birth naturally and may need a Caesarean birth, so take this into consideration if you are thinking of breeding from your French Bulldog.

Also consider The Bulldog (*see pages 74–75*) may be an option if you would prefer a larger dog. If the prick ears particularly appeal to you, the Boston Terrier (*see pages 72–73*) is an obvious alternative candidate – it is also slightly taller and less stocky in build, but it is bred in fewer colours than the French Bulldog.

Tech Spec

Features

A *Head:* Skull flat between the ears, with a well-defined stop; a deep broad muzzle

B *Eyes:* Widely spaced, round and medium-sized, set away from the ears

C *Ears:* Distinctive bat-eared appearance, set high; broad at the base, with round tips

D *Chest:* Deep and broad

E *Tail:* Set low and tapered along its short length; may be either straight or screwed

F *Bite:* Scissors bite

G *Height at shoulder:* 30.5cm (12 in)

H *Weight:* Up to 12.5kg (28 lb)

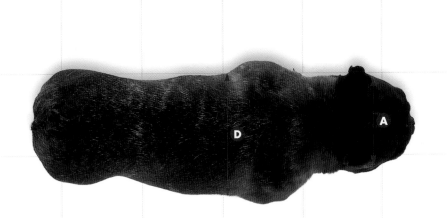

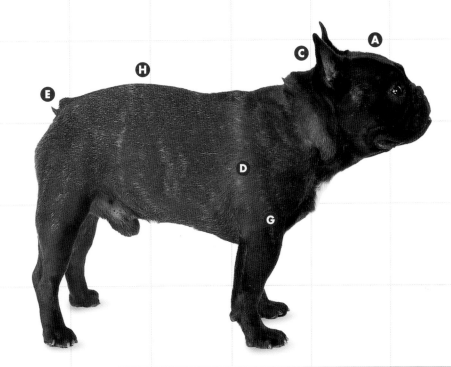

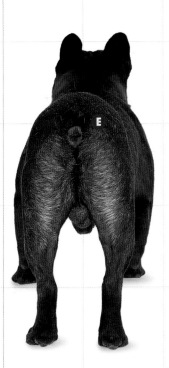

Keeshond

Overview

Recognition
North America, Britain and
FCI member countries

Life expectancy
10–12 years

Colour
A shaded mix of grey,
black and cream

Grooming

Feeding

Child friendliness

Exercise
A good daily walk is
essential

This breed has become recognized as the national breed of Holland. In the past it was a common sight on the canal barges there, guarding their cargo, and it is sometimes still known as the Dutch Barge Dog. Its name is pronounced as 'kays-hawnd', and the plural form is Keeshonden.

Origin The Keeshond probably gained its name from the nickname – Kees – of Cornelis de Gyselaer, the leader of an uprising in Holland against the established Royal House of Orange. De Gyselaer used his dog as his party's symbol and the breed fell out of favour for a period after the revolt was crushed. It survived as a working dog, but had largely ceased to be used by the end of the 19th century, switching to the show arena soon afterwards.

Appearance The Keeshond shows the characteristic features of a spitz breed, although its precise ancestry is unknown. It has a distinctive wolflike shaded colouring. The narrow muzzle is covered with relatively short hair, and the ears are pricked, giving an impression of alertness. The coat stands up, away from the body, and there is a paler ruff of long fur around the neck.

Personality Intelligent and watchful, the Keeshond makes a loyal companion, although it can be noisy and energetic, requiring regular exercise. These are wholeheartedly friendly dogs towards those they know well, settling down happily in the home.

Health and care Heart defects, especially those affecting the mitral valve, can be a congenital weakness in some Keeshonden, and a new puppy should be checked thoroughly by a vet. Another inherited trait associated with the breed is epilepsy, which may not develop until the dog is over 3 years old. Ongoing medication is usually required to treat it. Ask your breeder about the health of their breeding stock before buying a puppy.

As an owner This is a breed that needs regular grooming to maintain its attractive appearance, particularly in the spring when the thicker winter coat is shed. If you like the ruff, choose a male puppy – he will develop a more evident mane than a female. The characteristic shaded markings in the coat are also less apparent in a puppy, but develop as the dog matures.

Also consider The German spitz breeds exist in various sizes and may be possible alternatives. The largest form, the Giant German Spitz, is slightly smaller than the Keeshond, but is bred in a wider range of colours. If you would like a larger breed of similar appearance, the white-coated Samoyed (see pages 244–245) may be a good choice.

Tech Spec

Features

A *Head:* Well-proportioned and wedge-shaped from above, with an evident stop; medium-length muzzle

B *Eyes:* Almond-shaped, set obliquely, and dark brown with black rims

C *Ears:* Erect, set high and triangular in shape

D *Chest:* Strong deep chest

E *Tail:* Curled up and over the back

F *Bite:* Scissors bite

G *Height at shoulder:* Dogs 45.5cm (18 in); bitches 43cm (17 in)

H *Weight:* 25–30kg (55–66 lb)

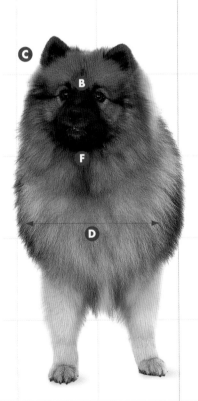

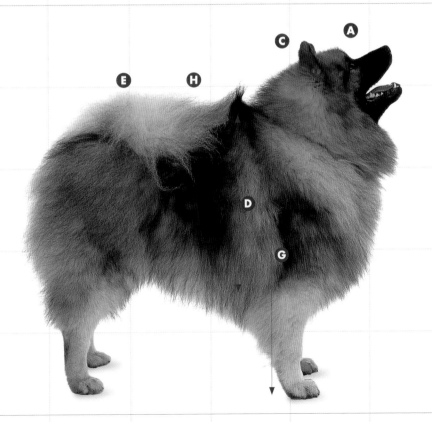

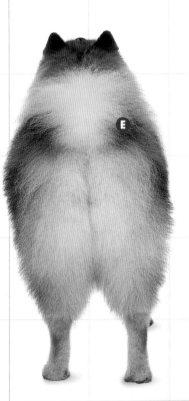

Lhasa Apso

Overview

Recognition
North America, Britain and
FCI member countries

Life expectancy
11–13 years

Colour
Any colour; may have dark
tips to the beard and ears

Grooming

Feeding

Child friendliness

Exercise
A reasonable daily walk
will be needed

This dog originated in one of the remotest areas in the world, where it was kept in isolation for thousands of years. In its Tibetan homeland, the Lhasa Apso's name translates roughly as 'hairy lion dog', referring both to its profuse coat and its distinctive character. It has now become a very popular companion breed.

Origin It is believed that the Lhasa Apso dog was bred by monks from small Tibetan Terriers. There was a belief that these small dogs were repositories for the souls of dead monks, and so they were viewed as sacred, given only occasionally to outsiders as gifts. Some reached England in the early 20th century, and the first examples seen in North America were presented as a gift by the Dalai Lama in 1933.

Appearance The Lhasa Apso's appearance has been shaped over the centuries by the landscape in which it evolved. Its long body allows it a good lung capacity, which is vital in the thin mountain air, and the dense coat offers good protection against the bitter cold of the night in this region. The thick covering of fur on its pads protects against rough, stony ground.

Personality The Lhasa Apso makes a good pet – quiet and measured in its responses, it can also be playful. On the other hand, these dogs have a stubborn side and will show a strong protective streak.

Health and care Inguinal hernias are common in Lhasa Apsos, and usually require surgical correction. Occasionally, puppies suffer from a brain disorder known as lissencephaly, which causes them to lose coordination. This disorder is most likely to occur in a bloodline with a history of the problem.

As an owner This small breed matures slowly, and young dogs do not show at their best until they are around 4 years old. These dogs need careful and diligent grooming; the long coat is usually parted down the middle of the back and combed smoothly down to the ground. The tail is sometimes slightly kinked under its long covering of hair, and this particular characteristic was traditionally believed to bring good luck.

Also consider Other similar breeds from the region share some of the same qualities as the Lhasa Apso. The Tibetan Terrier (*see pages 96–97*), which has a less profuse coat, and the Tibetan Spaniel (*see pages 94–95*) may both be considered as alternative choices. The Pekingese (*see pages 198–199*) is another possibility, as is the Kyi Leo, a modern breed from California that was created in 1972 and is descended from crossings between Lhasa Apsos and Maltese dogs.

Tech Spec

Features

A *Head:* Relatively narrow skull, with a medium-length muzzle and a medium stop

B *Eyes:* Medium-sized; not prominent or sunken into the skull

C *Ears:* Hang down over the sides of the face, with long feathering

D *Chest:* Medium, but with good rib cage

E *Tail:* Screw-shaped, carried up over the back and well-feathered

F *Bite:* Level or slightly undershot bite

G *Height at shoulder:* Dogs 25.5–28cm (10–11 in); bitches 23–25.5cm (9–10 in)

H *Weight:* 6–7kg (13–15 lb)

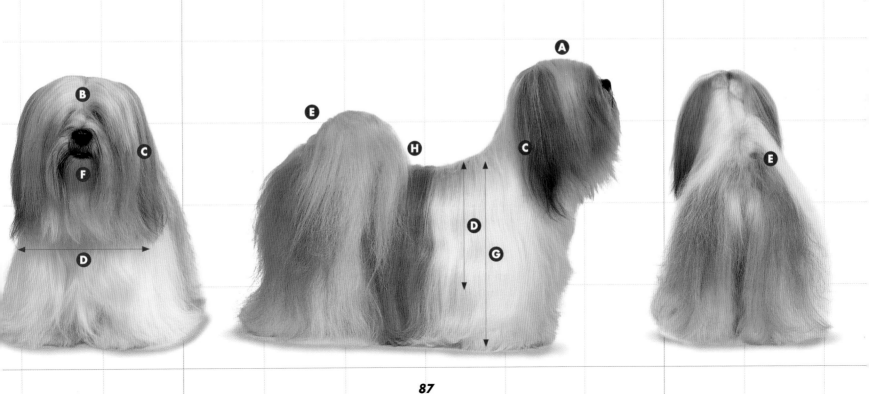

Schipperke

Overview

Recognition
North America, Britain and
FCI member countries

Life expectancy
13–16 years

Colour
Black

Grooming

Feeding

Child friendliness

Exercise
This lively dog needs
a good daily walk

This breed used to be a common sight on the canals of Flanders, often being seen on the barges plying their trade, acting as a watchdog on board, just like the Keeshond (see pages 84–85) in Holland. The name of the Schipperke should be pronounced 'sheep-er-ker', almost without sounding the final 'r'.

Origin The background of the Schipperke is a mystery. Its appearance suggests that it is descended from spitz-type stock, but it could be a scaled-down form of the Belgian breed of sheepdog called the Leauvenaar, which is now extinct. Schipperkes took part in probably the first-ever dog show back in 1690, at the Grand Palace of Brussels, wearing distinctive custom-made hammered brass collars, which traditionally they still wear today. The breed was first seen in North America in 1888.

Appearance Colouration is a distinctive feature of the Schipperke. These dogs are black in colour, with the undercoat often being slightly paler, although older individuals over 7 years old frequently turn grey around the muzzle. Their small oval eyes are brown, with their ears also being small and triangular in shape. This breed is often naturally tail-less, a feature that emphasizes its square profile.

Personality Lively, with an innate curiosity, the Schipperke also acts as an alert guard dog, barking without any hesitation at the approach of strangers. Outdoors, these dogs will also often display terrier-like ratting skills if they have an opportunity.

Health and care The Schipperke is a hardy breed, in spite of its relatively small size. The dense undercoat provides good insulation against the elements, and even if the coat becomes wet, water runs off readily, rather than penetrating down to the skin For show purposes, the quality of the coat is an important feature, and there must be clear differentiation between the two layers. Some Schipperkes may be born with a tail, which if not docked will be carried below the level of the body.

As an owner Be prepared for relatively long walks, because the Schipperke is a breed that possesses plenty of energy and thrives on exercise. This characteristic and its loyal nature makes it a good choice for a home alongside children, and it often forms a particularly strong bond with them. It also has a reputation for being a relatively long-lived breed, with individuals commonly living into their mid-teens.

Also consider The Keeshond (see pages 84–85) has a corresponding background but a slightly larger build. There is a similar Japanese breed called the Kai Dog, first brought to North America in 1951. It stands up to 58.5cm (23 in) tall, with the coat being shorter than that of the Schipperke. Puppies of this breed are all black at birth, with some ultimately becoming brindle.

Tech Spec

Features

A *Head:* Medium-width and tapering along the muzzle, which is slightly shorter than the skull, with an obvious stop

B *Eyes:* Dark brown, small, oval-shaped; directed forwards

C *Ears:* Small and triangular; set high and held erect

D *Chest:* Deep and broad

E *Tail:* May be born tail-less

F *Bite:* Scissors or level bite

G *Height at shoulder:* Dogs 28–33cm (11–13 in); bitches 25.5–30.5cm (10–12 in)

H *Weight:* 5.5–7kg (12–16 lb)

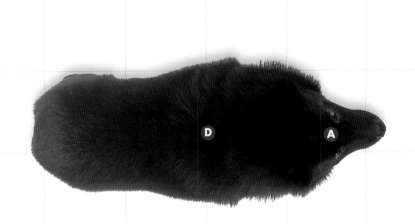

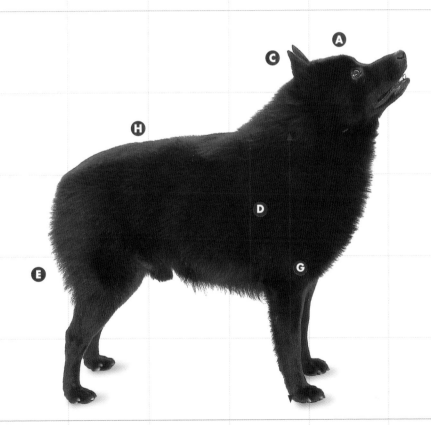

Overview

Recognition
North America, Britain and
FCI member countries

Life expectancy
11–13 years

Colour
Based on red, black, and
sesame, which has red
undercoat and black tips to
the fur, with a paler
undercoat and markings

Grooming

Feeding

Child friendliness

Exercise
A good period of daily
exercise is required

This breed is the most common native Japanese breed in its homeland. It is sometimes also known as the Brushwood Dog, based on the terrain in which it has traditionally worked, where it was used to hunt game birds. Today, however, it has become popular simply as a companion, and it is now seen frequently abroad as well.

Origin The ancestors of the Shiba Inu have been present in Japan for over 2,500 years. They developed their unmistakable spitz appearance following crosses with imported dogs around AD 200, and since then the breed has changed remarkably little in appearance. Their breeding was being actively encouraged by a special dogkeeper's office, which was set up around AD 600. However, numbers fell dramatically in the 1920s, as foreign breeds became popular.

Appearance The Shiba Inu ranks as the smallest of all Japan's native breeds, with its name actually meaning 'small dog'. It has an alert appearance, thanks to its triangular-shaped ears, which tilt forwards, and a kindly expression, due in part to its deep-set brown eyes. The coat is short, with a harsh topcoat above a soft, dense undercoat, which provides good insulation. The hair is longest on the curved tail.

Personality Highly alert and intelligent, the Shiba Inu makes a good companion, which helps to explain its rapidly increasing international popularity. It is a breed that has a long history of working alongside people, and it is responsive as a result.

Health and care The breed is generally healthy, but as with all dogs, it is important to keep their vaccinations up to date. The Shibu Inu may perhaps be more susceptible than many dogs to the distemper virus. Certainly, this infection almost wiped out the breed in its homeland after the end of World War II in 1945. Today's Shiba Inus are descended predominantly from the Shinshu bloodline as a consequence, with the Sanin and Mino Shiba lines having been largely decimated.

As an owner Be aware of the fact that these dogs have a strange call, more like a shriek than a conventional bark. There is also a slight difference in size between males and females, as occurs in larger spitz breeds, with males being bigger overall. They need to be adequately trained, since they do still retain an instinctive desire to hunt. A Shiba Inu will also be protective at home, proving to be a good watchdog.

Also consider The Akita (*see pages 212–213*) is a possibility if you are seeking a larger breed. These strong hunting dogs also originate from Japan. Less well-known internationally, being intermediate in size between these breeds, is the Ainu, also known as the Hokkaido Dog, based on the region of Japan where it was bred. It stands up to 56cm (22 in) tall at the shoulder.

Tech Spec

Features

A *Head:* Skull has a broad forehead and moderate stop, with a round, slightly tapering muzzle with a straight bridge

B *Eyes:* Deep-set, dark and triangular, slanting upwards towards the base of the ears

C *Ears:* Well-spaced, small, pricked, and triangular in shape, tilting forwards

D *Chest:* Deep

E *Tail:* Carried upward, over the back, either curled or sickle-shaped

F *Bite:* Scissors bite

G *Height at shoulder:* Dogs 37–42cm (14½–16½ in); bitches 34–39cm (13½–15½ in)

H *Weight:* Dogs 10.5kg (23 lb); bitches 7.75kg (17 lb)

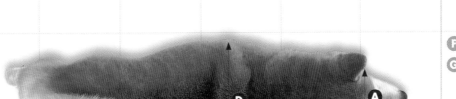

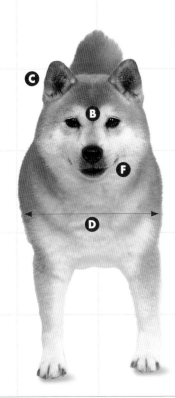

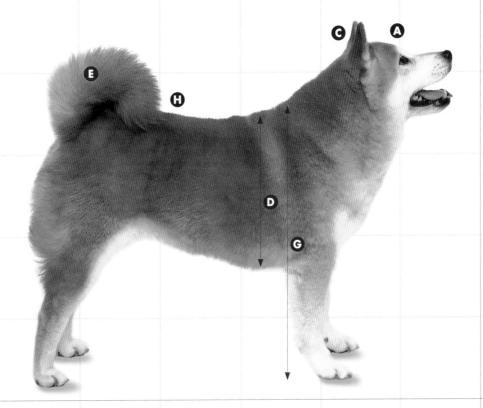

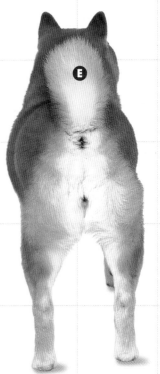

Standard Poodle

Overview

Recognition
North America, Britain and FCI member countries

Life expectancy
11–13 years

Colour
Solid colours, ranging from white to cream and apricot, to blue and black

Grooming

Feeding

Child friendliness ??

Exercise
This is a lively breed that needs a good daily walk

Poodles are now bred in three different sizes, but the standard is the oldest variety, created originally as a water dog. Its name comes from the German word *pudel*, which means 'to splash in water', and it was in Germany that the ancestors of the breed originated. In spite of the exotic appearance of a Standard Poodle in full show clip, these dogs make excellent pets.

Origin Dogs bearing a striking resemblance to the modern Standard Poodle are featured in drawings by Albrecht Dürer, dating back to the 15th century. The breed was trained as water retrievers, fetching shot waterfowl out of lakes and rivers. During the 19th century, trained poodles became popular as circus entertainers, impressing audiences with their agility and responsiveness. As show dogs their popularity has waned over the past 50 years, but they still attract a loyal following.

Appearance The most obvious feature of the Poodle is the way in which its coat is traditionally clipped, in one of a range of over 50 variations. The show clip looks decorative but derives from a utility cut, designed both to keep the dog warm while swimming and to reduce its drag in the water. Hair is left to form 'bracelets" on the lower limbs, to protect against rheumatism, and the pompon on the tail is used to locate the dog in water.

Personality Playful and responsive, the Poodle is an excellent companion, still ready to plunge into water if given the opportunity. It is easily trained, active by nature, and will enjoy retrieving games.

Health and care Standard Poodles are robust dogs, and tend to be fitter overall than the smaller varieties, with few inherited problems. The tear glands, which open on to the inner surface of each lower eyelid, may develop a drainage problem, causing tearstaining at the corners of the eyes. Epilepsy is a problem in some bloodlines. It can be confirmed by an EEG examination, and regular medication is usually needed for an affected dog. You should ask your breeder about any incidence of this condition in their breeding stock.

As an owner The grooming needs of the Poodle need not be elaborate – the coat of a pet can be maintained in a basic sporting clip, which is easily managed. It creates an appearance not dissimilar to that of a sheep, but retains the pompon on the tail. The Poodle does not shed its coat, and some people have found that the breed can be kept by those allergic to pet hair without provoking any allergic symptoms.

Also consider The Miniature Poodle, which measures up to 38cm (15 in) tall, or the Toy varieties (*see page 211*) of the Poodle are possible choices if you like the Standard form but feel that it is too large.

Tech Spec

Features

A *Head:* Long and fine, with a relatively narrow skull, moderate stop, and well-defined, protruding chin

B *Eyes:* Almond-shaped and dark; reasonably widely spaced

C *Ears:* Long, wide and set low, close to the sides of the face

D *Chest:* Deep and wide

E *Tail:* Set high, thick at its base, and carried away from the body

F *Bite:* Scissors bite

G *Height at shoulder:* 38cm (15 in) or more

H *Weight:* 20.5–32kg (45–70 lb)

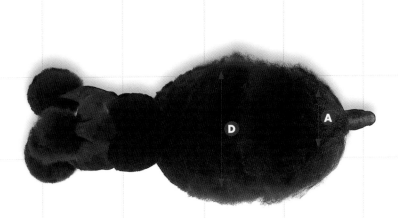

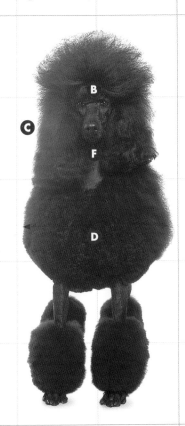

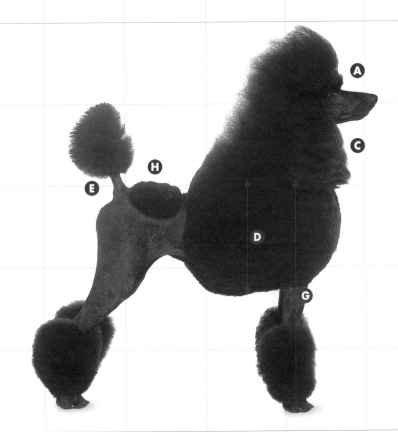

Tibetan Spaniel

Overview

Recognition
North America, Britain and
FCI member countries

Life expectancy
11–13 years

Colour
Any colour or combination
acceptable

Grooming

Feeding

Child friendliness

Exercise
A moderate daily walk
in the park will be enough

This breed is not related in any way to the European or American breed of spaniel, but simply acquired this name in the West because of its similarity in appearance to a toy spaniel breed. It has never developed a particularly strong following in other countries, which is a shame because these dogs have an appealing nature.

Origin This ancient Tibetan breed is closely linked with the monastic communities in its homeland. Its ancestors are believed to have been used to turn prayer wheels, which carried the words of a prayer on a scroll, enabling these to be constantly repeated by the monks. Early Tibetan Spaniels were variable in both size and appearance, with those near the Chinese border being more akin to the Pekingese in their muzzle shape. The breed first reached the West in the 1890s.

Appearance Today's Tibetan Spaniels have a much more standardized appearance, although they can still vary significantly in weight. The breed's forelegs are short and slightly bowed, supporting a relatively long body. The tail forms a plume, which is carried high over the body when the dog moves. The slightly domed head is small, and the muzzle is of medium length.

Personality An intelligent breed that relates well to people in its immediate circle, the Tibetan Spaniel is nevertheless suspicious of strangers. It also has an assertive side to its nature, but it is adaptable and does well in an urban environment.

Health and care Tibetan Spaniels tend to be sounder than the Pekingese to whose ancestry they contributed, partly because their facial shape is less extreme. They are hardy dogs as well, thanks to their dense, double-layered coat. This is an important feature in the show ring, and it must be allowed to lie naturally, without being clipped or otherwise modified. Their attractive appearance is easily maintained with standard grooming.

As an owner Be aware that the coats of male Tibetan Spaniel puppies are likely to become more profuse than those of bitches, forming a small mane around the neck. Much of their dense undercoat is shed in the spring. This is not a prolific breed, partly because bitches only normally come into season once a year, rather than twice. Litter sizes tend to be small, averaging just three puppies.

Also consider The Pekingese (*see pages 198–199*) is much better known. The Lhasa Apso (*see pages 86–87*) and Shih Tzu (*see pages 204–205*) are other small breeds from this part of the world, but again, like the Pekingese, will need far more grooming. Although unrelated, the Cavalier King Charles Spaniel (*see pages 178–179*) shares a similarity with the Tibetan Spaniel.

Tech Spec

Features

A *Head:* Slightly domed skull, with a small head in proportion to the body, a slight stop and medium-length muzzle

B *Eyes:* Medium-sized, well-spaced, dark, oval eyes, looking directly forwards

C *Ears:* Medium-sized, lifted slighted away from the skull, and set high

D *Chest:* Moderate in width

E *Tail:* Set high and carried over the back when on the move

F *Bite:* Undershot bite

G *Height at shoulder:* 25.5cm (10 in)

H *Weight:* 4–6.75kg (9–15 lb)

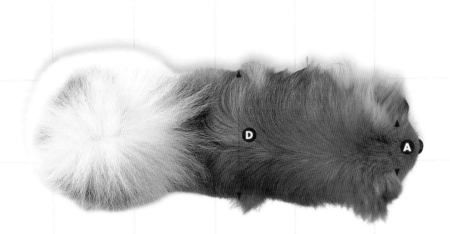

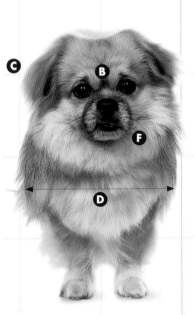

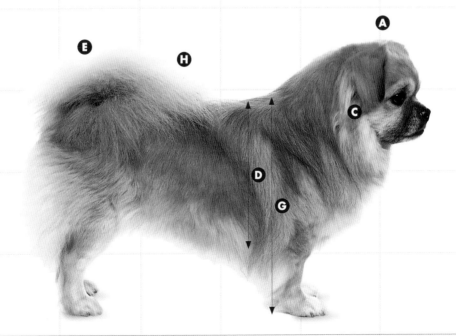

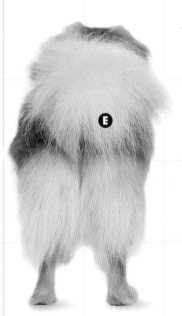

Group **Non-sporting**

Overview

Recognition
North America, Britain and
FCI member countries

Life expectancy
11–13 years

Colour
No restrictions at all

Grooming

Feeding

Child friendliness

Exercise
Provide a good daily walk

In spite of this breed's name, by which it is known in the West, the Tibetan Terrier was bred to herd sheep rather than for hunting vermin It can still be seen carrying out this role in Tibet today. This is a breed that deserves to be more popular than it has been, simply because it makes such a wonderful companion.

Origin It appears that there was no record of the Tibetan Terrier in Europe or North America until 1895, and little is known about its ancestry. Their long coats are clipped in the summer with those of the sheep, and used together with yak hair to make cloth. The number of Tibetan Terriers plummeted in the mid-1900s as a result of the Communist takeover in China, which led to dogs of all types being slaughtered in huge numbers as undesirable, even if they were working stock.

Appearance The Tibetan Terrier has been described as a miniature Old English Sheepdog, which gives some impression of its appearance. The breed is well-equipped to survive outdoors in the bitter winters of its homeland, thanks to its profuse, double-layered coat. The undercoat is woolly, which helps to trap warm air close to the body, and the outer coat is fine and, in some cases, wavy.

Personality This breed is affectionate, sensitive and responsive. Its loyalty is illustrated by one story in which a Tibetan Terrier saved its owner by driving off a rabid dog, and suffered a fatal bite as a consequence.

Health and care Tibetan Terriers are healthy dogs, and this can be linked directly to their working ancestry. Remarkably, they do not seem particularly bothered by climatic extremes, whether hot or cold, and this is probably a reflection of the climate in their homeland. Both sound health and temperament have long been regarded as important characteristics of this breed in Tibet.

As an owner Be prepared for puppies having much shorter coats, which are also likely to have a softer texture than those of adult Tibetan Terriers. Their coats will be single-layered at this stage; this is a serious flaw in older individuals. Like the Tibetan Spaniel (see pages 94–95), this breed is shown in a natural state, and the coat must not be sculpted at all.

Also consider The Old English Sheepdog (see pages 38–39) is an option if you like the profile of this breed, and possibly the smaller Bearded Collie as well (see pages 22–23). Another small sheepdog that may appeal is the Hungarian Puli (see page 45). Should you be looking for a smaller breed from this part of Asia, then the Lhasa Apso (see pages 86–87) represents a possibility.

Tech Spec

Features

A *Head:* Medium-length, with an evident stop in front of the eyes; neither broad nor massive

B *Eyes:* Widely spaced, large and dark

C *Ears:* V-shaped and medium-sized, hanging down loosely over the sides of the head

D *Chest:* Moderate in width

E *Tail:* Set high and curled over the back; well-feathered

F *Bite:* Level or slightly undershot

G *Height at shoulder:* Dogs 35.5–40.5cm (14–16 in); bitches 13–14 in (33–35.5cm)

H *Weight:* 20–30 lb (9–13.5kg)

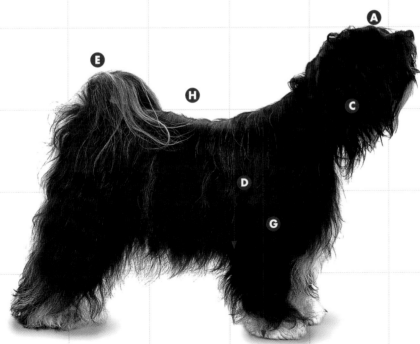

Pet Spec
American Eskimo

This attractive dog was created from various spitz-type breeds brought by European settlers to the US, including the German Spitz and the Volpino Italiano. During the early days of the breed's existence in the late 1800s it became very popular as a circus entertainer, not just because of its attractive appearance, but also because it could be trained easily. The Eskie, as the American Eskimo Dog is often known, makes a great companion.

Appearance Ideally, American Eskimo Dogs should be pure white in colour, but they may sometimes display pale biscuit-cream markings as well. They have a typical spitz appearance, with a foxlike face, pricked ears and a tail that curves up over the back. Unusually, however, they can display a wide variance in size, with three distinct categories being recognized, all of which are classed together in the same breed group.

Breed care and health Be prepared for regular grooming of the double-layered coat, particularly during the spring when these dogs shed their thicker, longer winter coat. You will also need to wipe away tearstaining, which is likely to become apparent at the corners of the eyes, using damp cottonwool.

As an owner You need to consider that male dogs tend to develop a more profuse mane of longer fur around the neck than bitches, which may influence your choice if you are seeking a pet. The American Eskimo Dog is a relatively easy breed to train, and will also make an alert watchdog around the home.

Also consider If you are seeking a slightly larger dog, then the Samoyed (see pages 244–245) will be an obvious choice. The white variety of the Giant German Spitz represents another possibility, as does the Pomeranian (see pages 200–201), which is available in a wide choice of colours.

Pet Spec
Czesky Terrier

The Czesky or Cesky (pronounced 'ses-ki") Terrier is a relatively new addition to the list of purebred dogs, created by a geneticist in what is now the Czech Republic. From 1949 he used a combination of Scottish and Sealyham Terriers to develop the Czesky, with the aim of creating both a superb hunting dog and a breed appealing enough to win in the show ring.

Appearance The Czesky combines the head shape of the Scottie with a body profile more reminiscent of the Sealyham, and is also characterized by a long neck. The coat has a silky texture, and in contrast to the traditional appearance of working terriers, the dog's tail is never docked, but hangs down close to the ground, tapering along its length.

Breed care and health The Czesky is a healthy breed. The coat needs to be clipped regularly and is kept short over the back of the head and the neck, and on the sides and rear of the body. The underbody is left long, as is the dog's beard.

As an owner The Czesky was bred partly for its hunting abilities and is still an effective ratter. It makes a good house dog. It is both an alert guard dog and more tolerant of children than many other terrier breeds.

Also consider The Sealyham (see page 173) and the Scottish Terrier (see pages 158–159), both of which contributed to the development of the Czesky, may be worth considering, as may the Dandie Dinmont Terrier (see pages 144–145). There is no larger terrier quite like the Czesky, although there is another native Czech breed, a gundog known as the Czesky Fousek, which is similar.

Pet Spec
Dogue de Bordeaux

This French mastiff breed became much more popular internationally after its appearance with Tom Hanks in 1989 in the popular film Turner and Hooch. Originally created as a fighting breed, with its strength being pitted not just against other dogs but also bulls and bears, it then became a drover's dog. Today this breed usually has a placid nature.

Appearance A huge head with an upturned nose and undershot jaw help to characterize this breed. Its ears are located well back on the head, in common with other breeds originally kept for fighting purposes. The skin on the face surrounding the eyes is furrowed. The coat is fawn, often with a white patch on the chest. It is also known as the French Mastiff.

Breed care and health The folds of skin on the face are susceptible to infections and should be cleaned regularly. These dogs should not be exercised during the hottest part of the day; their compact facial shape leaves them prone to heatstroke.

As an owner These dogs have a tendency to drool copiously, particularly in hot weather. Their powerful physique makes adequate training, both on and off the leash, essential.

Also consider The breed most similar in physical appearance is the Boxer (see pages 220–221). It is slightly smaller and considerably lighter, with less wrinkling of the skin on the face. The Dogue is also somewhat similar to the Olde English Bulldog, a breed re-created in North America in the 1970s to resemble the style of bulldog that was popular in Victorian England.

Height Toy 23–30.5cm (9–12 in); Miniature 30.5–38cm (12–15 in); Standard 38–48cm (15–19in)
Weight 9–18kg (20–40) lb
Exercise Enjoys playing when out for a walk

Height 25.5–36.5cm (10–14 in)
Weight 5.5–8kg (12–18 lb)
Exercise This dog needs active walks and will enjoy exploring in rural areas

Height 58.5–68.5cm (23–27 in)
Weight 36–45.5kg (80–100 lb)
Exercise Plenty of exercise is required, although this dog is a plodder, rather than a natural runner

Pet Spec
Finnish Spitz

This is an old breed, whose appearance was first described in 1812. Its native name is the Suomenpystykorva, and it was originally kept for hunting birds. It behaves like a pointer, flushing the birds into a tree and then 'marking' them by emitting a series of rapid and distinctive yodelling calls. The Finnish Spitz can make as many as 160 calls of this type per minute.

Appearance This breed is a typical member of the spitz group, with a foxlike face and pricked ears. Its long plumed tail is held curled forwards over the body and it has a ruff of longer fur across the chest and shoulders. The dark eyes make a distinctive contrast with its striking golden-red colouring. The Finnish Spitz occurs in no other colours.

Breed care and health Fit and healthy by nature, the Finnish Spitz is a robust if somewhat excitable breed. Its coat requires more grooming in the spring, when it is moulting its thicker undercoat. The depth of coat colour can vary widely.

As an owner Male Finnish Spitz are slightly larger than bitches and usually have a more impressive ruff. They can run fast when hunting, and will then wave their tail slowly while barking, originally as a way of distracting the bird from the hunter's approach.

Also consider There are a number of spitz-type dogs of Scandinavian origin to choose from, including the Norwegian Buhund (see pages 36–37), which can be found in a reddish cream shade and is heavier in build. The Norrbottenspets is a predominantly white Swedish spitz breed of similar proportions, and also originally bred as a gundog, but it is now much rarer.

Pet Spec
Löwchen

This breed is also described as the Little Lion Dog because of its appearance when it is clipped. It is actually a member of the bichon group of breeds and was a favourite among European aristocracy as early as the 15th century. The breed was not seen in North America until 1971, and it was added to the Non-sporting Group in 1999. As recently as the 1970s, it was considered one of the rarest breeds in the world, but it has been more widely bred since.

Appearance In traditional clip, the rear part of the Löwchen's body is shaved, as are the legs, leaving just pompoms of fur around the ankles. The coat is naturally long, soft and wavy and exists in a wide variety of colours. The ears are long and profusely covered with hair. They hang down the sides of the head, adding to the overall impression of the mane.

Breed care and health The Löwchen's ears should be checked regularly for infection. The skin exposed by clipping is naturally warm to the touch. A clipped Löwchen should wear a coat in cold weather. This dog does not shed its hair and needs regular grooming as a consequence.

As an owner If you want to show your dog, the distinctive lion trim is the only accepted show style for this breed.

Also consider If you like the clipped style, consider a poodle. In common with the Löwchen, this breed does not shed its coat, making it a tidy indoor companion. Other possibilities include various members of the bichon group, such as the Bichon Frise (see pages 174–175), or the Coton de Tulear (see pages 184–185), whose coat has a cottonlike texture. The hairless Chinese Crested (see pages 182–183) may be another option.

Pet Spec
Standard Mexican Hairless

There are records of hairless dogs originating in both Middle and South America, and this Mexican breed is currently the best-known example. Its native name is Xoloitzcuintli, and there are also miniature and toy varieties. Its original functions included serving as a bed warmer, and its body heat was believed to be helpful in curing fevers. These dogs were also once used as a source of food.

Appearance Contrary to its name, this breed is not completely hairless. There are usually traces of hair on the top of the head and the ears, as well as on the tip of the tail. The skin is dark brown in colour, often with darker mottling superimposed on it. The muzzle is pointed. The ears are widely spaced, and they are raised when the dog is alert.

Breed care and health The lack of fur leaves these dogs vulnerable in both cold and hot weather. This breed frequently lacks a full set of molar teeth at the back of the jaws. Puppies with full coats occasionally crop up in litters alongside their hairless siblings.

As an owner You need to wipe over the skin regularly with a damp cloth to keep it in good condition, and also apply a special canine sunblock when your dog goes out on sunny days. The lack of fur means that this breed rarely has flea infestations.

Also consider There has recently been an attempt to categorize the Mexican Hairless breed on the basis of size. The miniature variety, called the Tepeizcuintli, measures 33–45.5cm (13–18 in) tall and weighs 6–10kg (13–22 lb), and it is considered the medium-sized type, and the Toy is the smallest size, weighing just 4kg (9 lb). Other options include the rarer Peruvian Hairless breeds, or the much more widely kept Chinese Crested dog (see pages 182–183).

Height 38–51cm (15–20 in)
Weight 14–16kg (31–35 lb)
Exercise Woodland walks will encourage the Finnish Spitz to display its natural behaviour

Height 25.5–33cm (10–13 in)
Weight 4–8kg (9–18 lb)
Exercise Energetic by nature, this breed will need a daily run in the park

Height Over 45.5cm (18 in)
Weight Over 10kg (22 lb)
Exercise This dog has limited exercise needs but will require a daily run

Overview

Recognition
North America, Britain and
FCI member countries

Life expectancy
10–12 years

Colour
Any solid colour, with
or without tan points,
and parti-coloured,
including roans

Grooming

Feeding

Child friendliness

Exercise
This is not a lap dog; it will
need a good daily period
of exercise

Sporting dogs are usually bred to work effectively in particular terrain, seeking specific game. This helps to explain why the American Cocker Spaniel has evolved into a different breed from the English Cocker Spaniel (*see pages 106–107*). The breed has become immensely popular as a companion.

Origin During the 1870s, English Cocker Spaniels were seen with increasing frequency in North America, where they were used primarily to hunt game birds. Once the breed had been accepted for show purposes, it was developed into a quicker, scaled-down version of its English ancestor. Known in the United States simply as the Cocker Spaniel, it is now the smallest spaniel bred originally for sporting purposes. It has proved to be a versatile worker, both flushing game from brush and retrieving on land and in water.

Appearance Apart from its smaller size and lighter weight, the most obvious difference between the American Cocker Spaniel and its English relative is the much longer coat of the former. It also has particularly dense feathering on its legs. When seen in profile, its back is shorter, too, and the head is more domed and the muzzle blunter than those of the English Cocker Spaniel.

Personality Easy-going and enthusiastic, the American Cocker Spaniel is a tireless and talented worker in the field. It is affectionate, forms a close bond with those in its immediate circle and settles easily in the home.

Health and care Unfortunately, as with many other breeds that have had a surge in popularity, the soundness and temperament of the American Cocker Spaniel have suffered somewhat as a result. At least 25 different hereditary and congenital health problems have been recognized in the breed, although puppies from a reputable breeder will come from stock that has been screened for many of them. It is still strongly advised that you have your new pet checked by your vet.

As an owner These spaniels need to be groomed daily to maintain their coats in top condition, with particular attention paid to the long pendulous ears. The weight of hair means that the ears obscure the entrance to the ear canal, and this makes them susceptible to infections. Seek veterinary help promptly if your dog starts scratching in the ear area.

Also consider The English Cocker Spaniel (*see pages 106–107*) is a slightly larger alternative, and other members of the spaniel group may appeal, too. The Field Spaniel is the closest relative to the Cocker Spaniels – originally classed simply as a variety of the English breed in the 1890s, it is an ideal working companion.

Tech Spec

Features

(A) *Head:* Rounded, with a distinctive stop, a deep broad muzzle and square jaws

(B) *Eyes:* Round, pointing directly forwards, with the eye rims being almond-shaped

(C) *Ears:* Set low, from the base of the eye; long and well-feathered

(D) *Chest:* Deep, extending down the elbows

(E) *Tail:* Carries on with the top line of the back

(F) *Bite:* Scissors bite

(G) *Height at shoulder:* Dogs 38cm (15 in); bitches 35.5cm (14 in) but can vary 12mm (½ in) in each case

(H) *Weight:* 11–12.5kg (24–28 lb)

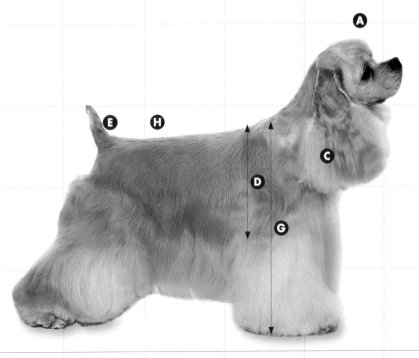

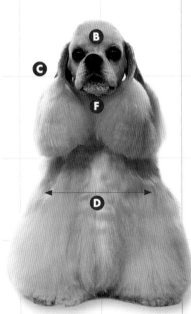

Brittany

Overview

Recognition
North America, Britain and
FCI member countries

Life expectancy
11–13 years

Colour
Orange or liver and white,
and maybe roan; any
black markings are
discouraged

Grooming

Feeding

Child friendliness

Exercise
Will play in a park but
prefers country walks

These lively gundogs have become very popular over recent years. Show and sporting stock are not formally divided, as is the case with many other sporting breeds, and examples of the Brittany have been recognized as Dual Champions, excelling both in the show ring and in field trials.

Origin The breed arose in northern France, in western Brittany. It was first kept as a spaniel, used to flush and retrieve game. It evolved into a true all-purpose gundog, following crossbreeding with setters and pointers, and although it is instinctively still a working spaniel, it is easily trained to point effectively, too. This is why the qualifying description of 'spaniel' has been dropped from its name. The Brittany was first seen in North America in 1931, and it was recognized for show purposes here three years later.

Appearance The colour of the Brittany is now more restricted in North America than in Britain, where the breed was only recognized in 1976. It has a fine, dense coat, with little feathering on the backs of the legs or fringing on the ears. Another point of distinction with true spaniels is that the lips are tighter, not tending to droop down. The Brittany has a very short tail, or may be completely tailless.

Personality Responsive and adaptable, the Brittany makes a good and affectionate companion. It has a determined side to its nature, combined with considerable stamina, but is usually keen to please, and it can be trained easily.

Health and care Some bloodlines are afflicted by the blood-clotting disorder known as haemophilia. As a result of the way in which this trait is passed from one generation to another, male dogs are most likely to be affected, but bitches can be carriers, transmitting the rogue gene to their offspring, while showing no signs of the illness themselves. If you are acquiring a Brittany, make sure the breeding stock has been screened. Care of the Brittany is straightforward and its coat is easy to groom, compared with those of true spaniels.

As an owner Brittanys need regular, off-leash exercise in the countryside. This allows your dog to exercise its natural instincts, such as flushing ground-dwelling birds. Always inspect the body of your dog if it has been working in undergrowth, because it may pick up burrs or ticks, and check your pet's feet for embedded grass seeds, which can puncture the skin and cause infection.

Also consider The Dutch Partridge Dog is another multi-purpose sporting dog, slightly larger than the Brittany, and unfortunately much rarer. An alternative Dutch sporting dog that may appeal is the Stabyhound. Like the Brittany, this breed has made a smooth transition from field work to companion dog, but it is still uncommon.

Tech Spec

Features

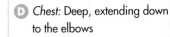

A *Head:* Slightly rounded and medium-length skull, with a sloping, not indented stop and a muzzle that tapers gradually

B *Eyes:* Set deep and emphasized by the eyebrows

C *Ears:* Triangular and short with rounded tips; set high above the eyes and lie flat against the sides of the head

D *Chest:* Deep, extending down to the elbows

E *Tail:* Set high, often naturally tail-less or extremely short

F *Bite:* Scissors bite

G *Height at shoulder:* 44.5–52cm (17½–20½ in)

H *Weight:* 13.5–18kg (30–40 lb)

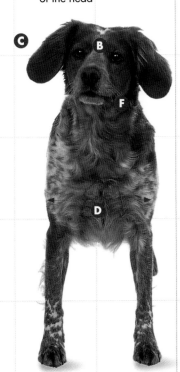

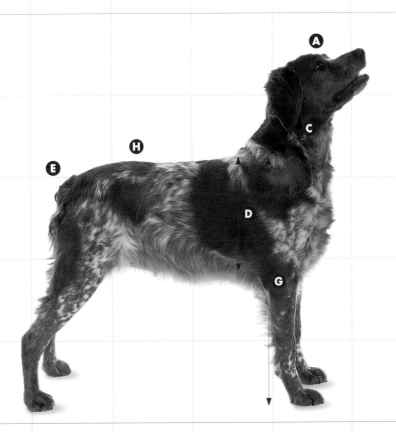

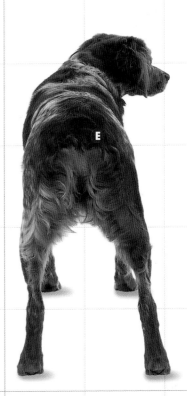

Chesapeake Bay Retriever

Overview

Recognition
North America, Britain and
FCI member countries

Life expectancy
10–12 years

Colour
Shades of brown
and sedge

Grooming

Feeding

Child friendliness

Exercise
Great stamina, so it needs
long walks and preferably
an opportunity to swim

As its name suggests, the Chesapeake Bay Retriever is a breed evolved to work in water, named after the area close to Washington, D.C., where it was created. Since then it has been seen in many other parts of the world, although it still ranks as one of the less common retrievers, probably because it is unsuited to urban life.

Origin The history of this breed traces directly back to 1807, when two Newfoundland puppies were rescued from a ship that was sinking off the coast of Maryland. They were mated with local retrieving dogs, laying the foundation for the modern breed. Other crosses, possibly including Irish Water Spaniels and Otterhounds, also contributed to the breed's subsequent development. Chessies are versatile today, and they are as effective retrieving on land as they are in water.

Appearance Signs of its Newfoundland ancestry are still evident in the Chessie's large head and powerful hindquarters. The double-layered coat is a particular feature of the breed, providing effective insulation against cold water. The outer layer is also oily and water-repellent, while the woolly undercoat serves to trap warm air close to the skin

Personality Strong and tireless, these retrievers display immense stamina, able to plunge repeatedly into choppy and often near-freezing coastal waters and retrieve as many as 200 ducks during a day's work.

Health and care These retrievers sometimes suffer from congenital eye problems. Entropion affects the eyelashes, causing them to rub on the surface of the eye, and it is likely to require surgery. Chessies can also develop progressive retinal atrophy (PRA), so check that any breeder from whom you are buying a puppy breeds only from screened stock. Generally, Chesapeake Bay Retrievers are extremely hardy dogs.

As an owner With this breed, always obtain a puppy rather than an adult dog. Chesapeake Bay Retrievers bond early with their immediate family, and it can be difficult to persuade them to transfer their affections at a later stage. They learn readily and are adaptable. They are exceptionally strong swimmers, ably swimming against strong tides and currents, but do not put your dog at risk when exercising him near water.

Also consider The Curly Coated Retriever (see page 134) has a distinctive appearance, and is also believed to have a part-Newfoundland ancestry. It is similarly well-adapted to retrieve from water. The popular Labrador Retriever (see pages 124–125) is another powerful swimmer, often slightly smaller in size than the Chessie and bred in different colours.

Tech Spec

Features

A *Head:* Broad, rounded skull and a medium stop, with a tapered muzzle of similar length

B *Eyes:* Widely spaced, relatively large and yellow or amber in colour

C *Ears:* Set high, hanging loosely on the sides of the head, and small

D *Chest:* Deep, wide and muscular

E *Tail:* Medium-length; straight or slightly curved, although not over the back

F *Bite:* Scissors bite preferable; level bite is accepted

G *Height at shoulder:* Dogs 58.5–66cm (23–26 in); bitches 53–61cm (21–24 in)

H *Weight:* Dogs 29.5–36kg (65–80 lb); bitches 25–32kg (55–70 lb)

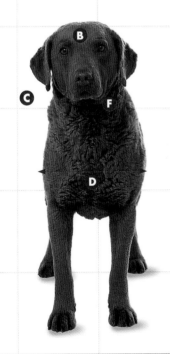

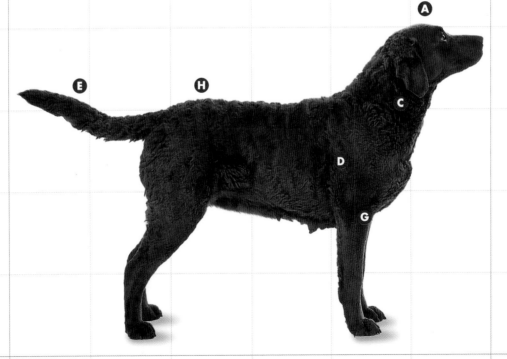

English Cocker Spaniel

Overview

Recognition
North America, Britain and
FCI member countries

Life expectancy
10–12 years

Colour
Solid red, liver or black,
and parti-colours, including
roans, are permitted, as
are tan markings

Grooming

Feeding

Child friendliness

Exercise
Walk daily and exercise
in a rural environment if
possible

There can be confusion between this breed and its American relative, both of which are sometimes simply described as Cocker Spaniels. English Cocker Spaniels have become popular in the show ring and as household pets over recent years, but they are also adept in field trials.

Origin The Cocker and Springer Spaniels share a common ancestry. Both types were originally described as Land Spaniels, but gradually a divergence in type emerged. This split had become evident over 200 years ago, with the English Cocker Spaniel already recognized by its smaller size. However, they were formally separated into two breeds only when the Kennel Club in England drew up official standards for both in 1893.

Appearance The English Cocker Spaniel creates an impression of greater power and strength than the American type; it is both taller and heavier. Although not especially fast on the move, the English Cocker Spaniel appears to move without obvious effort, propelled along easily by its powerful hind legs. The tail is usually held in a horizontal position, but it may occasionally be lifted slightly if the dog is especially excited.

Personality Friendly and responsive, the English Cocker Spaniel is a lively breed with an enthusiastic outlook on life. Thanks to their intelligence, they can be trained quite easily. They are keen to please and respond well to encouragement.

Health and care Although usually a genial dog, there is a disturbing condition known as the Rage Syndrome that occasionally afflicts solid (single)-coloured English Cocker Spaniels. Such dogs suddenly and inexplicably become aggressive, then revert equally fast to their previously docile personalities. There appears to be a genetic component associated with this behaviour, and it is important to check bloodlines carefully, not just for this condition but for other weaknesses, too, when you are looking for a pet.

As an owner These spaniels are full of energy, reflecting their sporting nature, and this makes them a good choice as a family pet alongside older children. The family may also like to share the daily task of grooming – this dog needs a good deal to keep it looking its best. English Cocker Spaniels need plenty of attention and opportunities to play to prevent them from becoming bored around the house.

Also consider The English Springer Spaniel (*see pages 110–111*), or the American Cocker Spaniel (*see pages 100–101*), which is slightly smaller in size, may be alternatives. Other possibilities are the Field Spaniel, a close relative of the English Cocker Spaniel, although with a heavier build, or the distinctive, stockier Sussex Spaniel (*see page 135*).

Tech Spec

Features

A *Head:* Arched and flattened skull with muzzle being of corresponding length, although narrower

B *Eyes:* Well-spaced, medium-sized, with a slight oval shape and tight eyelids

C *Ears:* Long and set low, lying close to the sides of the face

D *Chest:* Deep; moderate in width

E *Tail:* Carried horizontally and moving repeatedly when the dog is working

F *Bite:* Scissors bite

G *Height at shoulder:* Dogs 40.5–43cm (16–17 in); bitches 38–40.5cm (15–16 in)

H *Weight:* Dogs 12.5–15.5kg (28–34 lb); bitches 11.75–14.5kg (26–32 lb)

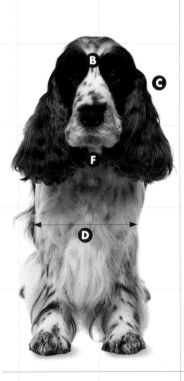

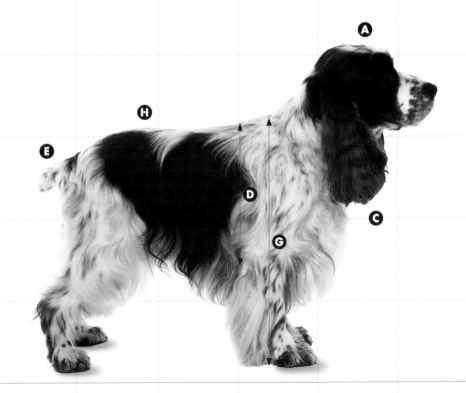

English Setter

Overview

Recognition
North America, Britain and FCI member countries

Life expectancy
10–12 years

Colour
Lemon with white, liver with white, black with white, or tricolour; sometimes seen in blue belton with tan evident above the eyes, on the muzzle and on the legs

Grooming

Feeding

Child friendliness

Exercise
Be prepared for lengthy walks

The word 'setter' is based on the original description of a 'setting spaniel', which explained the way in which these gundogs would sit ('set') quietly once they had found their game – game birds such as partridge, woodcock or pheasant. This would alert the sportsmen to the birds' presence without frightening the birds into flying off.

Origin A variety of breeds, believed to include the English Springer Spaniel, the Water Spaniel and the Spanish Pointer, contributed to the English Setter's initial development. Early in its history a number of different strains evolved, of which the most famous was that created by Sir Edward Laverack between 1825 and 1875. Another strain that made a lasting impact was the Llewellin bloodline, founded by Purcel Llewellin and renowned for its ability in field trials.

Appearance The colouring of this breed is unmistakable: its white coat is overlaid with darker hairs, creating a distinctive type of flecking known as 'belton'. The silky coat lies flat, with profuse feathering in the chest area and on the back of the legs and lower underparts. The tail tapers to a point, with longer hair on the underside. The pendulous ears are also feathered and set well back on the head. As they mature, the difference in appearance between dogs and bitches becomes pronounced, with the dogs appearing more square-set and masculine.

Personality A breed with great stamina, the English Setter is a good-natured gundog, and it makes an excellent companion provided that its need for exercise can be met. It is naturally intelligent and tends to learn quickly.

Health and care There are a number of hereditary conditions that can affect this breed. You should check that any dog you are thinking of acquiring comes from breeding stock that has been screened for hip dysplasia, a malformation of the hips that can be painful. A rare condition also found in English Setters is recessive juvenile amaurotic idiocy. Affected dogs show signs of deteriorating vision at 12 to 15 months, and the condition progresses to muscle spasms, and ultimately leads to seizures.

As an owner This is not a breed that will adapt to city life. The English Setter needs space to run, ideally in rural surroundings. If bored, these dogs are likely to become destructive around the home.

Also consider The Gordon Setter (see pages 120–121) or the Irish Setter (see pages 122–123), both slightly smaller than the English Setter, may be possibilities. Alternatively there are several rarer breeds originating from mainland Europe, such as the slightly smaller Picardy Spaniel (Épagneul Picard) from France.

Tech Spec

Features

A *Head:* Long, with a lean shape and clearly defined stop; the muzzle is long, level and square-shaped

B *Eyes:* Relatively large, almost rounded, and dark brown with dark rims

C *Ears:* Set low, at or below the level of the eyes, and far back; carried near the head

D *Chest:* Deep, with brisket reaching to the elbows

E *Tail:* Extended from the topline and tapered to a point; carried straight and level with the back

F *Bite:* Scissors bite preferable, but level bite acceptable

G *Height at shoulder:* Dogs 63.5cm (25 in); bitches 61cm (24 in)

H *Weight:* 25.5–30kg (56–66 lb)

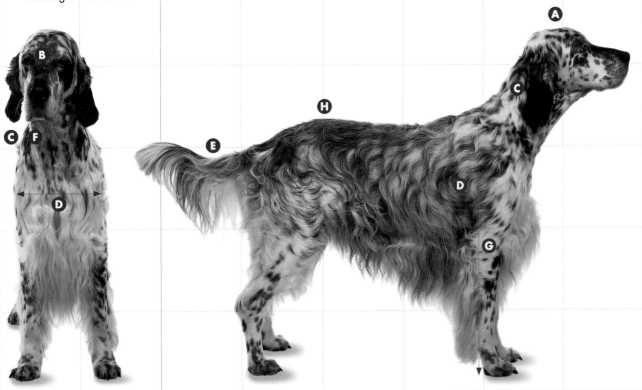

English Springer Spaniel

Recognition
North America, Britain and
FCI member countries

Life expectancy
11–13 years

Colour
Black and white or liver
and white, blue, or liver
roan, or tricolour – black or
liver and white with tan
markings

Grooming

Feeding

Child friendliness

Exercise
A breed with great
stamina, this dog needs
plenty of exercise

The description 'springer' relates not to the jumping abilities of these spaniels, but to the way in which they work, 'springing' game out of the undergrowth. This breed was known originally as the Wood Spaniel because it invariably worked on land rather than in water. In spite of its relatively small size, it has tremendous energy and stamina.

Origin The early Land Spaniel breed was divided into the English Cocker Spaniel (*see pages 106–107*) and this larger breed, which has existed in a recognizable form for over 350 years. It was a common sight on large estates and was highly valued by gamekeepers. The breed became well known in North America during the 1920s, and it was soon taking part in both field trials and shows, but gradually a divergence in type arose. Today, there tend to be two distinct strains of English Springer Spaniel, one of which is seen in the show ring while the other competes in field trials.

Appearance A medium-sized gundog, the English Springer Spaniel has a compact body with a head of proportional size, creating a balanced impression. The coat is of moderate length, with evident feathering. The long, pendulous ears are set well back on the head, in line with the eyes, and are well covered with hair. The upper lips hang down below the lower jaw line and the cheeks are flat.

Personality Exuberant by nature, the English Springer Spaniel is an industrious worker in the field and will always be keen to please. It relates well to people and is a lively companion. Its powers of concentration, whether learning or working, are good.

Health and care This breed is particularly susceptible to a range of congenital eye problems. It can suffer from inward- or outward-curling eyelashes, or even an additional row of eyelashes, and all these conditions may require corrective surgery. Glaucoma and PRA (progressive retinal atrophy) are also recognized weaknesses in English Springer Spaniels. You should therefore check the breeding stock of any dog you are planning to acquire.

As an owner This is a breed with extremely high levels of energy. You must be prepared to give it plenty of exercise, ideally in a country area where it can run off the leash every day. This applies equally to dogs from show or from hunting stock. Without enough exercise and stimulation, the English Springer Spaniel may become destructive around the home. It can easily be trained to retrieve balls and to play other fetching games.

Also consider The smaller relatives of the English Springer Spaniel, the English and American Cocker Spaniels (*see pages 106–107 and 100–101*) may be possibilities. The Welsh Springer Spaniel (*see pages 132–133*) is another option, as is the increasingly popular, although still uncommon, French Spaniel (Épagneul Français), which is taller and longer in the body than the English Springer Spaniel.

Tech Spec

Features

A *Head:* Relatively broad, medium-length skull, with a muzzle of corresponding length

B *Eyes:* Oval in shape and medium-sized, set relatively deep and well-spaced

C *Ears:* Set level with the eye and not far back; long and wide, hanging down on the cheeks

D *Chest:* Deep and of moderate width

E *Tail:* Carried horizontally or slightly vertically; wagged earnestly by the dog when working

F *Bite:* Scissors bite

G *Height at shoulder:* Dogs 51cm (20 in); bitches 48cm (19 in)

H *Weight:* Dogs 22.5kg (50 lb); bitches 18kg (40 lb)

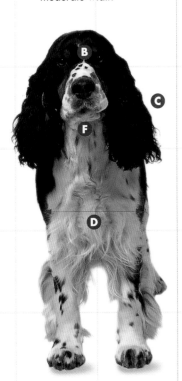

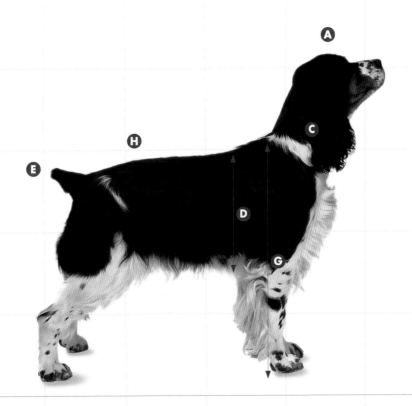

Flat Coated Retriever

Overview

Recognition
North America, Britain and FCI member countries

Life expectancy
11–13 years

Colour
Solid black or liver

Grooming

Feeding

Child friendliness

Exercise
An active breed that needs plenty of exercise

The popularity of the Flat Coated Retriever declined during the last century in the face of competition from what is now the better-known Labrador Retriever. As a result, relatively few of these gundogs are kept purely as pets today, but they tend to be valued most for their working abilities, and sometimes for their appearances in the show ring.

Origin It is thought that an ancestral form of the Labrador Retriever from Newfoundland, called the St John's Dog, was crossed with various setters to establish the foundations of this breed. The introduction of setter blood resulted in these gundogs becoming known as Wavy Coated Retrievers for a time, but this characteristic gradually disappeared and the breed became known under its current name. By the late 1940s it had become scarce, but it was being bred in increasing numbers once more by the 1960s.

Appearance The most striking feature of the Flat Coated Retriever is undoubtedly its straight, flat, glossy coat. The legs and tail are well-feathered, and the coat provides good insulation. The head of this dog is large, allowing it to carry game, such as hares or ducks, easily. It works both on land and in water; its muscular hindquarters make it an efficient swimmer.

Personality Friendly and well-disposed towards people, the Flat Coated Retriever is a breed that is diligent in the field and loyal at home. Its intelligent nature ensures that it is a quick learner, and it is adaptable and affectionate. Its excellent temperament and gentle mouth when retrieving were the factors that made it more popular and numerous than the Curly Coated Retriever in the late 19th century.

Health and care The Flat Coated Retriever is generally a healthy breed, although older dogs do seem to be susceptible to bone cancer. The coats of some individuals may still occasionally display a slight waviness.

As an owner This is not a dog that will thrive in a restricted urban space unless you can ensure that it has regular exercise each day in rural surroundings. When choosing a puppy, consider that adult dogs and bitches differ from one another in looks more than most breeds – males have a longer and more profuse chest mane.

Also consider Other breeds of retriever, including the Golden Retriever (see pages 118–119), are of similar size and may be possible alternatives. There is also a corresponding black form of the Labrador Retriever (see pages 124–125), which is usually slightly smaller than the Flat Coated Retriever, and which has a short coat that needs minimal grooming.

Tech Spec

Features

A *Head:* Flat skull with a slight stop and a long, powerful, deep muzzle

B *Eyes:* Almond-shaped, brownish, medium sized and widely spaced

C *Ears:* Set relatively high, small yet well-feathered; lie close to the sides of the head

D *Chest:* Deep

E *Tail:* Relatively straight, not curled; not carried significantly above the level of the back

F *Bite:* Scissors bite preferred but level bite accepted

G *Height at shoulder:* Dogs 58.5–62cm (23–24½ in); bitches 56–60cm (22–23½ in)

H *Weight:* 27–32kg (60–70 lb)

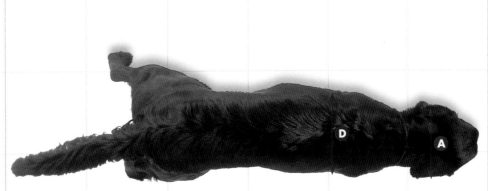

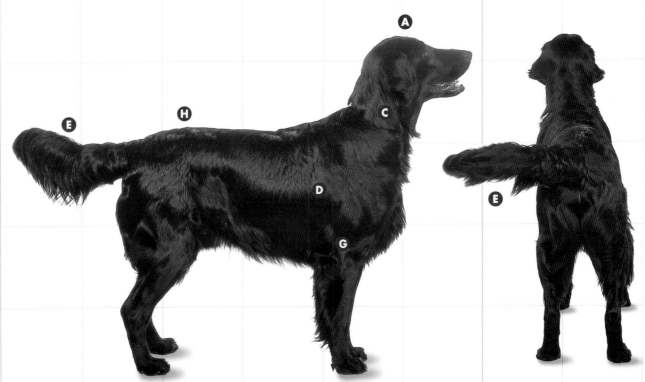

German Shorthaired Pointer

Overview

Recognition
North America, Britain and
FCI member countries

Life expectancy
12–16 years

Colour
Liver or liver-and-white
combinations

Grooming

Feeding

Child friendliness

Exercise
Daily walks off the leash
in country areas are
necessary

Lively and enthusiastic by nature, the German Shorthaired Pointer has all the characteristics of a sporting dog, and it is essential that it is kept in an environment where it can have plenty of exercise. Provided that the breed's needs can be met in this respect, it makes an excellent companion, adapting well in the home and acting as an alert guard dog.

Origin The ancestors of this breed were Spanish Pointers. These dogs have a rather ponderous gait, and so in the 19th century other breeds were introduced into the mix to develop the German Shorthaired Pointer into a faster, more athletic gundog. A variety of other breeds were used for this purpose, including the more agile English Pointer and the Bloodhound, both of which also improved its scenting ability, and also English Foxhound stock, which contributed greater pace and stamina.

Appearance This is a well-built dog, with a broad skull and strong legs. The tail is positioned high on the back and tapers along its length. Dogs are either solid liver or liver and white – in bicoloured dogs the upper parts of the body are coloured, with white areas predominating on the underparts. So-called roan colouring, in which dark and white hairs are merged together, is not unusual.

Personality Having evolved as a working gundog, this breed is responsive to training. It thrives in a country environment and will display considerable stamina, proving to be both a lively companion and a talented retriever, on land and in water.

Health and care As with many of the large breeds, hip dysplasia and weaknesses of the elbow joint can be problematic. Epilepsy is also linked with some bloodlines, so check carefully before purchasing a puppy. After walking in country areas, you should check your dog for ticks, as these blood-sucking insects can spread various diseases – Lyme Disease among them. Do not over-exercise puppies, because this can cause long-term damage to their joints.

As an owner You need to be an active, outdoor type to take on this breed. In return you will be rewarded with a loyal companion, which has only modest grooming needs. Mud should be left to dry and then brushed easily out of the coat. German Shorthaired Pointers can be nervous as adults unless they have been carefully socialized early with both other dogs and people, so make sure your puppy is introduced to new experiences in a controlled way while it is still young.

Also consider Various other types of pointer may be alternative choices. Not all have short coats, so if you would like a dog with a more tousled look consider the German Wirehaired Pointer (*see pages 116–117*). Another possibility is the German Longhaired Pointer, which has longer fur on the ears and tail, although its coat remains easy to groom overall.

Tech Spec

Features

A *Head:* Clean-cut; in proportion to the body

B *Eyes:* Medium-sized, lively and intelligent; level with the face, neither protruding nor sunken

C *Ears:* Long; should drop level with corners of the mouth

D *Chest:* Deep and powerful

E *Tail:* High and firm; still usually docked to 40 per cent

F *Bite:* Scissors bite

G *Height at shoulder:* Dogs 58.5–63.5cm (23–25 in); bitches 53–58.5cm (21–23 in)

H *Weight:* Dogs 25–32 kg (55–70 lb); bitches 20.5–27kg (45–60 lb)

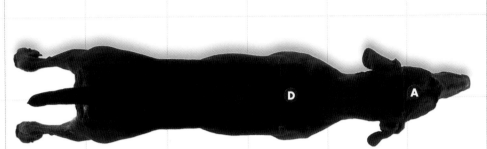

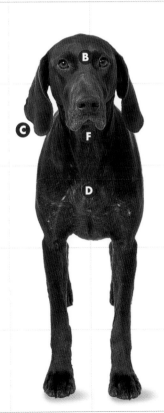

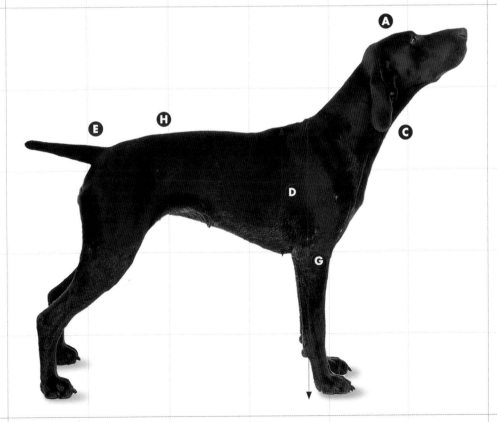

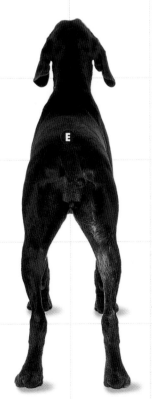

German Wirehaired Pointer

Overview

Recognition
North America, Britain and
FCI member countries

Life expectancy
11–13 years

Colour
Liver or liver-and-white
combinations

Grooming

Feeding

Child friendliness

Exercise
Daily walks off the leash
in country areas will be
necessary

This breed has been bred on slightly different lines from its shorthaired relative, and it is less inclined to be nervous in temperament. It is somewhat slower when working, but has a hardier constitution, and it has become a versatile and adaptable gundog. It is also known occasionally as the German Rough-Haired Pointer.

Origin Its precise origins are unclear, but it is likely that German Shorthaired Pointers played a central role in the development of the Wirehaired form, with crosses involving breeds such as the French Griffon. Some Airedale Terrier or Pudelpointer blood may have helped to develop its distinctive appearance. German enthusiasts wanted a sporting dog that could excel at all tasks, from pointing to retrieving.

Appearance The coarse beard of these dogs is a distinctive feature, standing out against the shorter hair of the head and ears. The rough coat has a wiry texture, but it lies close to the body and should be no more than 5cm (2 in) long. The quality of the coat is regarded as an important breed characteristic. The eyes are prominent, but the projecting eyebrows help to protect them.

Personality This breed has a reputation for being somewhat aloof as far as strangers are concerned, but it is loyal and affectionate towards people it knows well. Young dogs especially are enthusiastic and generally learn rapidly.

Health and care These pointers may suffer from hip dysplasia. Check that any dog you acquire comes from breeding stock that has been screened. Signs of lameness, resulting from underlying arthritis, will otherwise occur. The characteristic coat provides good protection against injuries in the field.

As an owner The dense undercoat of the German Wirehaired Pointer is shed in the spring, and much more time must be spent grooming for a short period. Generally, however, coat care is straightforward. If your dog swims or plays in water, the wiry top coat is water-resistant, so he can simply shake himself dry when he emerges.

Also consider Both the other breeds of German Pointer are possibilities, but if you particularly like the wirehaired appearance of this breed, the Czesky Fousek, originating from the Czech Republic, but becoming increasingly popular abroad, will be a good alternative. The Spinone Italiano (*see page 135*) has more profuse eyebrows and beard, and this breed is also becoming more widely known internationally.

Tech Spec

Features

A *Head:* Relatively long with a broad skull, medium stop and a relatively long muzzle

B *Eyes:* Medium-sized, oval and brown, with evident eyebrows

C *Ears:* Round and hanging close to the head

D *Chest:* deep

E *Tail:* Set high and carried either horizontally or above this level when dog is concentrating

F *Bite:* Scissors bite

G *Height at shoulder:* Dogs 61–66cm (24–26 in); bitches 56–58.5cm (22–23 in)

H *Weight:* 22.5–34kg (50–75 lb)

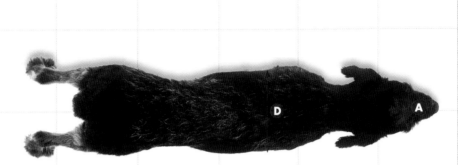

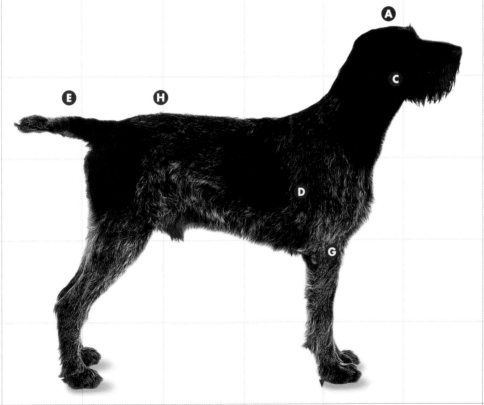

Overview

Recognition
North America, Britain and
FCI member countries

Life expectancy
10–12 years

Colour
Golden

Grooming

Feeding

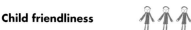

Child friendliness

Exercise
This dog needs plenty
of exercise

Consistently ranking as one of the world's most popular breeds, the Golden Retriever is highly valued – and not only as a companion. Its adaptable nature has also led to this dog working closely with people in a wide variety of situations, from guiding the blind to taking an active role in search and rescue operations.

Origin The founder of this breed was a golden-coloured puppy named Nous born in a litter of black Flat Coated Retrievers. Subsequent crossbreeding with the now-extinct Tweed Water Spaniel developed the bloodline, and the golden colouring became established. The first examples of the breed reached Canada in 1881 and were first seen in the United States nine years later, although it was not until the 1930s that the Golden Retriever started to establish a strong presence in show circles.

Appearance Lighter-coloured dogs are preferred in the show ring, and the golden colour of this dog's coat is often paler on the feathering. The coat can be flat or slightly wavy on top, and the dense undercoat acts as an effective barrier against the cold. The eyes are a warm brown colour and the nose is black or brownish black, as are the lips.

Personality Gentle, intelligent and affectionate, with a lively, exuberant side to its nature, the Golden Retriever is universally recognized as the ideal family pet, especially alongside older children. The breed makes a trustworthy and loyal companion.

Health and care As with many of the most popular purebreds, Golden Retrievers can develop a variety of hereditary problems, particularly those affecting the sight. Cataracts and other conditions affecting the eyelashes and eyelids are not uncommon. If you are considering buying a puppy, find a reputable local breeder and ask about the health of their breed stock.

As an owner The Golden Retriever is a reasonably straightforward breed to train, but the puppies tend to be exuberant. If you have no previous experience with dogs, it will be worthwhile attending training classes to master the basics. As adults, these dogs often excel in obedience trials and agility contests.

Also consider The short-coated Labrador Retriever (*see pages 124–125*) shares a coat colour with the Golden Retriever, although in the Labrador's case this is usually referred to as yellow. Another possibility is the Flat Coated Retriever (*see pages 112–113*). If you want a slightly smaller dog, the Nova Scotia Duck Tolling Retriever (*see page 134*) may appeal to you.

Tech Spec

Features

A *Head:* Broad with well-defined stop; straight, slightly tapering muzzle joining with the skull

B *Eyes:* Relatively large, set deep and ideally dark brown in colour

C *Ears:* Set above and behind the eyes, short, and extending near to the cheeks

D *Chest:* Broad and well-developed

E *Tail:* Thick and strong, carried either level with the back or slightly upward

F *Bite:* Scissors bite

G *Height at shoulder:* Dogs 58.5–61cm (23–24 in); bitches 54.5–57cm (21½–22½ in)

H *Weight:* Dogs 29.5–34kg (65–75 lb); bitches 25–29.5kg (55–65 lb)

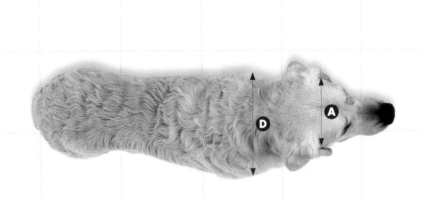

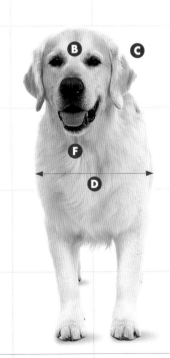

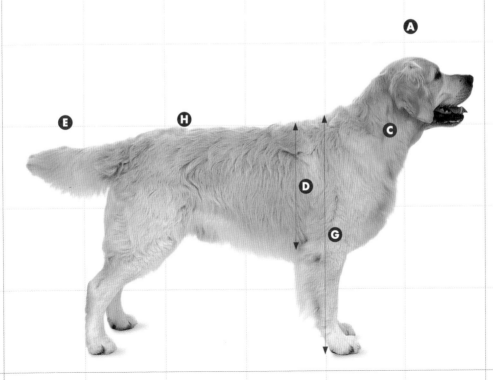

Overview

Recognition
North America, Britain and
FCI member countries

Life expectancy
11–13 years

Colour
Black with tan markings

Grooming

Feeding

Child friendliness

Exercise
Long daily walks are
essential

This breed is also known as the Black and Tan Setter, after its colouring. It was popular in the late 19th century, but is less often seen today. Its decline in popularity is a pity because it is both an attractive and an affectionate breed. Its adaptable nature means that, in addition to being a competent gundog, it can also make a well-tempered pet.

Origin The Gordon Setter is named after the Duke of Richmond and Gordon, who was responsible for its development in the 1820s on his Scottish estate in Banffshire. He wanted a setter that could hunt game birds, such as partridge and woodcock, effectively under more testing conditions than the English Setter. He therefore created a larger, more powerful breed, but he sacrificed some pace in the process.

Appearance Black and tan colouration is now a characteristic of the breed, although originally black- or red-and-white bicolours existed, as well as black, tan, and white tricolours. The Gordon Setter's glossy fur is often slightly wavy. The breed has a deep chest, with good lung capacity, and a broad nose with large nostrils, which aid its scenting ability.

Personality Hard-working and strongly devoted to those in its immediate circle, the Gordon Setter is far less inclined to accept strangers, serving as an alert watchdog. These dogs are intelligent and confident, and they also have admirable recall for learned training and for remembering people and places.

Health and care The only hereditary illness occasionally associated with this breed is progressive retinal atrophy (PRA), an incurable condition that ultimately leads to blindness. Breeding stock can now be screened in advance for PRA, and you should ask your breeder about this before obtaining a puppy.

As an owner The Gordon Setter is a breed that has more energy than other members of this particularly active group. It is not a suitable choice unless you can provide regular long walks, preferably in the countryside. If you are interested in taking part in competitions with your dog, note that a slight difference in type now exists between Gordon Setters seen at shows and the slightly smaller dogs used in field trials.

Also consider Both the English Setter (*see pages 108–109*) and the Irish Setter (*see pages 122–123*), each of which has distinctive colouring, may be possibilities. You may also want to consider a Munsterlander, a breed from Germany, which is available in both small and large sizes. The larger is similar in size to the Gordon Setter.

Tech Spec

Features

A *Head:* Deep, with a long but not pointed muzzle, which is the same length as the skull down to the obvious stop

B *Eyes:* Oval, dark brown and moderate-sized

C *Ears:* Large, folded and set low; carried close to the head

D *Chest:* Deep, but not particularly broad, extending to the elbows

E *Tail:* Short and tapered; carried horizontally or nearly horizontally

F *Bite:* Scissors or level bite

G *Height at shoulder:* Dogs 61–68.5cm (24–27 in); bitches 58.5–66cm (23–26 in)

H *Weight:* Dogs 25–36kg (55–80 lb); bitches 20.5–32kg (45–70 lb)

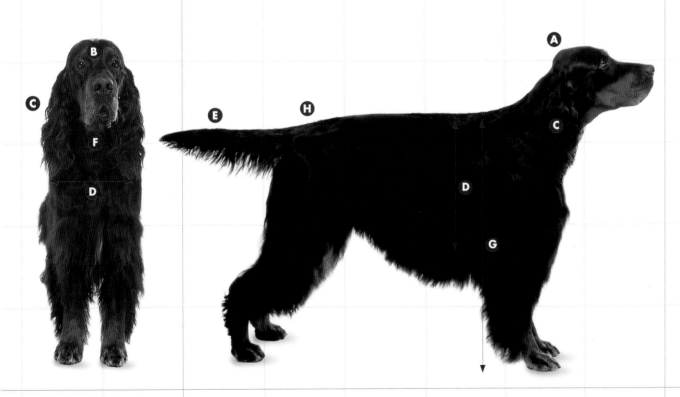

Irish Setter

Overview

Recognition
North America, Britain and FCI member countries

Life expectancy
11–13 years

Colour
Mahogany to rich shades of chestnut red

Grooming

Feeding

Child friendliness

Exercise
A good daily run, preferably in the countryside, is vital

The stunning chestnut-red colouring of this setter has guaranteed its huge popularity. It is sometimes even erroneously called the 'Red' Setter. Unfortunately, although it has a kindly disposition, its background and behaviour mean that it is not a good choice as a pet in a town or city environment.

Origin As its name suggests, the Irish Setter is a native of Ireland, developed from the Old Spanish Pointer crossed with various types of spaniels. It was originally used to hunt birds, ranging from pheasants to wild ducks, driving them into nets or flushing them for an accompanying falcon to catch overhead. After Irish Setters entered the show ring, they were crossed with Borzois to improve their elegance, with the side effect that they became taller, too.

Appearance It is not just the lovely colour of these dogs that is impressive, but also their smooth, powerful and elegant gait. The coat is at its shortest on the front of the forelegs and the head, and longer – and flat – elsewhere on the body. The backs of the legs and the thighs have long, fine feathering, and there is a longer, tapering fringe of hair on the underside of the tail.

Personality A true extrovert, the Irish Setter is an enthusiastic, energetic breed. These setters can be wayward, however, especially while they are young and not fully trained, and have a tendency to run off, so they should be thoroughly trained in obedience.

Health and care A problem that may arise in puppies of this breed results in the gullet becoming blocked by the incorrect development of the aorta, the body's major artery. It makes swallowing difficult, so an affected puppy may regurgitate its food. This is problem that may be helped by surgery. It is also a symptom of the inherited condition known as generalized myopathy, which is a form of muscle weakness. Other symptoms include an enlarged tongue and stiffness when moving.

As an owner Do not be seduced by this dog's beauty. You need to be able to give an Irish Setter plenty of exercise every day – a bored, unexercised Irish Setter can be destructive, especially if left alone for too long at home. Be patient when training your Irish Setter; this is a breed that can be slow to learn, but your dog will have good recall when it has mastered what is expected of it.

Also consider Two rare but striking alternative choices to the more dominant red form are the Red and White Irish Setter, which is identical to the Irish Setter in all respects other than its colour, or, even rarer, a variety from northwest Ireland called the Shower of Hail, because the white spots on its coat resemble hailstones.

Tech Spec

Features

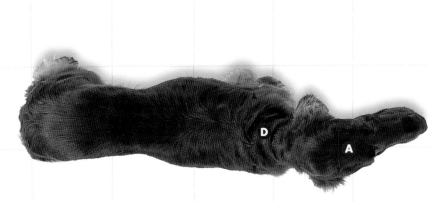

A *Head:* About twice as long as the width between the ears; the skull is oval and slightly domed

B *Eyes:* Well-spaced, medium-sized and almond-shaped

C *Ears:* Set at or below the level of the eye and well back, hanging close to the sides of the head

D *Chest:* Deep, extending to the elbows and medium-width

E *Tail:* Almost merges with the topline; broad at the base and tapered to a point

F *Bite:* Scissors or level bite

G *Height at shoulder:* Dogs 68.5cm (27 in); bitches 63.5cm (25 in)

H *Weight:* Dogs 32kg (70 lb); bitches 27kg (60 lb)

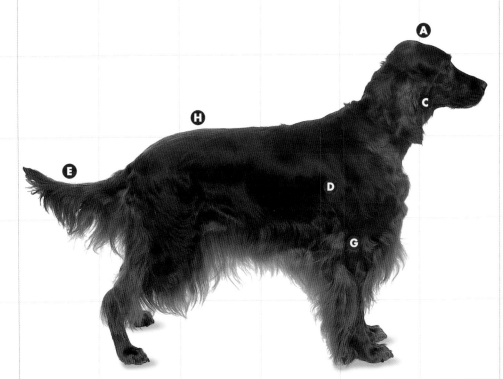

Overview

Recognition
North America, Britain and
FCI member countries

Life expectancy
10–12 years

Colour
Yellow, chocolate
and black

Grooming

Feeding

Child friendliness

Exercise
A good daily run is
essential

This gundog has become the most popular purebred dog in the world, thanks in part to its generous and loyal nature. It was originally bred to work closely with people, and it forms a strong bond with its owners. It is an ideal choice as a family pet.

Origin Although there is some dispute about its precise ancestry, the Labrador Retriever is known to have been bred originally by fishermen on the coast of Newfoundland in the 1830s. The dogs used their great strength to help the men haul in their nets, and the breed's enthusiasm for swimming remains evident. The breed was championed by the Earl of Malmesbury, who named it and introduced it to Britain, where it became a highly proficient gundog both on land and in water.

Appearance The overall impression of this breed is one of strength. Its tail is distinctive – thick, broad and relatively short – and is sometimes described as an 'otter tail' because it serves as an effective rudder in water. The distinctive glossy coat is short and water-repellent. Black was the original colour of the Labrador, but yellow Labradors are common today, and there is also the less widely seen chocolate variety.

Personality Labradors are lively and enthusiastic dogs. Intelligent and responsive, they are usually straightforward to train and keen to learn. The breed is also versatile, mastering new tasks easily.

Health and care Labradors are susceptible to hip dysplasia, a problem created by a malformation of the hip joints, causing severe pain Only purchase puppies from breeding stock that has been screened for this condition. Obesity is a major problem – this is a breed that is extremely fond of food – but it can be prevented with a strictly supervised and balanced diet and plenty of exercise. Older Labradors may benefit from a specially devised senior diet.

As an owner Do not rely too heavily on treats for training purposes, because this can be a contributory factor to your dog becoming too fat. With all Labradors, but especially with puppies, be aware of the dog's overwhelming urge to plunge into water – this may occasionally be dangerous, although the breed are strong swimmers. Labradors are powerful dogs and must be well trained to control their natural exuberance.

Also consider The longer-coated Golden Retriever (see pages 118–119) or the Flat Coated Retriever (see pages 112–113) would both be good alternatives. If you want a smaller dog, consider some of the spaniels, but be prepared for more grooming and for the fact they may be harder work to train

Tech Spec

Features

A *Head:* Clean and broad with a medium stop

B *Eyes:* Medium-sized and rounded

C *Ears:* Drop; set far back and low on the skull

D *Chest:* Good balance between width and depth

E *Tail:* Distinctive otter shape

F *Bite:* Scissors bite

G *Height at shoulder:* Dogs 57–62cm (22½–24½ in); bitches 54.5–59.75cm (21½–23½ in)

H *Weight:* Dogs 29.5–36kg (65–80 lb); bitches 25–32kg (55–70 lb)

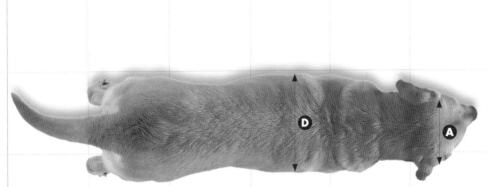

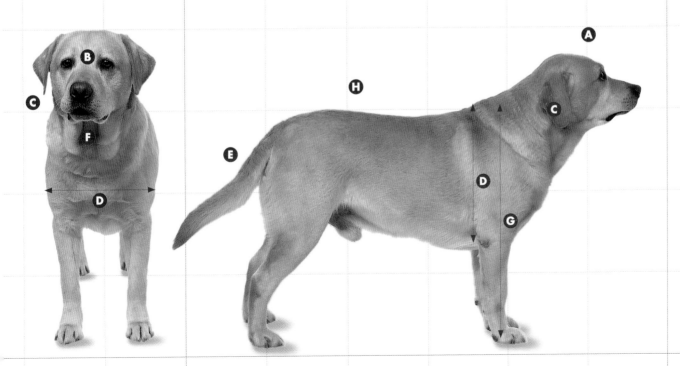

Overview

Recognition
North America, Britain and
FCI member countries

Life expectancy
11–13 years

Colour
Solid lemon, orange, liver
or black, or any of these
colours combined with
white

Grooming

Feeding

Child friendliness

Exercise
This dog must have a good
daily walk

These gundogs communicate with their owners in the field not by barking, but by freezing in a characteristic stance when they detect their game, revealing exactly where the birds are hidden in undergrowth. They are highly specialized and do not flush the birds up for the waiting guns.

Origin It is probable that the English Pointer is descended from one of the mainland pointer breeds from southern Europe, possibly the Old Spanish Pointer, which was brought to England in 1713. Crossings with the Foxhound and possibly Greyhounds increased the pace of these pointers, with the Bloodhound also contributing to the mix, enhancing their scenting ability. Conversely, a similar type of dog may already have existed in England in the 18th century, modified by matings with Spanish pointers.

Appearance This dog has an athletic, muscular build and a short, sleek coat. The muzzle is broad with wide nasal passages, helping the Pointer's ability to track scents. The upper lip hangs down below the level of the lower jaw. The tapering tail is long and is held horizontally, curling up toward its tip. Thick pads protect the feet, cushioning their movement over rough ground.

Personality Friendly, alert and sensitive by nature, the Pointer is an easy breed to train and enjoys working closely with people. This is a dog that displays considerable stamina and natural agility in the field.

Health and care Pointers may occasionally develop a hereditary condition known as neurotropic osteopathy, symptoms of which typically emerge when the dog is aged between 3 and 9 months. Affected individuals start gnawing at their toes and seem insensitive to the resulting pain The blood supply becomes affected, and changes occur in the spinal cord, too. However, a much more common cause of toe-biting is an infection arising from an infestation of harvest mites, especially in the summer, and this can be eliminated with medicated shampoo.

As an owner Pointers are easy to train. Puppies may even start to display their characteristic pointing stance as young as 8 weeks, with a front foot raised, the head extended and the tail quivering with concentration. Pointers have always been bred for their appearance, so that a working dog may excel in the show ring and a show dog in the field.

Also consider There are several other breeds of pointer to choose from. Of the German pointers, the Shorthaired variety (*see pages 114–115*) is closest to this English breed in appearance, although there are also Wirehaired (*see pages 116–117*) and Longhaired options to consider. The various Shorthaired French pointers are less well known internationally, but otherwise are similar in colour and temperament.

Tech Spec

Features

A *Head:* Medium-width with a pronounced stop; nose is slightly elevated compared with the start of the deep muzzle

B *Eyes:* Good size, round and dark

C *Ears:* Set at the level of the eyes, hanging down to below the lower jaw, with pointed tips

D *Chest:* Deep but not wide, with a bold breastbone

E *Tail:* Tapered along its length, with no curl; can reach down to the hocks, but not carried between the legs

F *Bite:* Even or scissors bite

G *Height at shoulder:* Dogs 63.5–71cm (25–28 in); bitches 58.5–66cm (23–26 in)

H *Weight:* Dogs 25–34kg (55–75 lb); bitches 20.5–29.5kg (45–65 lb)

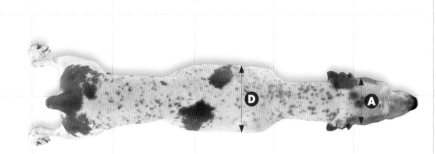

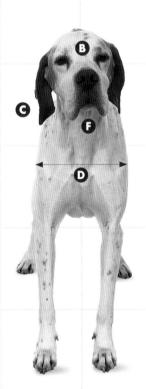

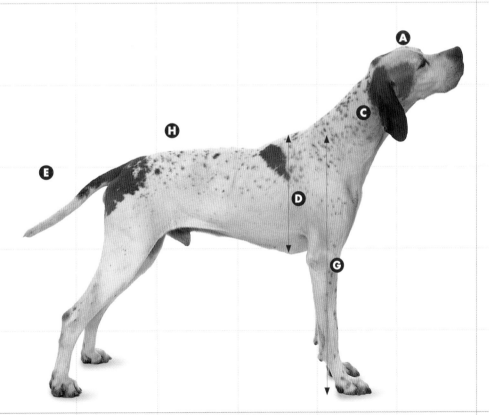

Hungarian Vizsla

Recognition
North America, Britain and
FCI member countries

Life expectancy
11–13 years

Colour
Solid golden-rust

Grooming

Feeding

Child friendliness

Exercise
This dog must be given a
good daily walk

Developed to work as a gundog on the open plains of central Hungary, the Vizsla is a breed that has been shaped much by the environment in which it evolved. This region has a continental climate, with hot summers and cold winters. The short-coated Vizsla is well adapted to work in the heat, possessing plenty of energy.

Origin The ancestors of today's Vizslas may have been kept in Hungary over 1,000 years ago. The breed served as a pointer, working in combination with falcons, which would seize birds that were flushed after the Vizsla had located them. By the 19th century, however, the number of Vizslas had declined to barely a dozen individuals, leaving the breed facing imminent extinction. It survived against the odds, and during World War II when Hungarian refugees fled abroad, a number took their Vizslas with them, helping to increase awareness of the breed internationally.

Appearance A sleek, short, shiny golden rust-coloured coat is an obvious feature of this breed. It has a large brown nose, and eyes of corresponding colour, with the muzzle tapering slightly along its length to a square end. The ears are thin and pendulous, lying close to the sides of the face, and the forehead has a natural furrow. The hindquarters are powerful, with muscular thighs.

Personality The Vizsla's expression emphasizes its gentle disposition. This is a sensitive breed with a lively nature, whose pointing skills are almost instinctive. It is also adaptable, and in recent times it has been trained for search-and-rescue work.

Health and care The lack of an undercoat does mean that Vizslas, unlike many gundogs, are liable to feel the cold. This breed may therefore need the protection of a coat in bad weather. Its grooming needs are modest. It suffers from few hereditary conditions, but some dogs, usually male, do inherit haemophilia, usually through their mothers who are carriers of a defective gene. It is worth checking with your breeder that this problem does not affect their stock lines.

As an owner Although this breed evolved originally as a pointer, it also became an effective retriever when shooting took over from falconry in the 19th century. Vizslas have proved themselves to be one of the most versatile of gundog breeds, and even if your pet does not work, it will still enjoy the opportunity to find and retrieve toys, such as balls or flying disks, when out on a walk.

Also consider The Wirehaired form of the Vizsla may appeal to you – it is identical in all respects other than its coat type. This form of the breed has a good undercoat and was used for hunting in the winter. It has a distinctive beard, but the eyebrows are not especially pronounced. An alternative smooth-coated breed, possibly related to the Vizsla, is the Weimaraner (see pages 130–131).

Tech Spec

Features

A *Head:* Muscular and lean with a moderate stop; square and deep muzzle corresponds in length to the skull

B *Eyes:* Medium-sized with lower eyelids, which neither turn out nor in

C *Ears:* Relatively long, round at the tips and set low, hanging against the cheeks

D *Chest:* broad, extending down to the elbows

E *Tail:* Set just below the level of the croup; thick at its base and carried almost horizontally

F *Bite:* Scissors bite

G *Height at shoulder:* Dogs 56–61cm (22–24 in); bitches 53–58.5cm (21–23 in), with a variance of 3.75cm (1½ in) in either case

H *Weight:* 22–30kg (49–66 lb)

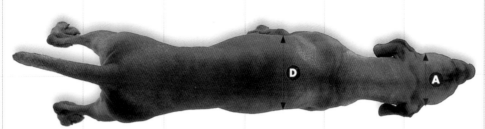

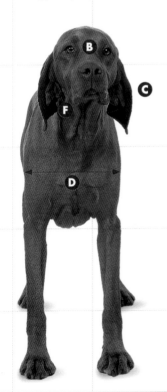

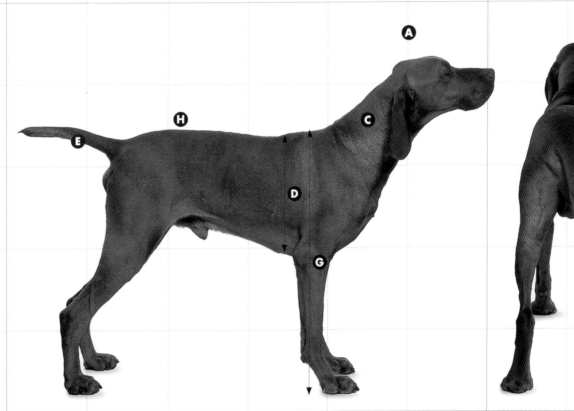

Weimaraner

Overview

Recognition
North America, Britain and
FCI member countries

Life expectancy
11–13 years

Colour
From silvery grey to a
darker mouse grey

Grooming

Feeding

Child friendliness

Exercise
This dog must have an
energetic walk every day

These elegant gundogs, with their distinctive silvery grey coats, were so highly prized in their homeland that they were not available to those outside the aristocracy until the 1930s. Weimaraners have since acquired a strong international following and are seen frequently at field trials and in the show ring.

Origin The Weimaraner was created at the court of Grand Duke Karl August of Weimar in about 1810. He sought to breed the ultimate hunting companion, using a combination of German pointers, with Bloodhounds for their scenting skills and French hounds to contribute pace and reinforce the breed's stamina. The Weimaraner's original game were large dangerous mammals, such as bears and wild boar. As such animals became scarcer in Europe, the breed evolved into a bird dog.

Appearance It is not just the Weimaraner's sleek glossy coat that is an unusual colour – the eyes are distinctive too, ranging from amber to grey or blue-grey. The head is long, and the ears are set high and slightly folded. The forelegs are both strong and straight, and the hindquarters are well-muscled, giving the Weimaraner an apparently effortless gait. The top line of the body should appear level in profile.

Personality The Weimaraner is not a gundog that is happy in kennels, having been bred much more as a companion breed. It is loyal and friendly by nature, and adaptable in terms of learning what is required, whether working on land or retrieving in water.

Health and care Check puppies for any swelling in the area around the umbilicus, because the breed can be prone to umbilical hernias, which may need surgical correction, although this should have no long-term effect on the dog's health. This breed is also prone to skin problems, often first indicated when the dog scratches or bites itself repeatedly. Parasites or even food intolerances may be the cause, and in this case the dog should be checked by a veterinarian.

As an owner This is a relatively large dog, and it needs reasonably spacious surroundings with a secure garden. It cannot be kept confined all day. The Weimaraner is responsive to training and is a good choice if you are interested in showing or competing with your dog. Coat care is straightforward. When grooming, use a hound glove to impart a good gloss.

Also consider There is a rarer longhaired variety of the Weimaraner, although this has yet to achieve such widespread recognition. The hair in this variety has a silky texture and is particularly profuse on the ears. It also has a feathered tail and, overall, is reminiscent of a setter in looks. If you prefer the sleek, short-coated look, then the Hungarian Vizsla (see pages 128–129) represents another option.

Tech Spec

Features

A *Head:* Relatively long with a medium stop; muzzle corresponds in length to that of the skull

B *Eyes:* Well-spaced, appearing almost black when the pupils are dilated

C *Ears:* Set high, slightly folded and long, with a lobular shape

D *Chest:* Deep and well-muscled

E *Tail:* Carried slightly vertically, conveying confidence

F *Bite:* Scissors bite

G *Height at shoulder:* Dogs 63.5–68.5cm (25–27 in); bitches 53–63.5cm (23–25 in), with a variance of 2.5cm (1 in) in either case

H *Weight:* 32–39kg (70–86 lb)

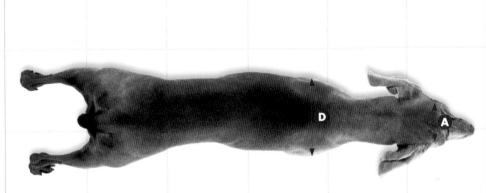

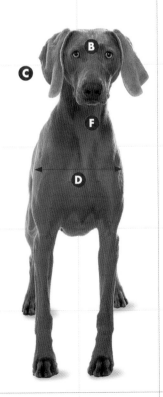

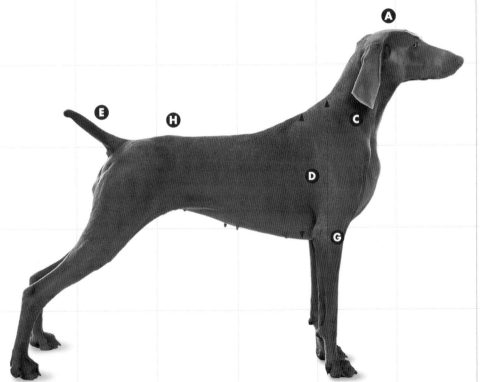

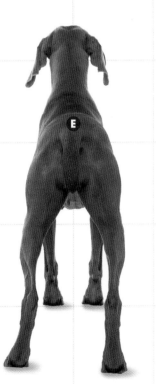

Welsh Springer Spaniel

Overview

Recognition
North America, Britain and
FCI member countries

Life expectancy
11–13 years

Colour
Red and white

Grooming

Feeding

Child friendliness

Exercise
An energetic breed that
needs plenty of exercise

This breed has retained a consistent following in Wales for more than a millennium and is still most likely to be seen there today, although it is found in many other countries around the world. Welsh Springers are lively and energetic, and they are happiest in rural surroundings, where they can locate and flush game in their traditional working style.

Origin It is possible that the Welsh Springer is the ancestral form of all British spaniels. There are records of these dogs in their homeland dating back to AD 900. Its origins are unclear, although they are possibly linked with those of the Brittany (see pages 102–103) from northern France. Until the late 19th century the breed was often called Welsh Cocker Spaniel, although it is a significantly heavier dog than its English counterpart. Welsh Springers were first introduced to North America at the end of the 19th century, and were officially recognized in 1906.

Appearance The dark red and white colouring of the Welsh Springer Spaniel is distinctive. Flecking – the intermingling of the red and white hairs – is permitted in the breed standard. The legs and underparts are heavily feathered and there is lighter feathering on the ears and tail. The Welsh Springer has a narrower head than most spaniels, and when viewed in profile the outline of the body is distinctly rectangular.

Personality Lively, active, and affectionate, the Welsh Springer is a breed that responds well to encouragement and is eager to please. It is an industrious dog that does not tire readily, and it will work with enthusiasm even in harsh conditions.

Health and care The coat of this spaniel is not so long that it would handicap it from working effectively, but it provides the dog with excellent protection. Nonetheless, you should groom your pet after any country walks or working excursions, combing out any burrs and thorns, and checking for ticks.

As an owner The Welsh Springer is a breed developed to work outdoors and is unsuited to urban living. Good training is essential to prevent the dog following its nose and disappearing after a scent when you are out for a walk, but these spaniels learn readily. They will settle well in a home, provided they can be given enough exercise, and they are good guard dogs.

Also consider Other spaniels that may appeal include the English Springer Spaniel (see pages 110–111), if you are looking for a larger dog, or the American Cocker Spaniel (see pages 100–101) or English Cocker Spaniel (see pages 106–107). The Brittany (see pages 102–103) is available in a similar colouring. You may also want to consider some of the other old breeds of French spaniels, such as the Épagneul Picard, or Picardy Spaniel.

Tech Spec

Features

A *Head:* Domed and medium-length with a clear stop; the muzzle may be as long as the skull

B *Eyes:* Dark, medium-sized and oval

C *Ears:* Lie close to the cheeks, set at the level of the eyes

D *Chest:* Muscular, with the brisket level with the elbows

E *Tail:* Extends the topline, lying virtually horizontal and raised slightly when excited

F *Bite:* Scissors bite

G *Height at shoulder:* Dog 45.5–48cm (18–19 in); bitches 43–45.5cm (17–18 in)

H *Weight:* 16–20.5kg (35–45 lb)

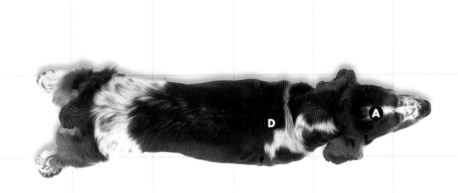

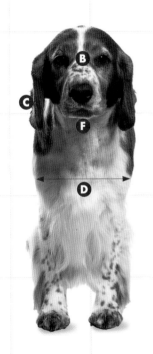

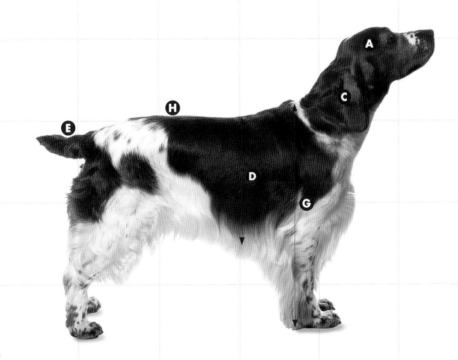

Pet Spec
Clumber Spaniel

Named after the Duke of Newcastle's estate at Clumber Park in the county of Nottinghamshire, where the breed is believed to have been created, this spaniel is something of a heavyweight. While not as fast when working in the field as some other spaniels, it nevertheless has great stamina and is a tireless worker. The Clumber is especially valued in areas of dense undergrowth, because it will plough through them without hesitation.

Appearance A stocky body with strong hindquarters is characteristic of this breed. It has a large, square-shaped head, with wide, pendulous ears that are said to resemble vine leaves in shape. The Clumber's broad muzzle enables it to retrieve a variety of game. The coat is predominantly white, with a silky texture, and may have lemon or orange markings.

Breed care and health This breed is vulnerable to ectropion, which causes the eyelids to hang down, leaving the eyes at risk of infection. The condition may need corrective surgery.

As an owner These spaniels rarely bark and are friendly towards most people, even complete strangers, so they cannot be trusted as watchdogs. The Clumber is gentle by nature and will make a good family pet. This breed has rather loose lips and therefore a tendency to dribble.

Also consider The colouring of the Clumber is unique in the spaniel group, but the Sussex Spaniel (*see page 135*) has a similarly massive head and rich golden-liver colouring, so it may be an alternative option. Another possibility, which is similar in head shape, but smooth-coated and with far less white in its coat, is the Portuguese Pointer, also known as the Perdigeuro Portugueso. It stands up to 56cm (22 in) tall, and can weigh up to 27kg (60 lb).

Pet Spec
Curly Coated Retriever

The distinctive curly coats of these dogs reflect an ancestry said to include the now-extinct English Water Spaniel. Later cross-breeding with both Labrador Retrievers and, subsequently, Poodles helped to shape the Curly Coated Retriever of today. Its popularity in the mid-19th century was such that it was one of the first breeds to be exhibited in shows in classes of its own.

Appearance The curls of this breed are tight and cover the whole body – only the face is smooth. It has a typical retriever profile and is usually black, although occasional liver examples are still seen. The hindquarters are strong, and the breed is both a fast runner and a strong swimmer. The tail, which tapers and is also covered in curly fur, acts as a rudder.

Breed care and health The coat of the Curly Coated Retriever requires little grooming and does not need to be trimmed. The coat is extremely water-resistant and, on emerging from the water, the dog can simply shake itself dry.

As an owner These retrievers are instinctively drawn to water, so care should be taken with where they are exercised, because some rough or deep water may be dangerous. On land, the dense coat also offers protection against thorny undergrowth. The Curly Coated Retriever is affectionate, loyal and responsive to training, but it is often reserved with strangers.

Also consider The curly coat is also a feature of the liver-coloured Irish Water Spaniel, which may also have contributed to its development. The Flat Coated Retriever (*see pages 112–113*) has a similar nature. It is slightly smaller than the Curly Coated, with a dense, flat and fine-textured black coat.

Pet Spec
Irish Water Spaniel

The tallest of all the spaniel breeds, the Irish Water Spaniel was originally bred to retrieve birds from water, rather than to flush game. It is strong enough to carry large birds, such as geese. Its ancestry is something of a mystery, but probably involved native Irish spaniels crossed with breeds such as the Poodle and the Portuguese Water Dog.

Appearance A tightly curled, liver-coloured coat is a characteristic feature of this breed. It also has a distinctive short, tapering tail, the first 7.5cm (3 in) of which is covered in short hair, with a bare tip. This tail type is called a rat tail and is set low on the back, ending above the hocks. The lower hind legs are covered with smooth hair.

Breed care and health The heavy ears may need occasional cleaning to reduce the risk of infection, but overall this is a very healthy breed that is not susceptible to hereditary weaknesses. Its grooming needs are also minimal.

As an owner These dogs are playful by nature and have plenty of energy. They sometimes display an independent streak, so they need to be trained thoroughly from an early age.

Also consider The Portuguese Water Dog (*see page 251*) may be an option. It has a less tightly curled coat, but shows a similar affinity with water, and it is bred in a wider range of colours. The hair over the hindquarters is often trimmed, with a long plume of hair left at the tip of the tail. A smaller alternative would be a Standard Poodle (*see pages 92–93*), which was also originally bred to retrieve from water.

Height 51cm (20 in)
Weight 25-38.5kg (55–85 lb)
Exercise This dog is not a runner, but its stamina means that long walks in the country are necessary

Height 63.5–68.5cm (25–27 in)
Weight 32–36kg (70–80 lb)
Exercise This gundog comes from a working background and needs plenty of exercise

Height 53–61cm (21–24 in)
Weight 20–29.5kg (45–65 lb)
Exercise This dog enjoys the opportunity to explore close to water, in a rural setting

Pet Spec
Nova Scotia Duck Tolling Retriever

Often described simply as the Toller, this breed was originally created for hunting waterfowl in the Canadian province after which it is named. It has an unusual working method – first it splashes around close to the shore chasing after sticks thrown by the hunters. It creates a lot of disturbance in the water but does not bark, and gradually ducks are attracted in towards the waiting guns. The dog will then wade in to retrieve any that are shot. This lively and agile breed is best suited to a rural environment.

Appearance The smallest member of the retriever group, the Toller is distinguished partly by its red colouring, which ranges from golden to a coppery shade. The feathering on the limbs, body and underside of the tail is always slightly paler. White patches sometimes feature on the chest, as a blaze between the eyes, on the feet below the pasterns and at the tip of the tail.

Breed care and health The coat of this retriever needs relatively little care, and it dries readily after becoming wet. Tollers should have powerful jaws with a tight scissor bite to enable them to retrieve waterfowl easily. The tail should not curl down so that it touches the back.

As an owner Tollers are determined gundogs, displaying high powers of concentration when working. They are affectionate, but they can be slightly withdrawn in unfamiliar situations. Puppies must be trained carefully to overcome any tendency to shyness.

Also consider The Golden Retriever (*see pages 118–119*) is a bigger breed, with a paler coat of similar length. Its temperament closely matches that of the Toller, and their overall care needs are similar. Both breeds display a natural affinity with water. The shorter-coated Labrador Retriever (*see pages 124– 125*) may be another option. These dogs are stockier and paler in colour, too.

Height 43–53cm (17–21 in)
Weight 16.25–23kg (37–51 lb)
Exercise Plenty of exercise is essential; this dog will enjoy any opportunity to swim or to play in water

Pet Spec
Spinone Italiano

This rough-coated Italian breed is a versatile hunting companion. Its prime function is still to serve as a pointer, although it will also retrieve game readily. Its thick, tousled coat allows it to work in dense undergrowth with little risk of injury. Its origins are unclear, but it is thought to be related to another popular Italian breed, the Segugio Italiano, and perhaps also to the French Barbet.

Appearance Long hair extends down over the jaws to create the impression of a beard. The large eyes vary from yellow to ochre in colour. The ears are long and hang down the sides of the head, and the coat has a wiry texture, as well as being thick. Although it may be slightly crimped, it should not be curly. The tail is carried below the level of the back. The dog is bred in a range of colours, but any black colouring counts as a fault in the breed standard.

Breed care and health The Spinone Italiano should not be immaculately coiffured before a show. These gundogs tend to be fit and strong, and they have no predisposition to any particular weaknesses.

As an owner This breed is an exceptionally versatile gundog and can display great stamina in the field. It is also a dog that needs plenty of attention – it 'talks' to its owner to attract notice. It makes a loyal and loving pet.

Also consider The Wirehaired Pointing Griffon, also known as the Korthals Griffon, may be an option. It is an ancient French breed that bears a similarity to the Spinone, but is slightly smaller, standing up to 61cm (24 in) tall. It has bushy eyebrows and a long beard. The Czesky Fousek is an effective working dog of equivalent size, but its coat is not as profuse. It is less suited in temperament to be a household pet.

Height 56–68.5cm (22–27 in)
Weight 32.25–37kg (71–82 lb)
Exercise Plenty of opportunity to exercise is essential

Pet Spec
Sussex Spaniel

Native to the English county of Sussex, this spaniel was developed in the 19th century, although its precise origins are unclear. On many occasions in the past the Sussex Spaniel has faced an uncertain future, but the breed has survived, although it remains rare. This is in part because it is slower in the field than other spaniels. It was introduced to North America in the 1880s.

Appearance These spaniels are of a highly distinctive rich golden-liver shade, the colour lightening at the tips of the hairs. The body is long and the legs short and powerful, creating a distinctly rectangular appearance. These features, combined with a broad chest, contribute to this spaniel's characteristic rolling gait. The skull is broad and the eyes have heavy brows, giving the dog a frowning expression.

Breed care and health This is a healthy breed. The ears need to be cleaned regularly, and the coat needs careful grooming to look its best. From a show perspective, the correct depth of colour in the coat is a critical feature.

As an owner Having evolved to hunt in dense cover, the Sussex is unusual in that it bays like a hound when it picks up a trail. This behaviour also suggests that hound blood may have contributed to its breeding mix.

Also consider The Field Spaniel is a possible option. It has a long body but is less broad in the head than the Sussex and is slightly taller. The Field Spaniel has been bred in a range of solid colours, but the richness of the Sussex colouring is unique. If you like the broad head, the Clumber (*see page 134*), which has a white coat with lemon or orange markings, may be another type to consider.

Height 33–38cm (13–15 in)
Weight 16–20kg (35–45 lb)
Exercise Walks in the country with the opportunity to explore will be necessary

Airedale Terrier

Overview

Recognition
North America, Britain and
FCI member countries

Life expectancy
12–14 years

Colour
Tan with black markings
forming a "saddle" on
the back

Grooming

Feeding

Child friendliness

Exercise
Active by nature, this breed
needs a long daily walk

The largest of the British terrier breeds, the Airedale is an impressive dog with an unmistakable appearance. It is versatile – in addition to being kept as a companion dog it has had a wide range of working activities, including herding stock, hunting, and serving in the Red Cross, seeing active service in World Wars I and II.

Origin The Airedale was developed in the 1840s, and its appearance and size suggest that Otterhounds probably contributed to the early breed. This view is reinforced by the fact that the breed grew up in close proximity to the Rivers Aire and Wharfe, in the northern English county of Yorkshire. Black and Tan Terriers were used, and this ancestry can still be seen in the Airedale's coat. Bull Terriers may have been involved in the early breeding mix, too. The breed was first seen in North America, where it became popular as a gundog, in 1881.

Appearance This breed has a long skull, which narrows only a little along its length. The Airedale's face ends in a distinctive beard, which hangs down over the jaws. The small ears are V-shaped and, like the head, must be tan in colour, with a black nose. The Airedale's coat is dense and has a hard, wiry texture, but there is a softer undercoat beneath.

Personality Bold and fearless, the Airedale has a strong personality, is energetic and can be playful, but it is not always friendly towards other dogs. The Airedale will also be alert to the presence of strangers and can make a formidable guard dog.

Health and care The Airedale is a breed at risk from umbilical hernias, so check a puppy's stomach around the umbilicus for lumps or pain. Minor surgery is usually needed to repair this muscle tear. Some young Airedales over 6 months old are affected by a nervous disorder that causes trembling in their hindquarters. This may be an inherited problem.

As an owner If you want to show your dog, remember that the Airedale is one of the most demanding breeds to prepare successfully for the show ring. Its coat must be hand-stripped, a job for a professional groomer. Airedales retain keen hunting instincts and will chase and kill small prey they encounter; they should be kept away from pets such as guinea pigs or rabbits. This breed needs a lot of training, but with patience on the part of their owner they can be taught to act as retrievers.

Also consider The smaller Welsh Terrier (*see pages 166–167*), which looks like a miniature form of the Airedale, is also usually black and tan and may be an option. The Lakeland Terrier (*see page 172*) might be a possibility, too. It is slightly smaller than the Welsh Terrier and is bred in a wider range of colours.

Tech Spec

Features

A *Head:* Similar length of skull and muzzle, with little evidence of a stop

B *Eyes:* Small and dark; they show intelligence

C *Ears:* Small and V-shaped; top line is above the level of the skull

D *Chest:* Deep chest extending down to the elbows

E *Tail:* Set high on the back, carried upright

F *Bite:* Scissors or level bite

G *Height at shoulder:* Dogs 58.5cm (23 in); bitches 56cm (22 in)

H *Weight:* 20–22.5kg (44–50 lb)

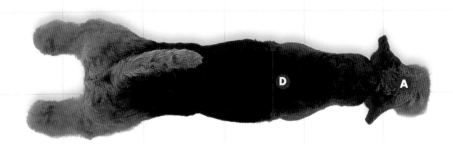

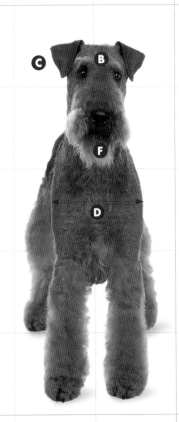

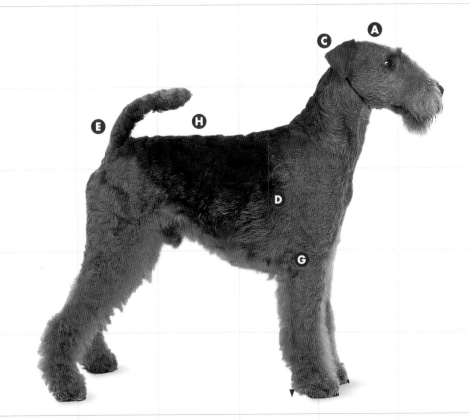

Australian Terrier

Overview

Recognition
North America, Britain
and FCI member countries

Life expectancy
12–14 years

Colour
Solid sandy or red; blue
and tan

Grooming

Feeding

Child friendliness

Exercise
Likes to explore on its walks

This hardy little terrier is one of the smallest working breeds. Early in its history it acquired a remarkable reputation for catching venomous snakes, leaping up and seizing them behind the head. 'Aussies', as these dogs are often known, will also hunt more typical terrier targets, including rabbits and rats.

Origin The breed developed in Australia from a wide variety of terrier breeds brought from Europe, ranging from the Dandie Dinmont to the Cairn (the latter contributed red colouring to Australian Terrier bloodlines.) The type of these terriers was established by the 1870s, but it was not until 1933 that the breed was recognized by the British Kennel Club, and it gained recognition in North America in 1960. Today the breed is widely represented internationally, but it is still seen most commonly in its homeland.

Appearance Seen in profile, this terrier has a long body in proportion to its height, and this may reflect the input of Skye Terrier stock to its ancestry. The head is also long, with a flat top to the skull. The erect ears are set high on the head and are small, with pointed tips. The outer coat has a harsh texture and is about 6.5cm (2½ in) long. The undercoat is soft and short, with a topknot of hair on the head.

Personality A confident dog in spite of its size, the Australian Terrier is naturally bold and inquisitive. It will form a strong bond with its owner and thrives on attention. These terriers' senses are finely tuned, ensuring that it is effective as a ratter.

Health and care Australian Terriers do not have any major inherited weaknesses, but it is important to ensure that they are adequately protected by vaccination against leptospirosis, a bacterial infection spread by rats, which can be fatal to dogs. Dogs can catch the disease from contaminated water, or through contact with rats' urine when they are hunting.

As an owner The Australian Terrier is highly recommended for the proud home owner, because it does not shed, even in warmer climates and seasons – it also does not require much grooming. These terriers will settle down well in the home, whether as part of a family or with someone living alone. Their keen senses make them alert watchdogs.

Also consider Other possibilities include the Australian Silky Terrier (see pages 206–207), which was developed in part from this breed, but has a softer, silky coat, or the Yorkshire Terrier (see pages 208–209). Although similar in colouring, the latter has a much more profuse coat, will need more grooming, and is usually considered more as a toy breed than a working terrier.

Tech Spec

Features

A *Head:* Long and powerful with a slight stop evident; the length of the skull corresponds to that of the strong muzzle

B *Eyes:* Well-spaced, small and dark

C *Ears:* Small, pointed and held erect; set high but well apart

D *Chest:* Extends below the elbows, with a deep keel

E *Tail:* Set high and carried upright, in an almost vertical position

F *Bite:* Scissors bite

G *Height at shoulder:* 25.5–28cm (10–11 in)

H *Weight:* 5.5–6.5kg (12–14 lb)

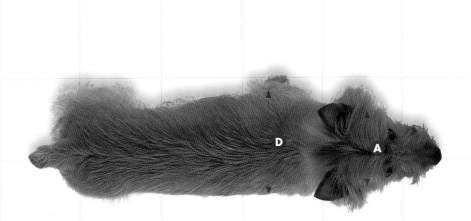

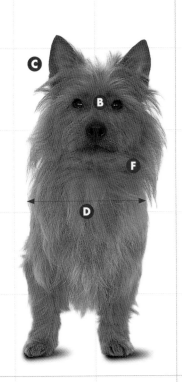

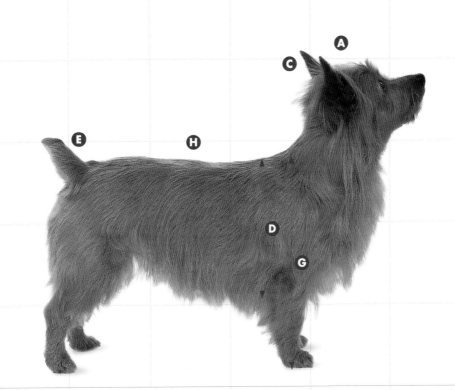

Border Terrier

Overview

Recognition
North America, Britain
and FCI member countries

Life expectancy
12–14 years

Colour
Blue and tan; wheaten;
red, grizzle, and tan

Grooming

Feeding

Child friendliness

Exercise
Active; needs a good
walk every day

The smaller working terriers have much greater stamina than their size would suggest, and they are different in temperament from toy dogs of similar size. They also tend to be more robust, as demonstrated in the case of the Border Terrier. This breed was exhibited at agricultural events before it was seen at dog shows.

Origin Created in the Borders, as the area around the English and Scottish border is known, this terrier has existed there for over 400 years. It was developed to run with the local hounds and yet to remain small and bold enough to venture underground and flush out a fox by itself. The Border Terrier was therefore a well-established working breed long before it was finally accepted by the Kennel Club in 1920. It was registered in North America for the first time a decade later.

Appearance The Border Terrier is a relatively long-legged breed with a compact body shape. Its head has been likened to that of an otter: it is broad, with a neat, dark muzzle. The otterlike appearance is reinforced by dark eyes. The ears are small and V-shaped. The topcoat is wiry, with a short dense undercoat, and the underlying skin is loose.

Personality Brave and fearless when working, the Border Terrier can be trained easily and is affectionate by nature. The breed has great stamina and is hardy, too, having evolved in an area where the weather can often be wet and stormy.

Health and care Border Terriers are sometimes born with holes in the walls of the ventricles of the heart, which may require surgical repair. Such dogs should not be used for breeding. In the case of mature male dogs, check that the testes descend into the scrotum; one or occasionally both may be retained within the body, and need to be removed surgically, as they can otherwise result in Sertoli cell tumours. For these reasons, you should have your Border Terrier puppy checked by a vet.

As an owner Having been bred to work closely in the company of hounds, Border Terriers are reasonably well-tempered towards other dogs, unlike some of the more antisocial terrier breeds. If you are considering breeding Border Terriers, you may need professional help – the bitches occasionally suffer from primary uterine inertia, meaning that there are no contractions to push the puppies out at birth.

Also consider The wirehaired type of the Parson Russell Terrier (*see pages 156–157*) is the breed that approximates most closely to the Border Terrier in terms of appearance. A breed that is similar in colour is the Norfolk Terrier (*see page 173*), but it has a broader body and shorter legs.

Tech Spec

Features

A *Head:* Otterlike, with a broad skull between the eyes and ears; short and preferably dark muzzle

B *Eyes:* Medium-sized, dark hazel, and not especially prominent or small

C *Ears:* Small and V-shaped, set on the sides of the face and falling forwards to the cheeks

D *Chest:* Neither deep nor narrow

E *Tail:* Short, tapered and not set high; held up when alert

F *Bite:* Scissors bite

G *Height at shoulder:* 25.5cm (10 in)

H *Weight:* Dogs 6–7kg (13–15½ lb); bitches 5.25–6.5kg (11½–14 lb)

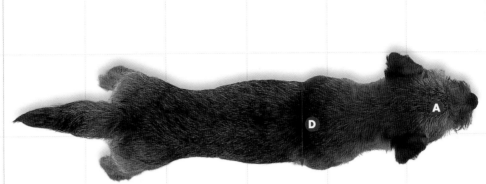

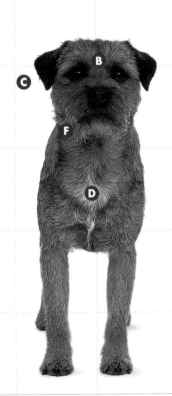

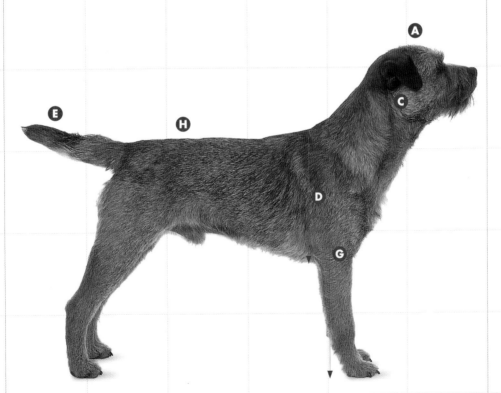

Cairn Terrier

Overview

Recognition
North America, Britain
and FCI member countries

Life expectancy
11–13 years

Colour
Any colour except white

Grooming

Feeding

Child friendliness

Exercise
Active; will need a good
daily walk

The Cairn is one of a number of working terrier breeds of Scottish ancestry. It is named after the piles of stones that were built up along the roadsides, both to mark boundaries and for ceremonial purposes, in many parts of Scotland. These provided ideal retreats for rats and even foxes, and farmers used terriers to drive unwelcome visitors out.

Origin The Scottish terrier breeds are all descended from similar ancestral stock, and the forerunners of today's Cairn have been known in the Western Highlands and on the Isle of Skye for over 400 years. The appearance of the Cairn Terrier has changed remarkably little over this period. Until 1909 it was called the Shorthaired Skye Terrier, but it was officially recognized as a breed under its current name by the Kennel Club in 1912, appearing for the first time in North America in 1913.

Appearance The Cairn is one of the smallest working terriers, and it still has workman-like looks, with a rough, slightly unkempt appearance. The breed stands taller in proportion to its overall size than its near relative, the Scottish Terrier, and a balanced appearance is considered essential for a show dog. The Cairn's double coat provides good protection against the elements; it is coarse on top with a short, soft undercoat.

Personality A typical terrier, with a bold, inquisitive nature and a strong character, the Cairn delights in human company, but is less keen on canine companionship. In spite of its size, this terrier is hardy and will expect to go out even in bad weather.

Health and care The breed suffers from a number of genetic problems, including haemophilia. A particular illness seen in puppies aged between 4 and 7 months is craniomandibular osteopathy. This affects the jaws and adjacent tympanic bullae, raises the puppy's temperature and makes eating painful. Treatment to lessen the inflammation and a diet of soft food will be necessary, and affected terriers recover uneventfully as they mature.

As an owner These terriers often enjoy swimming, and they may head off to a pond or river when you are out. The Cairn is a sturdy breed and has considerable energy, so although it may not run hard unless it is chasing or hunting, it will trot alongside you for considerable distances on a walk. If it does find something to chase, keep a watch to ensure that it does not disappear underground in pursuit of its game.

Also consider Related Scottish breeds, such as the West Highland White Terrier (*see pages 168–169*) or the long-coated Skye Terrier (*see page 173*) may be possibilities; the Skye Terrier, however, will need considerably more grooming. Originating from further south, the Norwich Terrier (*see pages 154–155*) is reminiscent of the Cairn, but has shorter legs.

Tech Spec

Features

A *Head:* Broad when compared with its length, with an evident stop; powerful but short muzzle

B *Eyes:* Sunken and well-spaced, protected by shaggy eyebrows

C *Ears:* Widely spaced, small and pointed; carried erect

D *Chest:* Moderate

E *Tail:* Held vertically, but not curled over the back

F *Bite:* Level bite

G *Height at shoulder:* Dogs 25.5cm (10 in); bitches 24cm (9½ in)

H *Weight:* Dogs 6.5kg (14 lb); bitches 6kg (13 lb)

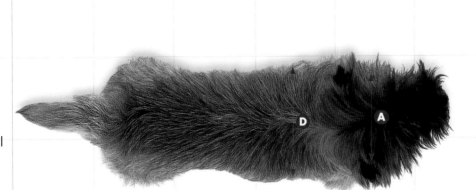

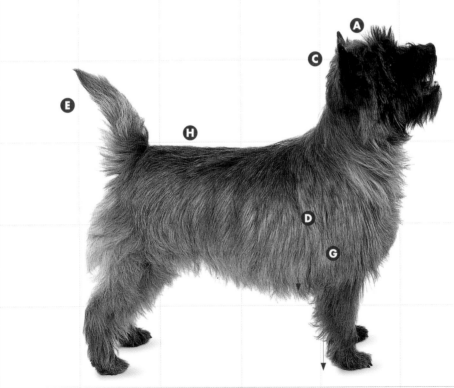

Dandie Dinmont Terrier

Overview

Recognition
North America, Britain
and FCI member countries

Life expectancy
11–13 years

Colour
Mustard or pepper

Grooming

Feeding

Child friendliness

Exercise
A good daily stroll around
the park should be enough

This is the only breed of dog that owes its name to a character in a popular novel. Sir Walter Scott featured Dandie Dinmont, the owner of one of these terriers, in *Guy Mannering*, published in 1814. As a result, the breed was soon being referred to as Dandie Dinmont's Terriers, and the name was ultimately shortened to the form used today.

Origin The Dandie Dinmont Terrier was bred from native terriers in the southern borders of Scotland in the early 18th century. Although it is tempting to suggest that Dachshunds may have played a part in the development of this low-slung breed, there is no evidence for this, in spite of similarities in their appearance and the fact that Dandie Dinmonts were also used to hunt badgers. After its appearance in Scott's novel, the breed's popularity grew, and King Louis Philippe of France was among notable Dandie Dinmont owners.

Appearance The Dandie Dinmont has a long, low-slung body and a topknot of silky hair on the head. The ears are pendulous and set well back, lying against the cheeks. The neck is muscular, suitable for a hunting breed that was expected to cope with game of much larger size. The breed's colouring is described as being either pepper – shades between silvery Grey and blue-black – or mustard, ranging from fawn to reddish brown.

Personality This breed is intelligent but reserved, although it can sometimes display a more extrovert, playful side. It is tenacious and bold, and it is not easily intimidated even when it encounters much larger dogs.

Health and care In common with the Dachshunds, the Dandie Dinmont's long body makes it susceptible to back problems, in particular to intervertebral disk conditions. These disks normally act as cushions between the vertebrae, but they can sometimes become displaced (this is commonly known as a slipped disk) and place pressure directly on the spinal cord. The symptoms depend on which part of the spinal cord is affected, and in the worst cases the problem can ultimately lead to paralysis, sometimes with loss of bowel and bladder tone. In many cases, however, careful nursing and treatment may lead to recovery. Grooming is considered important to maintain this breed's unique appearance. A professional groomer will hand-pluck the coat.

As an owner Try to minimize the risk of your dog developing back problems. Exercise your pet using a harness instead of collar to reduce pressure on the vulnerable neck region, and do not encourage it to jump up on furniture or to climb stairs. Use a stair guard, like those used to guard toddlers, if necessary.

Also consider The Skye Terrier, which has a similar body shape but a more profuse coat (*see page 173*), may be an alternative. The Yorkshire Terrier (*see pages 208–209*) represents another possibility, while from outside the terrier group, Wirehaired Dachshunds (*see pages 58–59*), in either a standard or miniature form, are other options that may appeal to you, as may the taller and distinctive Bedlington Terrier (*see page 172*).

Tech Spec

Features

A *Head:* Broad skull, tapered slightly between the eyes, with a well-domed forehead and evident stop; a deep, powerful muzzle

B *Eyes:* Large, round and widely spaced; set low and directly forwards

C *Ears:* Long, widely spaced and set well back, hanging down close to the cheeks

D *Chest:* Well-developed, extending between the forelegs

E *Tail:* Thicker for a distance from the base, then tapered; carried in a scimitar-like curve

F *Bite:* Scissors bite

G *Height at shoulder:* 20–28cm (8–11 in)

H *Weight:* 8–11kg (18–24 lb)

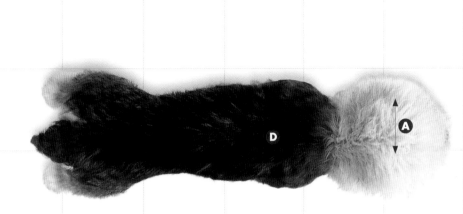

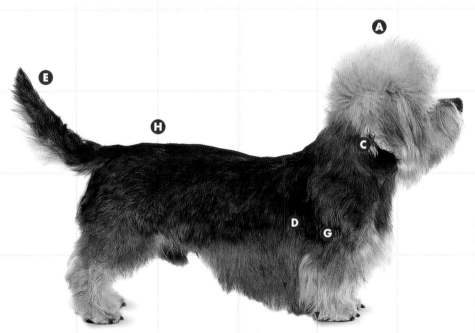

Overview

Recognition
North America, Britain
and FCI member countries

Life expectancy
12–14 years

Colour
Wheaten, blue or brindle

Grooming

Feeding

Child friendliness

Exercise
A lively daily excursion
in a park should be enough

Although it is an old breed, the Glen of Imaal has only come to international prominence over the past 20 years or so, finally achieving full American Kennel Club registration in 2004. It has changed remarkably little in appearance from its earliest days. The name comes from its place of origin in County Wicklow, Ireland.

Origin The original ancestors of this terrier were native Irish breeds, probably crossed with a basset hound of some type brought over from France over 400 years ago. The Glen of Imaal Terrier has been versatile, undertaking roles as various as that of turnspit dog (turning the wheel connecting to the spit roasting meat over a kitchen fire), fighting dog and hunter of badgers. Despite this checkered past, this breed has always been a genial companion dog, and the Irish Kennel Club recognized it in 1933.

Appearance Long-bodied and low-slung, but broad, the Glen of Imaal Terrier has a harsh, weather-resistant top-coat of medium length, with a softer undercoat beneath. It is often wheaten, but in a wide range of shades from cream through to a reddish tone. The front feet turn naturally outward.

Personality Unlike many terriers, the Glen of Imaal is not excitable but quiet by nature. It can be surprisingly athletic and run fast, which may be a sign of some hound ancestry. It settles down readily as a family pet.

Health and care These terriers are generally fit and hardy. The natural deviation in the position of their front feet means that their toenails may wear unevenly, and a Glen of Imaal Terrier that spends most of its time at home is likely to have overgrown claws, which will need to be trimmed back. This is a job for a professional groomer, because it can be difficult to see where the quick starts on the black nails.

As an owner Although the unkempt appearance of this terrier looks natural, it is usually attained by hand-stripping the harsh coat. You can learn this skill yourself, but most owners use a professional grooming service. Despite its comparatively quiet personality, remember that the Glen of Imaal is still a terrier, so it needs to be socialized with other dogs early to limit any tendency to fight.

Also consider The taller but similarly coloured Soft Coated Wheaten Terrier (*see pages 162–163*), which also originated in Ireland, may be one possibility. Others include the Norfolk Terrier (*see page 173*) or the Norwich Terrier (*see pages 154–155*). Both breeds exist in a wheaten form, although other colours are available.

Tech Spec

Features

A *Head:* Strong, with a broad, slightly domed skull and a slightly shorter but powerful muzzle

B *Eyes:* Well-spaced, round, brown and medium-sized

C *Ears:* Small and widely spaced; can be rose or half-pricked when dog is alert, lying back at rest

D *Chest:* Strong, wide and deep, reaching below the level of the elbows

E *Tail:* Strong and carried above the level of the back

F *Bite:* Scissors bite preferred, but level bite accepted

G *Height at shoulder:* 31.5–35.5cm (12½–14 in)

H *Weight:* 16kg (35 lb)

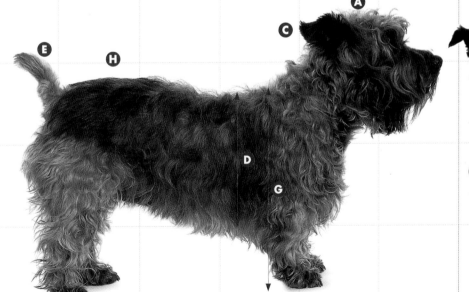

Overview

Recognition
North America, Britain and FCI member countries

Life expectancy
13–15 years

Colour
Blue-Grey, sometimes with darker or black points

Grooming

Feeding

Child friendliness

Exercise
A good daily walk, with the opportunity to explore off the leash, is essential

Originating in County Kerry, this breed is officially regarded as Ireland's national dog. The Kerry Blue is a versatile terrier with a good nose, and works effectively as a retriever. It has even worked as a herder as well as carrying out more typical terrier tasks, such as vermin control.

Origin The origins of the Kerry Blue Terrier are unknown. It may be descended from indigenous old terrier breeds, perhaps crossed with Bedlington Terriers. It became popular in its homeland in the late 19th century and was known internationally by the 1920s, appearing for the first time at leading American shows. This was the breed's heyday – since then, its popularity has faded somewhat in comparison with other types of terrier.

Appearance The colour of the Kerry Blue is an important feature of the breed. It can vary from blue-Grey to Grey-blue and should ideally be evenly distributed all over the dog, although the extremities – muzzle, ears, and feet – are often darker, or even black. The coat should be dense, soft, and wavy. The head is long but in proportion to the body, as are the V-shaped ears. The puppies are black at birth, but their colour lightens over the first year or so, a process that is described as 'clearing'.

Personality This is an intelligent and adaptable breed with strong working instincts. It also has a playful side, revels in human company and is a willing pupil.

Health and care Puppies typically aged between 9 and 16 weeks occasionally develop signs of a disorder of the nervous system. This manifests itself in tremors of the head and a stiffness of the forelegs, and it ultimately results in paralysis. Another unusual health problem associated with the breed are tumours of the hair follicles, which tend to afflict older Kerry Blues. These appear as swellings, which are noticeable during grooming.

As an owner Be careful with your terrier around cats, as this breed often displays a strong dislike of them that is hard to train out. Kerries are patient with children and make good watchdogs.

Also consider The Irish Terrier (see page 172) has a somewhat similar appearance, but is a different colour, with a wiry rather than a silky coat. Another Irish breed, with a more profuse coat, is the Soft Coated Wheaten Terrier (see pages 162–163). If you like the Kerry's beard, the Miniature Schnauzer (see pages 152–153) may also appeal to you.

Tech Spec

Features

A *Head:* Long yet in proportion, with a flat top to the skull and slight stop; the muzzle is of equal length to the skull

B *Eyes:* Small, dark and not especially prominent

C *Ears:* Small, V-shaped and lying close to the cheeks, with the tops being just above the skull

D *Chest:* Deep and broad

E *Tail:* Medium-length, straight and carried above the back

F *Bite:* Scissors or level bite

G *Height at shoulder:* Dogs 45.5–49.5cm (18–19½ in); bitches 44.5–48cm (17½–19 in) preferable, but a 2.5cm (1 in) variance is permitted

H *Weight:* 15–18kg (33–40 lb), with bitches being lighter than dogs

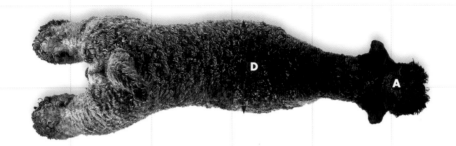

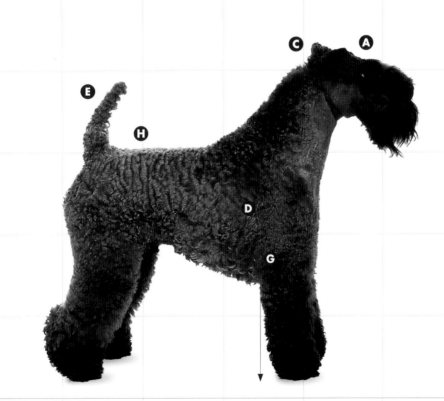

Overview

Recognition
North America, Britain
and FCI member countries

Life expectancy
10–12 years

Colour
White, fawn, red, black/
brindle, and bi- and
tricolour of all these shades

Grooming

Feeding

Child friendliness

Exercise
Lively, and needs a good
daily walk, but watch for
possible conflicts with
other dogs

There is no mistaking either the Standard or the Miniature Bull Terrier, thanks to the large egg-shaped face that characterizes the breed. It has a big personality to match its appearance, nd makes an excellent companion. Bull Terriers may sometimes display pointing behaviour , inherited through past crossings with gundogs.

Origin The full-size Bull Terrier arose directly as a result of the ban placed in England, in 1835, on bull-baiting with dogs. Enthusiasts then turned to dogfighting. Bulldogs were not suited to dogfights, because they were too slow and lacked sufficient instinctive aggression, so the hunt for a fighting dog led to crosses between Bulldogs and some types of terrier, the latter to introduce the necessary ruthless, aggressive streak. Further matings with Dalmatians were made to increase the new breed's power and stamina. Miniature Bull Terriers were bred later, from the runts of Bull Terrier litters, and were used for ratting, not fighting. Although they stand about 10cm (4 in) shorter at the shoulder than the standard version and are treated as a separate breed, they have all the same characteristics.

Appearance Everything about this breed serves to emphasize its strength. Its long head is supported by a thick powerful neck, which in turn is linked to a broad muscular chest. The body is short and strong, with broad ribs providing for a good lung capacity. Although the dog is bred in a number of different colours, the familiar white-coated type, broken with dark spots on the face, is believed to be a reflection of its Dalmatian ancestry.

Personality In its day the Bull Terrier was reportedly a ferocious fighter, but the modern dog, in both its Miniature and Standard versions, has a gentle, affectionate side to its personality. Although these dogs can still be roused to fight – and are difficult to dissuade if they decide to act – great efforts have been made by breeders to reduce aggressive traits.

Health and care The white-coated variety of the Miniature Bull Terrier is susceptible to skin cancer, triggered by extensive exposure to hot sun. Avoid exercising these dogs in the middle of the day in hot weather, and rub a canine sunblock on their prominent ears if they have to be outdoors for any length of time in sunshine. Pure-white Bull Terriers may also suffer from inherited deafness, a congenital problem linked to their colour.

As an owner Bear in mind that, even in its Miniature package, the Bull Terrier is a powerful dog. It must be properly trained from a young age, ideally in puppy classes, which will have the added advantage of helping to socialize your pet with other dogs. Although Miniature Bull Terriers are friendly towards people, they may enter into disputes with other dogs, and they are capable of inflicting serious injuries. It is crucial that your pet is obedient to your commands.

Also consider If you want a bigger dog – and an even bigger challenge – consider the full-sized Bull Terrier. The Staffordshire Bull Terrier (*see pages 164–165*), which has a head shape like that of a mastiff, and a similar character, is another possibility.

Tech Spec

Features

A *Head:* Egg-shaped appearance, curving gently from the skull down to the tip of the nose

B *Eyes:* Small, dark and well-sunken, placed obliquely and close together, up high

C *Ears:* Small and close together; may be held erect

D *Chest:* Broad and powerful, with brisket nearer to the ground than to the belly

E *Tail:* Low-set, short and tapered; carried horizontally

F *Bite:* Level or scissors bite

G *Height at shoulder:* 53–56cm (21–22 in)

H *Weight:* 23.5–28kg (52–62 lb)

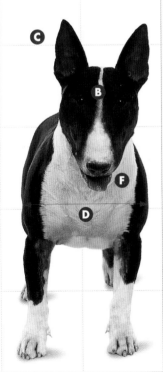

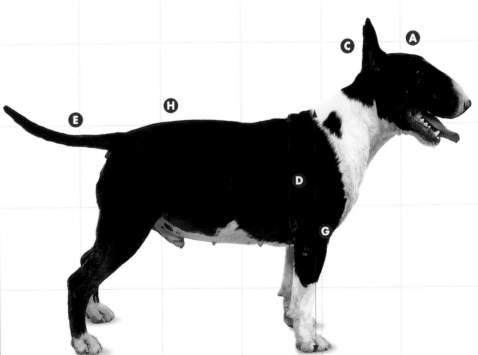

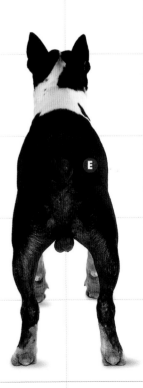

Group **Terrier**

Overview

Recognition
North America, Britain
and FCI member countries

Life expectancy
12–14 years

Colour
Salt and pepper, black and
silver, black

Grooming

Feeding

Child friendliness

Exercise
Needs the opportunity for
an energetic run around
the park every day

This is not simply a scaled-down version of the Schnauzer breed, but a working dog in its own right, bred originally to hunt rats. With a different heritage from that of other breeds classed as terriers, however, the Miniature Schnauzer is not inclined to go to ground in pursuit of its game.

Origin It is believed that the process of miniaturization leading to the development of this breed began with the selective breeding of the smallest puppies produced in Schnauzer litters. In the late 19th century Miniature Schnauzers were crossed with Affenpinschers to scale down the breed further. The Miniature Schnauzer was first exhibited in 1899.

Appearance The unusual colour combinations seen in the Miniature Schnauzer result from alternating light and dark banding running down the individual hairs. The hindquarters of this breed are especially angular, and in its show stance the hock joints of the legs extend further behind the body than the tail.

Personality Lively, playful and alert, the Miniature Schnauzer is a breed that can be trained with little difficulty. It relates well to children and, unlike some terriers, it is usually tolerant of other dogs.

Health and care In contrast with many breeds that have become less sound as the result of becoming smaller, the Miniature Schnauzer is generally healthy. Puppies are occasionally afflicted by a congenital narrowing of the pulmonary artery. Breathlessness and lack of energy are typical symptoms, and the problem requires surgical correction if possible. This weakness was probably inherited from the Schnauzer.

As an owner Coat care in this breed is demanding because it requires careful stripping to maintain the breed's distinctive appearance. If a Miniature Schnauzer is simply clipped, the characteristic banding in the top coat will be lost and the undercoat will show through. This breed has a bark that sounds like that of a much larger dog. It makes a good guard dog.

Also consider The Schnauzer (see pages 248–249) is a much larger dog with an identical appearance. If you like the long face of the Miniature Schnauzer but prefer a short-coated dog, the Smooth Fox Terrier (see pages 160–161) is an option. The Wire Fox Terrier (see pages 170–171) is another possibility.

Tech Spec

Features

A *Head:* Rectangular and powerful, with flat top to the skull, a slight stop and a strong, blunt muzzle

B *Eyes:* Set deep, dark brown, oval and small

C *Ears:* Set high, small, V-shaped, and naturally folded alongside the skull

D *Chest:* Moderate

E *Tail:* Set high and carried upright

F *Bite:* Scissors bite

G *Height at shoulder:* 30.5–35.5cm (12–14 in)

H *Weight:* 6–6.75kg (13–15 lb)

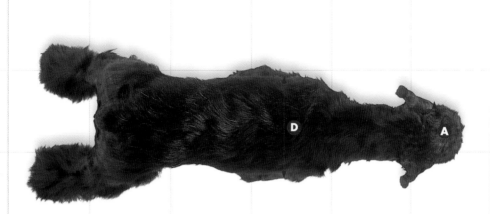

Norwich Terrier

Overview

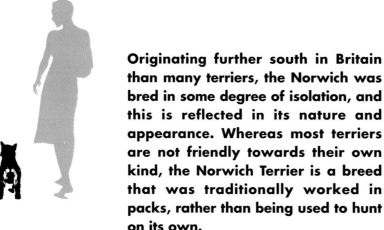

Recognition
North America, Britain
and FCI member countries

Life expectancy
12–14 years

Colour
Any shade of red,
wheaten, grizzle or
black and tan

Grooming

Feeding

Child friendliness

Exercise
A daily trot around the
park will be adequate

Originating further south in Britain than many terriers, the Norwich was bred in some degree of isolation, and this is reflected in its nature and appearance. Whereas most terriers are not friendly towards their own kind, the Norwich Terrier is a breed that was traditionally worked in packs, rather than being used to hunt on its own.

Origin The Norwich Terrier started with terrier stock kept at a livery stable in the heart of the city of Cambridge and became popular with undergraduates at the university there in the 1880s. One of these terriers, known as Rags, was given to another stable near Norwich in about 1900. Fourteen years later a direct descendant of Rags, called Willum, was taken to Philadelphia, where the breed was named after its British breeder, becoming known as the Jones Terrier. It gained show recognition in 1936.

Appearance Norwich Terriers have a lively, perky appearance, thanks in part to their erect, pointed ears. The coat has a harsh, wiry texture and forms a ruff around the neck and shoulders, but it is much shorter on the head, muzzle and ears. The front legs are short but strong, and the hindquarters muscular. The feet are rounded and the nails are black. The topline must be level.

Personality Friendly by nature, and with a more extrovert personality than many terriers, the Norwich has enjoyed a close relationship with people since its earliest days. It makes an ideal companion dog, although it can have an assertive nature.

Health and care This is a tough, hardy breed, which has altered little since its earliest days and is not susceptible to any particular weaknesses. The relative lack of standardization is reflected by the variance in its size, particularly its body length, which is still apparent in the breed today. The weatherproof coat needs little attention in terms of grooming, even for show purposes, for which it must not be styled in any way, although a little tidying up is allowed.

As an owner Be prepared for your dog to dig holes in your garden. Although the Norwich may represent an offshoot from the northern terrier lineage, it still displays this fairly characteristic terrier behaviour, particularly if left outdoors on its own for any length of time. Check that fences are on secure foundations, too, to ensure your terrier cannot burrow its way out of your garden.

Also consider The Norfolk Terrier (*see page 173*), which is a close relative of the Norwich, has dropped rather than pricked ears and may appeal. If the facial shape of these terriers appeals to you, another possibility is the West Highland White Terrier (*see pages 168–169*).

Tech Spec

Features

A *Head:* Broad and rounded, with a powerful, wedge-shaped muzzle, which is significantly shorter than the head

B *Eyes:* Small, well-spaced, oval and dark with black rims

C *Ears:* Well-spaced with pointed tips, carried upright when alert

D *Chest:* Wide and deep

E *Tail:* Level with the topline and held erect

F *Bite:* Scissors bite

G *Height at shoulder:* 25.5cm (10 in)

H *Weight:* 5.5kg (12 lb)

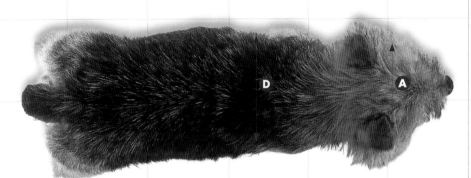

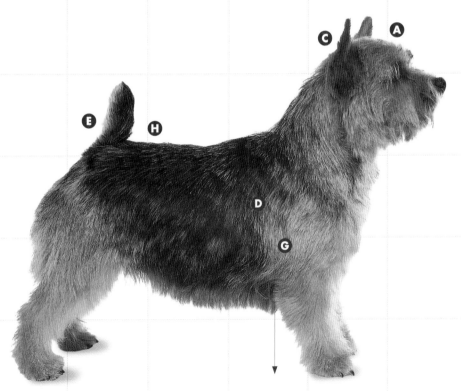

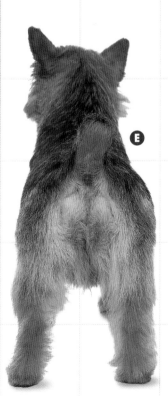

Parson Russell Terrier

Overview

Recognition
North America, Britain
and FCI member countries

Life expectancy
12–14 years

Colour
White and black, or tan
and white, or tricolour in
all three colours

Grooming

Feeding

Child friendliness

Exercise
Displays good stamina; will
enjoy working, walking,
and games

For many years, Parson Russell Terriers were bred more for their working abilities than their appearance, and there was no serious attempt to standardize them, despite the fact that they were the most popular terrier in their English homeland. They make personable companions, but they are often keen diggers.

Origin This breed commemorates the name of its founder, a sporting parson who lived in the southwest of England. He used Fox Terriers in its development, which took place in the mid-19th century, but it was not until 1989 that a standard was agreed. Only in 2004 did the breed obtain American Kennel Club recognition. These terriers were originally bred to dig foxes out from underground, working alongside hounds.

Appearance Under the breed standard, the Parson Russell Terrier is noticeably taller than many Jack Russell Terriers, but in other respects it is similar. The coat can be either broken or smooth, and coat care is straightforward. This terrier does not have a beard or bushy eyebrows, and the nose is black. The breed's small chest enables it to go underground easily, and the jaws are strong and rectangular – capable of inflicting a painful bite.

Personality Bold, lively and excitable, this is a breed that retains strong working instincts. The Parson Russell is not particularly patient and may express frustration by nipping, which means that it is not an ideal choice for a home with young children.

Health and care The varied ancestry and lack of standardization associated with these terriers until recently means that they are hardy and need little grooming. Their height now more closely approximates to that of the original strain, which was bred to be athletic, and it is able to run easily alongside Foxhounds. These terriers can be combative, both with their own breed and with other dogs. They are also often skilled escape artists, good both at digging and at jumping surprisingly high, so a carefully escape-proofed garden for this pet is essential.

As an owner Remember that these terriers have a strong and recent working ancestry. This means that they will still readily 'go to ground' where they investigate tunnels and rabbit holes. When out in the countryside, keep a watch on your pet to ensure that you know where it is, because there is a risk that it may get stuck if it ventures underground. Retrieving a trapped terrier can be a difficult operation.

Also consider If you are looking for a sound working terrier, the ordinary Jack Russell Terrier, which is still widely kept, may be an option. The Fox Terrier breeds that contributed to its ancestry (see pages 160–161 and 170–171) are other possibilities. There are also several rarer localized terrier breeds kept for working purposes in England, such as the Plummer Terrier, bred from Jack Russell Terrier stock.

Tech Spec

Features

A *Head:* Flat skull, broad between the ears and narrowing to the eyes, with a well-defined stop and a powerful, rectangular muzzle

B *Eyes:* Dark, medium-sized and almond-shaped

C *Ears:* V-shaped, small, and folded at the top of the skull or sometimes above it

D *Chest:* Narrow, yet of moderate depth, creating an athletic appearance

E *Tail:* Not set high, so maintaining a level topline; carried high

F *Bite:* Scissors bite

G *Height at shoulder:* Dogs 35.5cm (14 in); bitches 33cm (13 in)

H *Weight:* 6–7.75kg (13–17 lb)

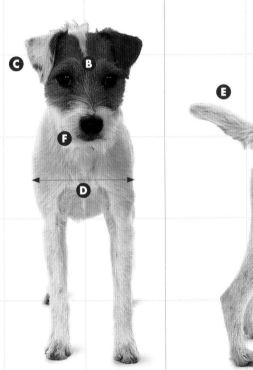

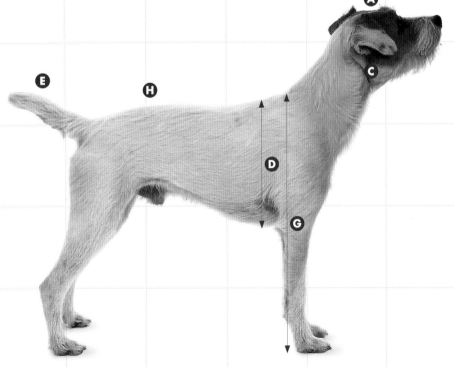

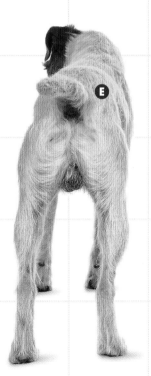

Scottish Terrier

Overview

Recognition
North America, Britain
and FCI member countries

Life expectancy
12–14 years

Colour
Black, wheaten or brindle

Grooming

Feeding

Child friendliness

Exercise
A walk around the local
park is usually adequate

Affectionately known as the Scottie, this terrier has an unmistakable appearance and a distinctive gait. Its back remains straight as it moves, and its legs are often mostly hidden by its trailing coat. The Scottie is often not tolerant of other dogs, and it may pick a fight if not restrained.

Origin It is thought that the Scottie may be the oldest of all Britain's terrier breeds; there are records of this terrier stretching back over 500 years. Confusingly, however, it was called the Skye Terrier for a time, but its name became established as the Scottish Terrier in 1879. The breed remained unknown in North America until it was first imported here in 1883, but it has since become more popular here than in its homeland. President Roosevelt boosted its popularity with his well-known pet Scottie, Fala, which lived in the White House.

Appearance Scotties have an elongated head, with a long, square muzzle. The small pricked ears are set high on the skull, and the nose is always black. The chest is broad and deep, and the body comparatively short. The hindquarters are powerful, and end in a tapering tail of about 18cm (7 in), carried high. The coat is hard and wiry, with a soft undercoat.

Personality Determined and loyal, a Scottie will make an excellent companion for someone living alone. These are affectionate dogs, although they do not have a highly extrovert nature. The breed is famously headstrong and stubborn, so it needs a strong-minded owner.

Health and care Scotties may be afflicted by a genetic weakness known as Scottie cramp. This manifests itself in short, painless seizures, lasting up to 30 seconds, during which time the dog's limbs, back and tail become rigid. The head may be held down between the front legs during a seizure, but recovery is rapid. Medical treatment can be given to control the problem, but will not cure it. Do not encourage a Scottie to sunbathe, because the breed is vulnerable to skin cancer. Scotties have a tendency to develop deafness, too, so if your pet appears unresponsive, you should have its hearing checked.

As an owner Try to socialize a Scottie as much as possible from an early age. Do not be surprised if a Scottie hunts small prey when off the leash, because the breed was originally bred as ratters. Scotties are not commonly kept as working terriers today.

Also consider Other Scottish breeds of terrier that may share similar ancestry include the Cairn Terrier (*see pages 142–143*) and the West Highland White (*see pages 168–169*). If you like the Scottish Terrier's facial shape but would prefer a larger breed, the Kerry Blue Terrier (*see pages 148–149*) or the Welsh Terrier (*see pages 166–167*) are possible alternatives.

Tech Spec

Features

A *Head:* Long, with a smooth skull; the muzzle is of equivalent length and tapered a little to the nose

B *Eyes:* Dark, small and almond-shaped, well-spaced under the brow

C *Ears:* Small, pricked and pointed, with the outer edges forming straight lines from the side of the skull

D *Chest:* Broad and deep, extending down between the front legs

E *Tail:* Thick, tapered along its length, and covered in short hard hair

F *Bite:* Scissors or level bite

G *Height at shoulder:* 25.5cm (10 in)

H *Weight:* Dogs 8.5–10kg (19–22 lb); bitches 8–9.5kg (18–21 lb)

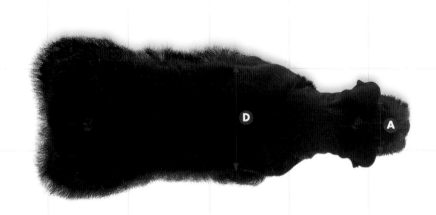

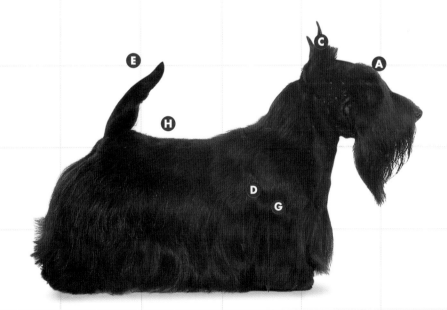

Overview

Recognition
North America, Britain
and FCI member countries

Life expectancy
11–13 years

Colour
Mainly white, broken
by black or tan

Grooming

Feeding

Child friendliness

Exercise
Lively, and will need
energetic but carefully
supervised walks

This terrier was developed for its courage and tenacity as a working breed, capable of going underground to drive foxes out from their lairs. Since their heyday in the late 19th century, Smooth Fox Terriers have become much less common, mainly because they have not transformed successfully into easily managed household companions.

Origin A surprisingly diverse group of breeds, including Beagles and Greyhounds, contributed to the development of these terriers, but the major influence was the Black and Tan Terrier. Bull Terriers also played a part, and the Fox Terrier's type had become established by the 1860s. At that date the wirehaired and smooth-haired forms were grouped together. By the beginning of the 20th century, the Smooth Fox Terrier was one of Britain's most popular breeds, but in the past 100 years its popularity has declined dramatically.

Appearance Predominantly white colouration became a characteristic feature of the breed at an early stage. This prevented these terriers from being confused with foxes when they emerged from below ground. The coat is smooth and lies flat, but has a relatively hard texture. Working Smooth Fox Terriers are not penalized for scars in the show ring.

Personality The breed's decline can be linked directly to its temperament. These Fox Terriers display a strong independent streak and are not therefore easily trained. They are lively companions, but may sometimes be snappy by nature.

Health and care A number of congenital problems have been recorded in this breed, with some, such as a lack of teeth, becoming apparent soon after birth. Symptoms of recessive ataxia, another inherited problem, emerge in puppies at between 2 and 6 months. It causes a degeneration of the spinal cord, and affected dogs lose the ability to walk. No treatment is possible; be sure to ask your breeder about its incidence in their breeding stock.

As an owner This is an independent breed that will undoubtedly seek to explore on its own when out. Take particular care in areas where there may be underground burrows, because your terrier may go to ground. You may want to obtain a special collar that will allow you to locate your pet underground.

Also consider The Wire Fox Terrier (see pages 170–171), which is closely related to the Smooth type, may be an alternative choice. Other terrier options include the Parson Russell Terrier (see pages 156–157) or its non-standardized variants, some of which are smaller. The American Fox Terrier, also known as the Toy Fox Terrier (see page 211), is another possibility that may appeal.

Tech Spec

Features

A *Head:* Skull flat and not wide, narrowing between the eyes, with little sign of a stop; tapered muzzle

B *Eyes:* Small, dark and virtually circular; set deep

C *Ears:* V-shaped and small; topline above the level of the skull and drops forwards sclose to the cheeks

D *Chest:* Deep, but not broad

E *Tail:* Strong and high-set, not curled or extended over the back

F *Bite:* Level bite

G *Height at shoulder:* 38–39cm (15–15½ in)

H *Weight:* 8–9kg (18–20 lb)

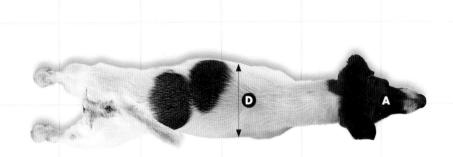

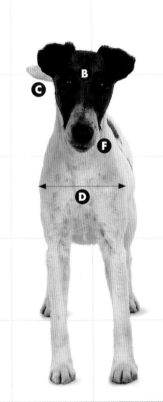

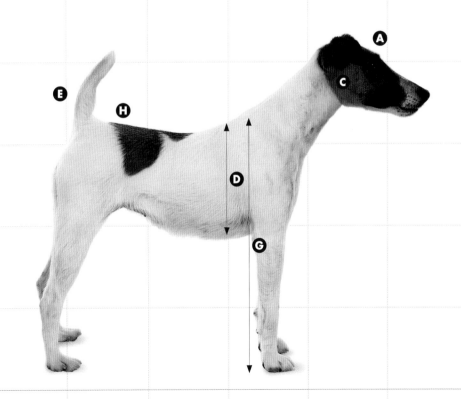

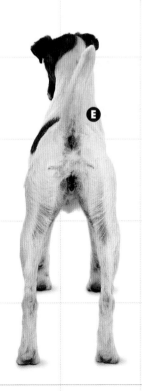

Soft Coated Wheaten Terrier

Overview

Recognition
North America, Britain and FCI member countries

Life expectancy
12–14 years

Colour
Clear wheaten

Grooming

Feeding

Child friendliness

Exercise
A good daily walk in the park or the countryside is necessary

Originally called the Irish Wheaten Terrier, this breed has been versatile as a working dog. As well as hunting game and killing rats and mice, it herded livestock and was also an alert guard dog. As a result of this mixed role, it is an ideal choice if you like the liveliness of terriers, but are looking for a more tolerant character than is found in most terrier breeds, especially in its relations with other dogs.

Origin The Soft Coated Wheaten is believed to be the oldest of today's four existing Irish terrier breeds, with an ancestry extending back over 200 years, but its exact origins are obscure. Surprisingly, it was not officially recognized in its native country until 1937. It was taken to North America for the first time nine years later. Soft Coated Wheaten Terriers only achieved full recognition from the American Kennel Club in 1973, and even now this is not a common breed.

Appearance As its name would suggest, this medium-sized breed has a soft, silky coat, which can be any shade of wheat. The coat is wavy in adults but lies flat in the young terriers. The shape of the head is rectangular. The skull is flattened between the ears, which hang slightly forwards. The nose is black and large, and the dog also has black lips.

Personality Friendly and self-confident, this breed is hardy, easy to care for and makes a superb companion – it deserves to be more popular as a pet. It will adapt well to various surroundings, although it tends to be happier in a rural environment.

Health and care The Soft Coated Wheaten Terrier tends to be a healthy breed. Although the coat is single-layered, it is effective at protecting these terriers from the elements. In addition, even for show purposes, grooming is more straightforward than for most longhaired terrier breeds, and neither plucking nor clipping is permitted. It will take up to 18 months for the coat of Soft Coated Wheaten Terriers to lighten and lose any darker markings, and for its distinctive texture to develop fully.

As an owner Although this breed is significantly larger than many other terriers, it can be trained easily. It is playful by nature, and, unlike some other terrier breeds, it is tolerant of children. If you are interested in showing a terrier, the Soft Coated Wheaten is a good choice. Few breeds are as versatile, or are better suited to living in a family environment.

Also consider The short-legged Glen of Imaal Terrier (see pages 146–147) may be descended from the Soft Coated Wheaten and would be a possible alternative. The Irish Terrier (see page 172) is of similar size, with a long face, but has a much shorter, wiry coat. A breed that, despite its name, is from a different group, and which has a profuse coat and often similar colouring, is the Tibetan Terrier (see pages 96–97).

Tech Spec

Features

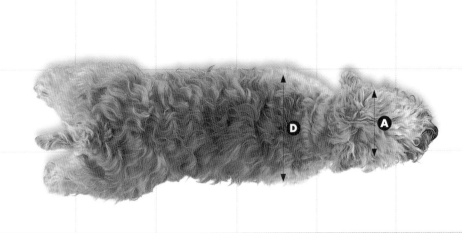

A *Head:* Rectangular and long, with a flat top to the skull, well-defined stop and strong muzzle

B *Eyes:* Medium-sized, almond-shaped, brown and well-spaced, with dark rims

C *Ears:* Small or medium-sized and level with the skull; hang slightly forwards, with inner edge against the cheek pointing to the ground

D *Chest:* Deep

E *Tail:* Well-set, held upward, not extended over the back

F *Bite:* Scissors or level bite

G *Height at shoulder:* Dogs 45.5–48cm (18–19 in); bitches 43–45.5cm (17–18 in)

H *Weight:* Dogs 16–18kg (35–40 lb); bitches 13.5–16kg (30–35 lb)

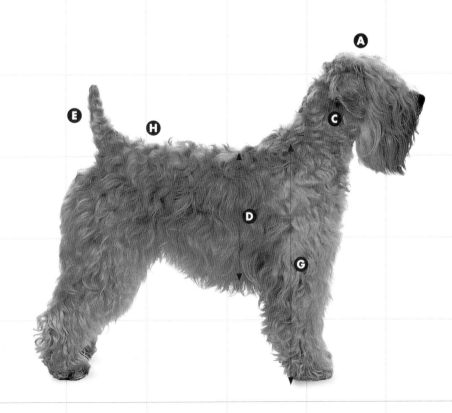

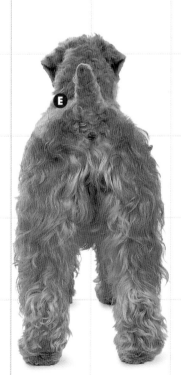

Staffordshire Bull Terrier

Overview

Recognition
North America, Britain
and FCI member countries

Life expectancy
11–13 years

Colour
White, fawn, red, black
or blue, all with or without
white; also brindle or
brindle and white

Grooming

Feeding

Child friendliness

Exercise
Enjoys a run and playing
a game, but try to avoid
crowded parks with
other dogs

This breed, often known as the Staffie, has become popular over recent years. However, owning one of these terriers can be a tiring experience, notably when you encounter other dogs. Bred from former fighting stock, Staffies often do not get along with other dogs, although they frequently make excellent companions for people.

Origin The Staffie shares its origins with the Bull Terrier, both breeds originally resulting from matings between Bulldogs and Black and Tan Terriers. Whereas the head shape of the Bull Terrier altered dramatically with further crosses, that of this breed stayed the same, with broad jaws suggestive of mastiff stock. To distinguish between them, this breed was given the name of the English county where it was especially popular when it was first recognized in 1935.

Appearance Smooth-coated and with a thick set and an extremely muscular appearance, the Staffordshire Bull Terrier has a broad chest and straight, powerful legs. The head is square and broad, too, with a short stop and powerful jaw muscles. The front legs should display good bone structure, although the most obvious power of these dogs is seen in their thick hind legs.

Personality Strong, intelligent and tenacious, these dogs are loyal and often playful at home with their families, but they can cause problems with other dogs, because their level of aggression towards them is often, although not invariably, high.

Health and care This breed does sometimes develop cataracts as the result of a hereditary recessive gene. The smooth coat is easy to keep in good condition, but you should not allow a Staffie, especially one with a predominantly white coat, to stay outside in bright sunlight for long periods, because this can lead to skin cancer, particularly in older dogs. Male Staffies that are not used for breeding should be neutered to lessen the risk of aggressive behaviour.

As an owner Ensure that you are in charge of your dog at all times, particularly when outside. If your dog attacks another, you may be left facing a large and expensive problem. If your pet is aggressive with other dogs, you can fit it with a muzzle, or exercise it when it is unlikely to meet other dogs. Like many heavy, muscular dogs, Staffordshire Bull Terriers have a tendency to become fat if they are overfed and underexercised, so keep an eye on your dog's weight.

Also consider The English Bull Terrier may be an alternative, in either its standard or miniature (*see pages 150–151*) forms. Their temperament is similar to that of the Staffie, although their facial shape is different. If you would like a bigger dog, the American form of the Staffordshire is a larger, heavier breed, standing about 5cm (2 in) taller. A more sociable dog that will mix better with others, the Boxer (*see pages 220–221*) may be another possibility.

Tech Spec

Features

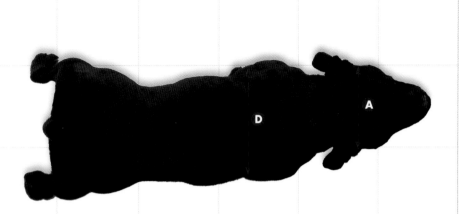

A *Head:* Short, broad skull, evident cheek muscles, a clear stop and a powerful, broad muzzle

B *Eyes:* Round, medium-sized and directed forwards

C *Ears:* Small; rose or half-pricked in appearance

D *Chest:* Broad, with a deep brisket

E *Tail:* Set and carried low; tapering to a point and medium in length

F *Bite:* Scissors bite

G *Height at shoulder:* 35.5–40.5cm (14–16 in)

H *Weight:* Dogs 12.5–17kg (28–38 lb); bitches 11–15.5kg (24–34 lb)

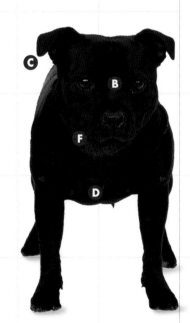

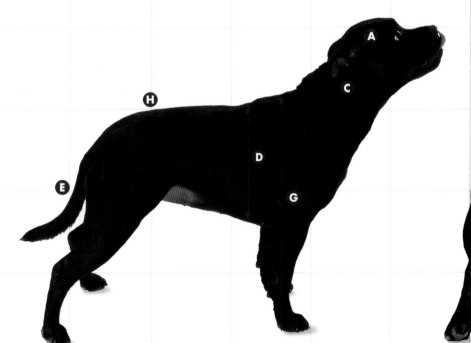

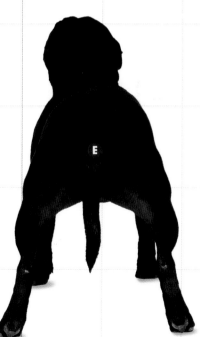

Overview

Recognition
North America, Britain
and FCI member countries

Life expectancy
11–13 years

Colour
Black and tan, or grizzle
and tan

Grooming

Feeding

Child friendliness

Exercise
This dog needs a good
walk every day

The friendly disposition of these terriers, coupled with their attractive appearance, has helped to ensure their popularity. Resembling a smaller version of the Airedale, the Welsh Terrier is a much easier breed to manage, thanks to its more tolerant nature. It is probably also the easiest of the terriers to train.

Origin This dog is descended principally from the Black and Tan Terrier, having being bred in Wales since the 18th century. Some subsequent crossings with both Lakeland and Airedale Terriers also played a part in its development. Welsh Terriers were expected to go underground and drive out game such as foxes. The long legs of the breed helped it to keep up with the hounds, ensuring the game had little chance of escape.

Appearance This breed was originally known as the Welsh Black and Tan Rough-coated Terrier, a name that reflects its appearance accurately. The black area covers the back, extending up to the neck and down to the tail, forming what is often described as a jacket. The tan areas are of a reddish shade. In some dogs, however, the black colouring may be replaced by grizzle (bluish-grey) markings.

Personality Lively and bold by nature, as its background would suggest, the Welsh Terrier is generally a more easy going household companion than some of the more assertive members of the terrier group. It usually gets along well with other dogs.

Health and care Welsh Terriers are a hardy, healthy breed. However, a dog that hunts and that stands any likelihood of coming into contact with vermin should be immunized regularly against leptospirosis. This potentially deadly infection is carried by rats and causes failure of the liver and kidney functions.

As an owner The Welsh Terrier is very playful and is happy to chase after and catch toys. If the opportunity presents itself, it is also a competent ratter. Hand-stripping – or possibly trimming a dog that is not shown – will be necessary about twice a year, and brushing will keep the harsh, wiry coat looking immaculate at other times.

Also consider If you are looking for a slightly smaller breed, the Lakeland Terrier (*see page 172*), may be a possibility; if you want a slightly larger one, consider the Airedale (*see pages 136–137*). Bear in mind, however, that this latter breed is likely to be more temperamental than the Welsh Terrier. Another possibility is the Irish Terrier (*see page 172*), which is slightly taller and lacks the black area seen on its Welsh cousin.

Tech Spec

Features

A *Head:* Rectangular in shape, with the muzzle half of the total length of the head, measured from the tip of the nose to the occiput

B *Eyes:* Set deep, widely spaced, small and dark brown

C *Ears:* Small and V-shaped; fold just above the topline of the skull, carried forwards near the cheeks

D *Chest:* Medium-width, with a deep brisket

E *Tail:* High-set and carried upright

F *Bite:* Scissors bite preferred, but level bite acceptable

G *Height at shoulder:* Dogs (15–15½ in) 38–39cm, with bitches sometimes smaller

H *Weight:* 9kg (20 lb)

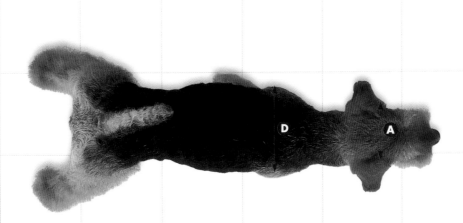

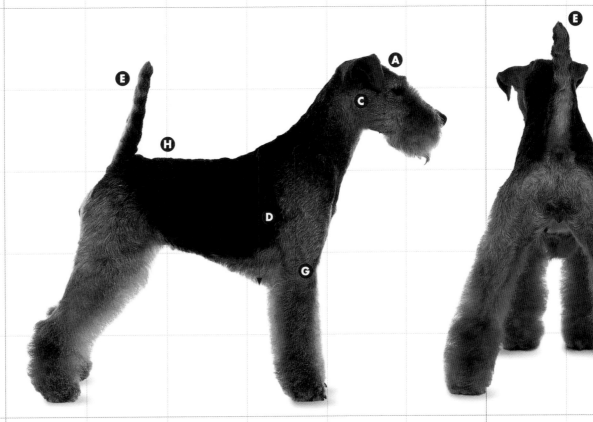

West Highland White Terrier

Overview

Recognition
North America, Britain
and FCI member countries

Life expectancy
11–13 years

Colour
White

Grooming

Feeding

Child friendliness

Exercise
A good daily walk is
recommended

These small dogs, frequently known as Westies, are typically strong-willed terriers, known for personalities much larger than their size would suggest. They are also keen working dogs and today are seen frequently not just in the show ring, but participating in agility competitions as well.

Origin This breed came about as the result of a tragic accident. On the Scottish moors, a Colonel Malcolm shot at what he thought was a fox, only to find that he had killed his beloved Cairn Terrier. He set out to create an unmistakable white strain, starting with the paler puppies in litters of Cairns. These dogs were originally called Poltalloch Terriers, after Malcolm's Argyllshire estate, but as other strains began to develop, they ultimately all became known as West Highland White Terriers.

Appearance A rounded yet broad head, tapering slightly to the eyes, is a feature of the breed. The pricked ears are small and widely spaced. The front legs are short, but strong, straight and covered in hair. The hind limbs are correspondingly short, and the back feet are smaller than the front ones. The thighs are muscular. As the name suggests, these terriers must be entirely white in colour.

Personality Bold and alert by nature, the Westie makes a fearless guard dog in the home. These terriers are energetic, too, in spite of their size, but they may be combative with other dogs, especially of their own kind.

Health and care Westies are susceptible to a number of inherited conditions, although signs may not become apparent until a dog is several months old. Pain when eating, combined with a fever, is indicative of craniomandibular osteopathy, a juvenile problem that should resolve itself when the dog is about a year old. Stiffness in the pelvic region and a loss of coordination can indicate the progressive illness that is known as Krabbe's Disease.

As an owner A Westie needs a considerable amount of grooming to look at its best in the show ring. A visit to the grooming salon every two months, combined with regular brushing of the breed's hard top coat at home, should be adequate for a Westie kept as a pet. It can be hard to keep the white coat pristine, especially as Westies enjoy both games and energetic walks.

Also consider The Cairn Terrier (see pages 142–143) is the closest relative of this breed, but the unrelated Norwich Terrier (see pages 154–155), has a feisty personality and is of a similar appearance and size, although a different colour. The Sealyham Terrier (see page 173) is another possibility – Westies contributed to its development, although its facial shape is different.

Tech Spec

Features

A *Head:* Round at the front, slightly domed on top, with a broad skull longer than the blunt muzzle

B *Eyes:* Medium-sized, widely spaced, almond-shaped and dark brown

C *Ears:* Widely spaced on the top outer edges of the skull, small, erect and pointed

D *Chest:* Deep, reaching the elbows, with breadth reflecting the individual dog

E *Tail:* Short, carrot-shaped, straight and covered with hard hair; carried upright

F *Bite:* Scissors or level bite

G *Height at shoulder:* 25.5–28cm (10–11 in)

H *Weight:* 6.75–10kg (15–22 lb)

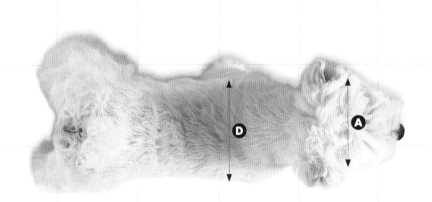

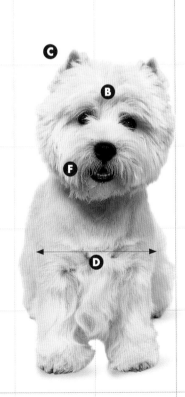

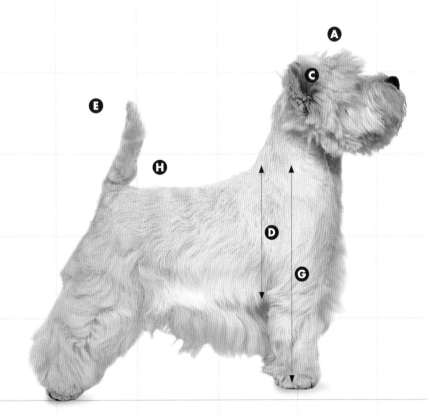

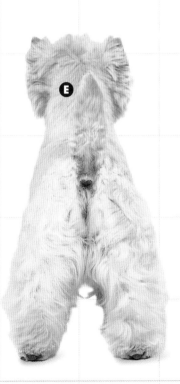

Overview

Recognition
North America, Britain
and FCI member countries

Life expectancy
11–13 years

Colour
Predominantly white, often
marked with tan or black.
No red, liver, brindle or
slate – blue markings are
allowed

Grooming

Feeding

Child friendliness

Exercise
Needs plenty of activity
and daily walks

In the early stages of their development, Wire and Smooth Fox Terriers were frequently bred together, but today they are treated as separate breeds. However, like its smooth-coated cousin, the Wire Fox Terrier is not a good choice as a pet in a home with young children, because it can be short-tempered.

Origin Although the Wire Fox Terrier is now closely related to the Smooth form, it is believed that the two breeds had different ancestries at the beginning, that of the Wire Fox Terrier being based to a much greater extent on the old rough-coated Black and Tan Terriers. Over time, however, the two types were mated together so often that they now essentially differ only in their coat type. The Wire Fox Terrier was originally slower to gain show recognition, but it now tends to be more popular.

Appearance The outer coat is dense and feels wiry, with a soft undercoat beneath. It should be longest over the back and sides of the body. The hairs may twist but should not be curly. The coat should be predominantly white in colour. In the show ring, the length of the head is deemed highly significant in both breeds, and is measured using callipers. It should be between 18 and18.5cm (7–7¼ in) in a dog, and slightly shorter in a bitch.

Personality An alert but independent-minded breed, the Wire Fox Terrier can be willful on occasions. These are fearless dogs and make excellent guard dogs, but they can be noisy, barking at the slightest sound.

Health and care The close links between this breed and its smooth-coated relative has resulted in the same congenital defects, including a higher-than-usual incidence of deafness. This should be suspected, and tested for, in a fox terrier puppy that appears to be unresponsive to voice commands or the sounds around it. Be alert to any swelling in the neck region, which may be indicative of the thyroid gland disorder described as goitre, to which both breeds are susceptible.

As an owner Wire Fox Terriers are very enthusiastic about digging, and they can tunnel their way out of any but the most securely fenced backyard. They are also keen and able ratters, being both fast and agile. Professional trimming of the coat will be needed to maintain their attractive appearance.

Also consider The Smooth Fox Terrier (*see pages 160– 161*) may be an option, differing from the Wire only in coat type and needing much less grooming. Other breeds resembling the Wire Fox Terrier include the Lakeland and Irish Terriers (*see page 172*), as well as the Welsh Terrier (*see pages 166–167*), although they do not correspond in colour.

Tech Spec

Features

A *Head:* Almost flat top to the skull and narrowing slightly towards the eyes; large muzzle, with the total length up to 18.5cm (7¼ in) in a dog, less in a bitch

B *Eyes:* Small, set deep and virtually circular; not widely spaced

C *Ears:* V-shaped, small and set high; dropping forwards near the cheeks

D *Chest:* Deep, yet not too broad; excessive depth impedes a terrier going to ground

E *Tail:* Strong, set high and held upright

F *Bite:* Level bite

G *Height at shoulder:* Dogs 39cm (15½ in); bitches 37cm (14½ in)

H *Weight:* 7.25–8kg (16–18 lb)

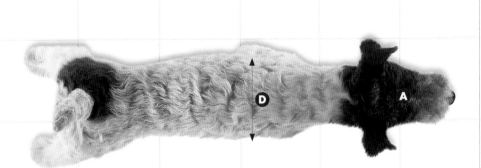

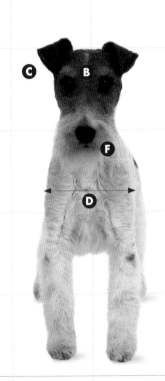

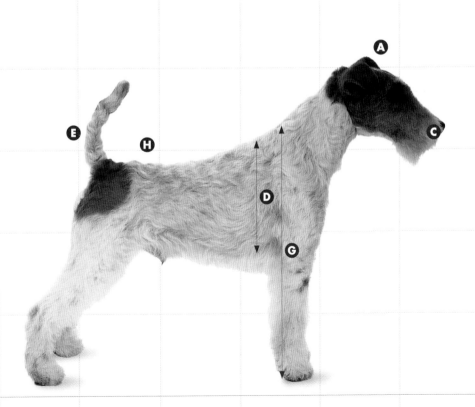

Pet Spec
Bedlington Terrier

Originally known as the Rothbury Terrier, today the Bedlington is named after a village in the northern English county of Northumberland where it was first bred in the 1820s. Its distinctive profile is the result of an ancestry that includes not just terrier stock, but crossings with Whippets, too, which have left an indelible mark on the breed. It is less common in the show ring than some terriers because of its grooming needs.

Appearance In its early days, the Bedlington tended to be liver in colour, although today blue individuals are more common. The topknot of longer fur on the head is always paler than that on the body. The whippet influence is clearly evident in the distinctive curve of the Bedlington's topline, often described as a roached back. The coat is both crisp and curly.

Breed care and health The breed can develop an inherited condition in which the dog is unable to metabolize copper in its diet, with fatal effects on the liver. Check that any puppy you acquire has been bred from stock that is free of this problem.

As an owner The Bedlington is one of the more active terriers, and can run at pace. It makes a loyal and friendly companion, although it is not an especially social breed as far as other dogs are concerned.

Also consider If you like the overall profile of the Bedlington Terrier, but would prefer a short-coated breed, the Whippet (see pages 68–69) will be a good choice. The colour range of the Whippet is not the same as that of the Bedlington, although you can choose from bicoloured examples in both cases. If you would prefer a larger dog, the Airedale (see pages 136–137) may be an option.

Pet Spec
Irish Terrier

First bred in the latter half of the 19th century, the Irish Terrier is the oldest of that country's four terrier breeds. It used to be bred in a range of colours, but red gradually became the characteristic colour associated with it. The breed saw active service as a messenger dog in World War I.

Appearance The Irish Terrier has a long head, and it must have brown rather than yellow eyes – the latter are deemed a serious breed fault. The ears are darker then the rest of the body and are small and folded at the top. The depth of red colouring varies between individuals. The coat is harsher along the back.

Breed care and health This breed can be vulnerable to an inherited condition called cystinuria, a painful problem that causes stones to form in the urinary tract. Check that the breeding stock is clear of this problem before you buy a puppy.

As an owner Irish Terrier puppies sometimes have black hairs mingled in with red, but these shed with age, and the dogs should be solid red by the time they are mature. The coat should be so dense that it is hard to see the skin when you part it.

Also consider The Kerry Blue (see pages 148–149) is a breed with a similar profile but in a different colour, and with a longer, soft, silky coat rather than a wiry one. By contrast, the smaller Lakeland Terrier (see right), another possibility, is a breed with a similar coat colour and texture. The Welsh Terrier (see pages 166–167) is a third option, although this breed does not occur in a pure red.

Pet Spec
Lakeland Terrier

This breed arose in the Lake District in northwest England about 200 years ago. Working in harsh upland terrain, Lakeland Terriers were brave and tenacious, often going underground. They were highly valued by farmers as a way of curbing the fox population, and they were originally judged on their working abilities as well as their looks.

Appearance Unlike some terriers, this breed exists in a wide range of coat colours. Some individuals are a solid colour while others may display darker, so-called saddle markings over the back. Grizzled Lakeland Terriers have intermingled colouring.

Breed care and health This is a tough, hardy breed, but puppies are occasionally born with an additional row of eyelashes, a condition called distichiasis. This causes inflammation and requires surgical correction.

As an owner The Lakeland Terrier is characterized by its double-layered coat, which has a hard outer layer and a soft undercoat. For show purposes, this breed needs to be hand-stripped. The coat on the body is traditionally left longer than that on the extremities, and the hair extends over the eyes, highlighting the rectangular shape of the head.

Also consider The larger Airedale Terrier (see pages 136–137), with its distinctive saddle marking, is a possibility to consider. Another breed with variable colouring and a somewhat similar profile is the Wire Fox Terrier (see pages 170–171) – and if you are looking for a smooth-coated option, the Smooth Fox Terrier (see pages 160–161) is another possibility. Both breeds are similar to the Lakeland in size. A Welsh Terrier (see pages 166–167), too, is an option.

Height 38–43cm (15–17 in)
Weight 7.75–10.5kg (17–23 lb)
Exercise Lively and energetic by nature, Bedlingtons need a daily run off the leash

Height 45.5–48cm (18–19 in)
Weight 11.5–12.25kg (25–27 lb)
Exercise This breed has plenty of stamina and will benefit from good walks

Height 35.5–38cm (14–15 in)
Weight 7–7.5kg (16–17 lb)
Exercise Will be keen to explore when out for a walk

Pet Spec
Norfolk Terrier

Originating from East Anglia, on the eastern coast of England, the Norfolk Terrier was developed as a working breed. Its small size and powerful jaws are both useful when it goes to ground after small prey, such as rats and rabbits. In North America it was known for many years as the Jones Terrier, after the breeder who popularized the breed, which was first recognized here in 1936.

Appearance Red in various shades tends to be the predominant colour of these terriers, although black-and-tan and grizzled variants are seen, too. Unusually, scarring incurred while working does not prohibit these terriers from being shown. The outer coat is wiry, measuring up to 5cm (2 in) long in places. The folded ears lie close to the cheeks and are covered with short hair of a velvety texture.

Breed care and health There are no breed weaknesses generally identified in Norfolk Terriers. The thick undercoat helps to protect against injury.

As an owner This breed digs enthusiastically and does not always distinguish between a field and the garden. It is an alert guard dog and a loyal companion.

Also consider The most obvious choice to consider is the Norwich Terrier (*see pages 154–155*), which is identical in appearance, but with pricked rather than drop ears. Both terriers are bred in similar colours. If you want a slightly larger dog, the Glen of Imaal Terrier (*see pages 146–147*) may appeal to you, while the sleeker profile of the Border Terrier (*see pages 140–141*) offers another option.

Pet Spec
Sealyham Terrier

Named after the estate in southwest Wales owned by its creator Captain John Edwardes, the Sealyham's origins can be traced back to the 1850s, although its exact ancestry is unclear. West Highland White Terriers may have been used in its development. It has since grown slightly in size and developed a much more friendly disposition than the original working strain.

Appearance Most Sealyhams are pure white, but the standard allows for individuals with lemon, badger or tan markings on the ears. The nose should be black. These terriers should give an impression of strength – they were bred to tackle foxes and badgers underground. The double-layered coat helps to protect against the elements.

Breed care and health These terriers are at risk from an inherited eye weakness called retinal dysplasia, which results in blindness. Be sure to ask your breeder about its incidence in their breeding stock.

As an owner Sealyham Terriers are strong-willed dogs and can be stubborn. On the other hand, they are much more tolerant of children than some of the other terrier breeds. They have a larger-than-life bark.

Also consider In terms of size and colour, the West Highland White Terrier (*see pages 168–169*) represents another option. If you find the Sealyham's long face and beard appealing, the taller Wire Fox Terrier (*see pages 170–171*) shares these characteristics. Larger, but paler in colour and with a softer coat, the Soft Coated Wheaten Terrier (*see pages 162–163*) is also an option.

Pet Spec
Skye Terrier

Originating on the Isle of Skye, off the west coast of Scotland, this breed has existed largely unchanged for over 400 years. During the 19th century, the Skye Terrier became a favourite of the English monarch Queen Victoria. Greyfriars Bobby, an Edinburgh dog which, in the later 19th century, guarded his late owner's grave for 14 years, and whose story is immortalized in films and books, is probably the most famous representative of the breed.

Appearance A long, low-set body, with a flowing coat that trails down to the ground, is characteristic of the breed. The ears can be dropped, but are more usually pricked, and they are profusely covered with hair. The coat colouration is unusual. The coat must be a single colour, but is shaded over the body, and the ears, muzzle and tail tip should be dark. A small white area is permitted on the chest.

Breed care and health Some puppies are born with a kink in the tail, causing it appear hooked at the tip. In some, the voice box, or larynx, may be narrowed, affecting the dog's ability to bark. The breed is also susceptible to digestive problems resulting from ulcerative colitis.

As an owner The Skye Terrier may try to go to ground after rabbits or other prey, so keep a watch on your dog when it is off the leash.

Also consider Although smaller and lighter, the Yorkshire Terrier (*see pages 208–209*) has a similarly flowing coat. The Dandie Dinmont Terrier (*see pages 144–145*) is another low-slung possibility and is almost certainly related to the Skye Terrier, while the Cairn (*see pages 142–143*) – which used to be known as the Short-Coated Skye Terrier – has a similar facial shape, but is slightly taller and has a less profuse coat.

Height 25cm (10 in)
Weight 5–5.5kg (11–12 lb)
Exercise Vary your route to add interest when walking one of these lively, curious terriers

Height 26.5cm (10½ in)
Weight 10–11kg (22–24 lb)
Exercise More adaptable than many terriers, but still requires a good daily walk

Height 24–25cm (9½–10 in)
Weight 8.5–10.5kg (19–23 lb)
Exercise This is not a lap dog but a working terrier, with matching exercise needs

Bichon Frise

Overview

Recognition
North America, Britain and
FCI member countries

Life expectancy
11–13 years

Colour
White

Grooming

Feeding

Child friendliness

Exercise
An opportunity to exercise
every day in a local park
is essential

The name of this popular toy breed is pronounced 'Bee-shon Free-zay.' 'Bichon' is a contracted form of Barbichon, which means 'small Barbet', and the Barbet is a French breed of water spaniel. 'Frise' refers to the dog's soft curly coat. The Bichon Frise still bears a slight resemblance to its larger ancestors.

Origin The Bichon Frise originally became popular as a ladies' companion in royal circles, first in France during the early 16th century and then in Spain. From here, the breed was taken to Tenerife in the Canary Islands. The Bichon Frise remained popular until the late 19th century, but then it fell from favour. It was not until the breed was taken to North America in the mid-1950s that its popularity started to revive, and it is now the best-known member of the bichon group.

Appearance The attractive dark eyes of the Bichon Frise are emphasized by dark matching rims, in contrast to its characteristic snow-white coat. Great importance is placed by breeders on the texture of the coat. The soft thick under layer is overlaid by a curly, coarser top coat to give a springy texture that feels somewhat like velvet. The Bichon Frise is trimmed to show off its physique, with longer furnishings on the head and on the tail. The pads are black, as is the nose.

Personality A small dog with an appealing nature, the Bichon Frise is a natural entertainer and clown that thrives on attention. This is why it became a popular choice with street performers when it fell out of favour in royal circles.

Health and care Like many other toy breeds, the Bichon Frise sometimes suffers from a weakness of the kneecaps, which is likely to require surgical correction. Epilepsy is also a problem in some bloodlines, and affected dogs usually need regular medication to avoid fits. The Bichon Frise's coat needs to be trimmed regularly to maintain its distinctive powder-puff appearance. In accordance with the breed standard, the nails need regular clipping to keep them short. As with many smaller breeds, their nails can become overgrown.

As an owner You can develop a very close relationship with a Bichon Frise, thanks in part to the breed's playful nature. They are gentle dogs and are very suitable for a home where there are younger children. Trimming and bathing may be best carried out at a professional grooming salon to ensure that your dog's high-maintenance coat is kept in good condition.

Also consider The Bichon group has other appealing members, including the Maltese (*see pages 190–191*), and the rarer Havanese and Bolognese. Only the Bichon Frise has a double coat, so the coat texture and appearance of these other breeds is different. If you like the trimmed style of the Bichon Frise, a Toy Poodle (*see page 211*) is an option.

Tech Spec

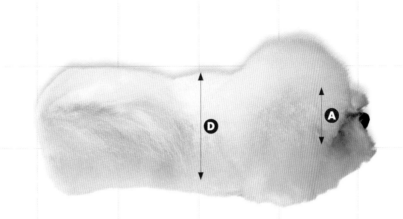

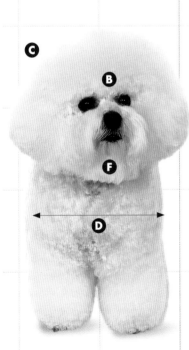

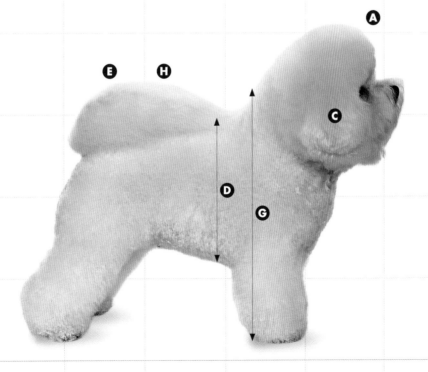

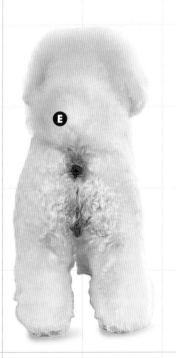

Griffon Bruxellois

Overview

Recognition
North America, Britain and
FCI member countries

Life expectancy
12–15 years

Colour
Red, occasionally with
some black on the muzzle;
black; black and tan;
belge–a black and reddish-
brown colouring, with
black on the head

Grooming
(Depending on coat type)

Feeding

Child friendliness

Exercise
A daily walk in the park
will be sufficient

Also sometimes known as the Brussels Griffon, these small terrier-like dogs have been popular in their Belgian homeland for more than 600 years. Their facial shape has modified through the years, and the breed now has quite a human expression, emphasizing the appeal of these lively dogs.

Origin Griffons Bruxellois were originally kept by the aristocracy, but soon gained wider popularity. Kept around stables, they proved to be proficient ratters. In the early stages of their development, they were more terrier-like in appearance, but in the 19th century, crossbreeding, with the Pug in particular, flattened their facial shape, and also created the smooth-coated Brabançon, which is identical to the Griffon apart from its coat. The breed then found favour once again as an aristocratic companion.

Appearance The head of the Griffon is large compared with its body, and its eyes are large, round and dark in colour. The coat has a harsh, wiry texture and is longer on the head of the Griffon (although in the case of the smooth-coated Brabançon, it must be short, straight and sleek). White areas in the coat in either variety are not permitted, apart from 'frosting' on the muzzle.

Personality Lively and alert, the Griffon is playful and easy to train, but has a rather sensitive nature. It has the reputation for sometimes being difficult to walk on a leash, so training should begin early.

Health and care The reproductive rate of the Griffon Bruxellois has fallen significantly over the past 80 years, with many bitches simply failing to conceive. In the case of those that become pregnant, the birth can be difficult, too, and litters quite frequently consist of just a single puppy, which has to be born by Caesarean section. The wire coat requires hand-stripping to keep it looking neat and tidy, but grooming of the smooth-coated Brabançon variety is straightforward.

As an owner Be prepared to devote sufficient time to a Griffon Bruxellois, because it thrives on attention and will form a close bond with members of its immediate family. A Griffon is a good choice if you have a cat, since these small dogs will usually live in harmony with a feline companion. This breed is less suitable for a home where there are young children because they do not enjoy boisterous play.

Also consider The smooth-coated Brabançon needs much less grooming. If you like a longer coat, the slightly taller Affenpinscher (*see page 210*), which played a part in the Griffon's development, is a further possibility.

Tech Spec

Features

A *Head:* Large and round, with a flat top to the skull and good width between the ears

B *Eyes:* Large, round and dark in colour with black rims

C *Ears:* Small and set high; held semi-erect

D *Chest:* Relatively deep and wide

E *Tail:* Angled at 90 degrees from the back, carried high

F *Bite:* Undershot bite

G *Height at shoulder:* 20cm (8 in)

H *Weight:* Ideally 3.5–4.5kg (8–10 lb); must not exceed 5.5kg (12 lb)

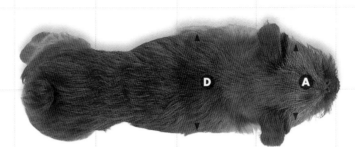

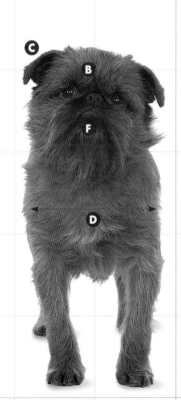

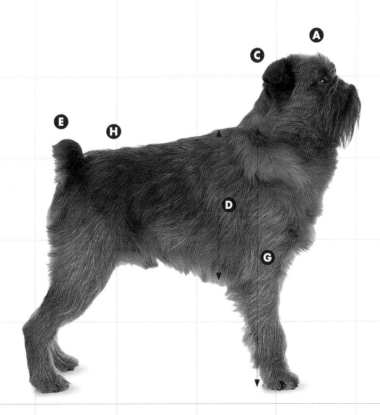

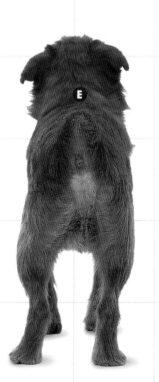

Cavalier King Charles Spaniel

Overview

Recognition
North America, Britain and
FCI member countries

Life expectancy
10–12 years

Colour
Chestnut and white (known
as 'Blenheim'); black and
tan; red (known as 'Ruby');
tricolour

Grooming

Feeding

Child friendliness

Exercise
Short daily walk needed

This spaniel now ranks as one of the most popular of all toy breeds worldwide, and it is seen far more frequently than the closely related King Charles Spaniel, with which it is sometimes confused. However, there is a very distinct difference between the two breeds – the Cavalier has a significantly longer facial shape.

Origin King Charles II of England enjoyed the company of King Charles Spaniels at his court in the second half of the 17th century. Over time, selective breeding gave these spaniels an increasingly flattened face. In 1926, the American Roswell Eldridge offered large cash prizes at Cruft's Dog Show for the next five years to try to encourage a return to a longer-faced type.

Appearance Eldridge was successful, and breeders selectively bred Cavalier King Charles Spaniels that gradually became slightly larger. The shape of the face and their size are the main features distinguishing the separate breeds today. The different colourations have separate names, in recognition of the other varieties of King Charles Spaniels that no longer exist, but which are now incorporated into these breeds.

Personality A friendly, well-adjusted nature is characteristic of the breed, which delights in human company of any age. Cavaliers are not especially athletic compared with larger spaniels, but they will still display a playful side to their natures, especially if encouraged to take part in games from an early age.

Health and care These spaniels are greedy and prone to obesity. This, in turn, may predispose them to diabetes, to which the breed is susceptible, so it is important not to allow Cavaliers to become overweight. They need regular grooming to keep their flowing, silky coats in good condition. Some Cavaliers have a strange nervous condition that causes them to jump up occasionally, as though they were trying to catch nonexistent flies.

As an owner Do not rely on food treats when training your Cavalier, because of the breed's tendency to put on weight – or, alternatively, use healthy options, such as pieces of carrot or apple. Apart from the risk of diabetes, obesity may worsen heart problems, to which these spaniels are also susceptible, especially in later life.

Also consider The King Charles Spaniel (*see page 211*), better known as the King Charles Spaniel elsewhere, is a possibility. The most obvious difference is a more compact facial shape, but it also has a clearly domed skull when compared with the Cavalier. Other possibilities include the Papillon (*see pages 196–197*), a continental toy spaniel, although this is more delicate in appearance.

Tech Spec

Features

A *Head:* Relatively flat top to the skull, with little sign of a stop, and a tapering muzzle

B *Eyes:* Round, large, dark in colour and well-spaced

C *Ears:* Set high on the skull, long, and hanging down the sides of the head

D *Chest:* Medium-sized

E *Tail:* Balanced in proportion to the body, generally carried low

F *Bite:* Scissors bite

G *Height at shoulder:* 30.5cm (12 in)

H *Weight:* 5.5–8kg (12–18 lb)

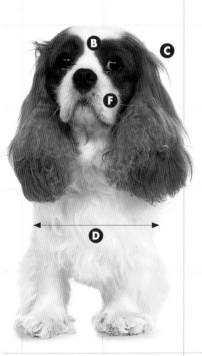

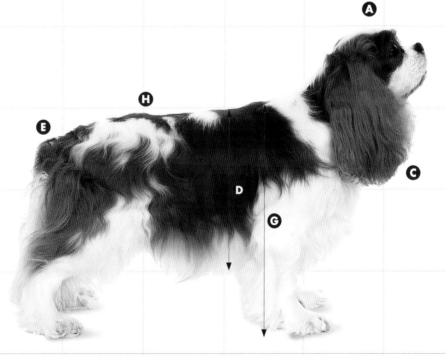

Group **Toy**

Overview

Recognition
North America, Britain and
FCI member countries

Life expectancy
12–15 years

Colour
Any colour or pattern
is acceptable

Grooming
(Depending on coat type)

Feeding

Child friendliness

Exercise
A modest daily walk in a
city park should be enough

Chihuahua

Apart from its fame for being regarded as the smallest breed of dog in the world, the Chihuahua is unusual in many other ways. Since it became popular in North America in the mid-19th century, it has changed significantly in appearance – it used to have a longer face and larger, more batlike ears.

Origin A native of Mexico, named after the province where it may have originated, the Chihuahua's more remote past is mysterious. Some claim its ancestors were brought from Europe by early Spanish settlers, or even that it came from China, but it is more likely that the Chihuahua is descended from dogs kept by the ancient Aztecs. In spite of its reputation for delicacy, the breed was brought to Central America in the 1850s, and it became a fashionable pet.

Appearance The Chihuahua has a large, domed head – the skull sometimes has an unprotected gap at its centre, known as a molera, and in consequence these tiny dogs must be handled carefully. The traditional form of the Chihuahua is smooth-coated, with sleek, glossy fur, but there is also a longhaired variety that has an equally soft coat, which is sometimes slightly curly, a long plume of hair on the tail and fringed ears.

Personality Lively and noisy, with a bark much larger than its size, the Chihuahua has a bold, fearless, somewhat terrier-like nature. These dogs form close bonds both with each other and with their owners. They may sometimes shiver with excitement, although the shorthaired variety is also sensitive to the cold.

Health and care Chihuahuas can suffer from a range of inherited ailments, some of which may not become apparent until later in life, whereas others – such as hydrocephalus, which causes an abnormally swollen head – will be evident at birth. It is important not to allow Chihuahuas to become fat, because this leaves them vulnerable to a narrowing of the airway to the lungs. This usually occurs at around 7 years old, and can be corrected only by surgery.

As an owner The smooth-coated form of the Chihuahua requires far less grooming than its long-coated counterpart. Check the mouths of puppies of this breed to ensure they are losing their milk teeth, because these are sometimes retained as the permanent teeth push through, and they will have to be removed by your vet. Chihuahuas can be somewhat fussy about their food.

Also consider The Chihuahua is a unique breed, so no other resembles it closely. One of the spirited, smooth-coated terrier breeds, such as the English Toy Terrier (see pages 192–193) or a Toy Fox Terrier (see page 211) might be an option. Other breeds from Central America, such as the toy form of the Mexican Hairless, may also be of interest.

Tech Spec

Features

A *Head:* Characteristic apple-domed skull, with a clear stop and a slightly pointed, short nose

B *Eyes:* Well-spaced and round in shape

C *Ears:* Large and positioned at an angle of about 45 degrees on the sides of the head

D *Chest:* Prominent with a deep brisket

E *Tail:* Medium-length and carried over the back; curled and tapered to a point

F *Bite:* Scissors or level bite

G *Height at shoulder:* 15–23cm (6–9 in)

H *Weight:* 1–1.75kg (2–4 lb) preferred, but can be up to 2.75kg (6 lb)

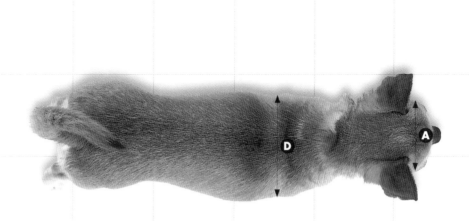

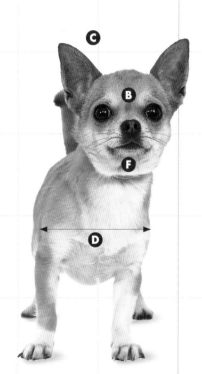

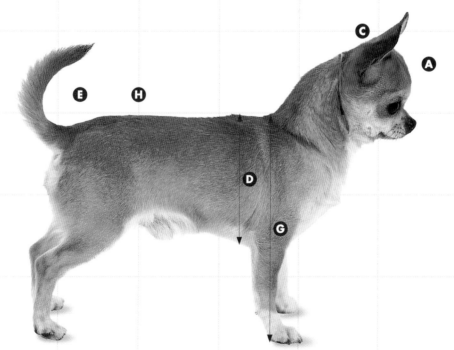

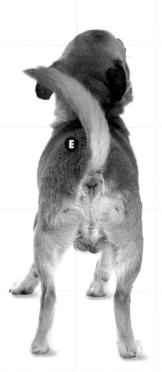

Chinese Crested

Overview

Recognition
North America, Britain and FCI member countries

Life expectancy
10–12 years

Colour
Any colour or pattern acceptable

Grooming

Feeding

Child friendliness

Exercise
Requires a walk in the park every day

The highly unusual Chinese Crested occurs in two forms, both of which may be born in the same litter. The most desirable puppies are the so-called Hairless; those with a full coat are called Powderpuffs. It is normal for the skin of these dogs to feel very warm to the touch.

Origin Hairless breeds of dog have cropped up at various times on different continents. The existence of the Chinese Crested was documented in England as early as 1686, but the breed may not actually have been imported here until the 1850s. The first examples of the breed were being shown in North America in the late 19th century, and the Chinese Crested achieved a good deal of publicity because the famous striptease artiste Gypsy Rose Lee chose to breed this near-naked dog!

Appearance In spite of being described as 'hairless', there is some hair on the Chinese Crested's head and tail, as well as 'socks' of hair on the lower legs and feet. The hair on the head is known as the crest, and that on the tail is described as the plume. In contrast, the Powderpuff variety has a true double coat, which is long, with a silky texture.

Personality A playful nature, combined with a pleasing personality, win over even those who instinctively dislike the idea of a hairless dog. The Chinese Crested is lively by nature, with an agile, trotting gait. The Powderpuff does not differ in its nature from the Hairless variety.

Health and care The hairless gene in dogs is usually linked to a reduction in the number of teeth. This characteristic is evident in the Hairless Chinese Crested, which lacks premolars, although Powderpuffs usually display a full complement of teeth. One of the advantages of a lack of fur is the fact that the breed does not tend to attract fleas, although they are not unknown. As you would expect, the grooming needs of the Hairless Chinese Crested are minimal, but the Powderpuff needs regular brushing and combing.

As an owner You need to protect your pet from both heat and cold. Your dog should wear a coat or special sweater – or even both – in cold or wet weather to help it retain its body heat. Apply a special canine sunblock outdoors on hot days to guard against sunburn, which can lead to skin cancer, especially on the paler areas of skin.

Also consider There are other breeds of hairless dog, such as the Mexican, which is available in three different sizes, from Toy to Standard. The Peruvian Hairless Dog is another possibility that may appeal, although it is considerably rarer. If you prefer the Powderpuff form of the Chinese Crested, you might be interested in a Papillon (see pages 196–197).

Tech Spec

Features

(A) *Head:* Balanced skull, measuring the same from the stop to the occiput as to the tip of the nose

(B) *Eyes:* Widely spaced, almond-shaped, with eye rims matching the colour of the dog

(C) *Ears:* Large and erect, with the base of the ear set at the same level as the outside edge of the eye

(D) *Chest:* Deep brisket, but breastbone is not prominent

(E) *Tail:* Slim and tapered, forming a curve and reaching to the hock; carried erect and slightly forwards when moving

(F) *Bite:* Scissors or level bite

(G) *Height at shoulder:* 28–33cm (11–13 in)

(H) *Weight:* up to 5.5kg (12 lb)

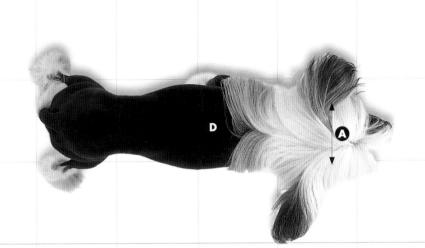

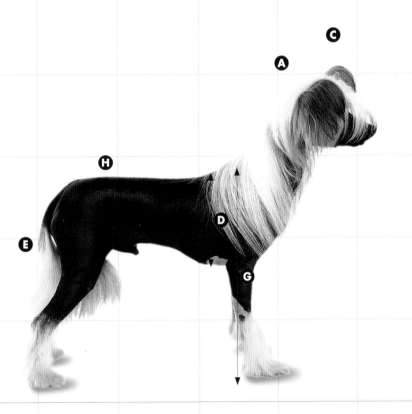

Coton de Tulear

Overview

Recognition
FCI member countries

Life expectancy
10–12 years

Colour
Pure white, bicolour (white and cream or white and black) or tricolour (white, cream and beige)

Grooming

Feeding

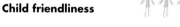

Child friendliness

Exercise
Appreciates a daily walk, with the opportunity to run

The Coton de Tulear is unusual in that it was kept in almost complete isolation for many centuries. Its origins lie on the small island of Reunion in the Indian Ocean. In the 18th century, French settlers brought some small Bichon-type dogs with them, which interbred with the local canine population, laying the foundations for the Coton de Tulear breed.

Origin Dogs originating in Reunion were traded at the port of Tulear on Madagascar (hence the breed's name today). It became a fashionable and exclusive pet among wealthy families on Madagascar, but it remained unknown elsewhere until the mid-20th century, when a few examples were taken to Europe. The breed reached North America in 1974, when a group of dogs were sent by a visiting biologist to his parents in New Jersey.

Appearance The white fluffy coat of this breed has a texture like cotton, as its French name suggests. It has a soft, light feel, and it is not moulted in a traditional way. Although white tends to be favoured, individuals with cream, or even black, patches are not unknown. The Coton de Tulear has a profuse covering of hair on the head, extending over the eyes. Both the nose and the claws are black.

Personality The rising popularity of this breed is a reflection of the fact that it has been developed solely as a companion, and it is ideally suited to domestic living. It has a placid, friendly temperament, but it also has a playful side to its nature.

Health and care The Coton de Tulear has proved to be a very healthy dog, although there are worries over its long-term future, because relatively few of these dogs have founded the bloodlines in Europe and North America. Breeding stock on Madagascar itself is limited, and the islanders are understandably reluctant to allow the export of their native breed. The dogs can suffer from overgrown claws, particularly if they do not walk on pavements or similar hard surfaces, and therefore may need regular trimming.

As an owner The Coton de Tulear is one of the rarer breeds you could choose, so you may have to wait until a puppy becomes available. Neutering is not advisable, because the availability of stock is limited, and your puppy may be needed as part of a future breeding programme.

Also consider Any of the Bichon breeds, such as the Bichon Frise (*see pages 174–175*), the Maltese (*see pages 190–191*) or the Havanese, may be possibilities – they are similar in terms of size and colouring. Unfortunately, this dog's ancestor from Reunion, sometimes called the Chien Coton or the Coton de Reunion, has already died out on its native island.

Tech Spec

Features

A *Head:* Skull is longer than the muzzle, with the head in proportion to the body

B *Eyes:* Medium-sized, relatively round and dark

C *Ears:* Narrow and hang closely down the sides of the head; held forwards when the dog is excited

D *Chest:* Deep brisket and well-developed

E *Tail:* Carried raised; curled loosely over the back, with only the hair touching it

F *Bite:* Scissors bite

G *Height at shoulder:* 25.5–30.5cm (10–12 in)

H *Weight:* 5.5–7kg (12–15 lb)

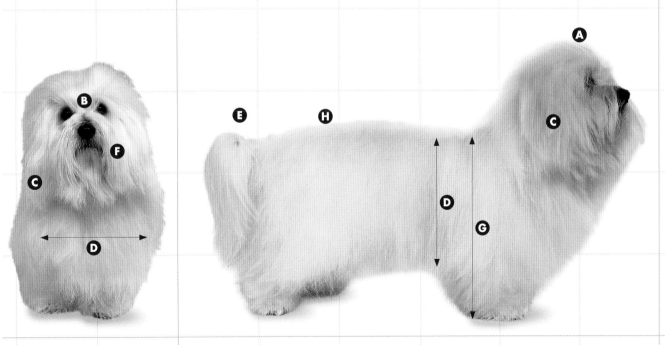

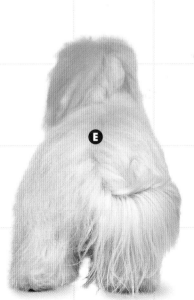

Italian Greyhound

Overview

Recognition
North America, Britain and
FCI member countries

Life expectancy
11–13 years

Colour
Virtually any colour is
acceptable, but brindles
and those with conventional
black and tan patterning
cannot be shown

Grooming

Feeding

Child friendliness

Exercise
These small greyhounds
are sprinters rather than
marathon runners—they
need the opportunity for
a short fast run

This toy breed may represent the earliest example of selective breeding in the dog world – it was created as a miniature version of a much larger hound. Italian Greyhounds were probably never used for serious hunting purposes, but were simply kept as companions around the home, like other toy breeds today.

Origin The Italian Greyhound has a long heritage, dating back over several thousand years. The mummified remains of similar dogs have been discovered in the tombs of the ancient Egyptian pharaohs. Later the breed was especially favoured as a companion by the nobility and was a frequent sight at the royal courts of Europe. It is shown in portraits dating back to the 15th century. The breed seems to have been introduced to North America in the 1880s, but it is still uncommon here today.

Appearance A scaled-down version of its larger relative, the Italian Greyhound has a deep chest and arched, sloping back that help it to run fast on its slender legs. The coat is thin, short and slightly glossy. The breed exists in a wide range of colours, often with white present on the chest, or forming a blaze between the eyes. The tail tapers along its length and is carried low.

Personality This breed can be shy and nervous with strangers, but socialization from an early age should help to overcome problems. Italian Greyhounds are gentle, trustworthy dogs and make excellent companions.

Health and care As often happens with deliberate miniaturization, the soundness of the Italian Greyhound was compromised by the late 19th century. Now, thanks to careful breeding, these small hounds are again robust. Italian Greyhounds prefer to run fast on flat ground, so try to find some open country to exercise your dog.

As an owner Italian Greyhounds feel the cold and dislike the wet. They should wear coats for protection in bad weather. They need minimal grooming – they have no undercoat, but the lack of insulation makes them especially sensitive to the elements. On the move, Italian Greyhounds have a distinctive, high-stepping gait not seen in their larger relatives.

Also consider The Whippet (*see pages 68–69*) is similar in overall appearance, but slightly larger; the other obvious choice if you are looking for an even larger dog is a true Greyhound (*see pages 60–61*).

Tech Spec

Features

A *Head:* Flat, long and narrow, with a fine muzzle

B *Eyes:* Bright and relatively large

C *Ears:* Soft, set back on the head and rose-shaped

D *Chest:* Narrow and deep

E *Tail:* Fine, relatively long, and carried low

F *Bite:* Level bite

G *Height at shoulder:* 33–38cm (13–15 in)

H *Weight:* 3.5kg (8 lb)

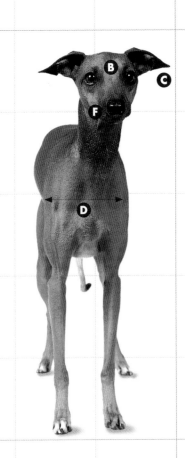

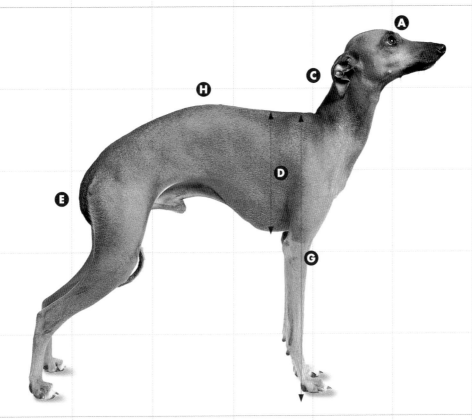

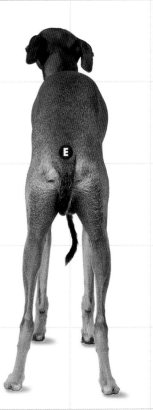

Japanese Chin

Overview

Recognition
North America, Britain and
FCI member countries

Life expectancy
11–13 years

Colour
Bicolour – this can be black
and white, with or without
tan points, or red and
white, the 'red' being any
shade from lemon through
to sable, and sometimes
overlaid with black

Grooming

Feeding

Child friendliness

Exercise
Regular walks in the local
park will be sufficient

It is often claimed that this is a dog that acts like a cat. In terms of its behaviour, the Japanese Chin often displays a feline side, particularly in its climbing ability and the way in which it uses its front feet. It can climb well and is a nimble jumper.

Origin The Japanese Chin is a very ancient breed, whose origins date back over a millennium. It may be descended from dogs that came from China or possibly Korea, and it has been suggested that it may share a common ancestry with the Pekingese. It was a pet of the Japanese nobility and was unknown in the West until the 17th century, when it was brought to Europe by Portuguese seafarers. The breed was not seen in North America until 1882, and it was initially known as the Japanese Spaniel.

Appearance A flattened face and an upturned nose are obvious features of this breed, and the very long ears hang far down the sides of the head. The coat is long and has a silky texture. Feathering occurs on the back of the front legs, with short hair in front, while the feet are hare-shaped (long and narrow). A clear white blaze between the eyes extending down over the muzzle is favoured. The tail arches forwards over the body.

Personality A breed that forms a close bond with people it knows well, the Japanese Chin is shy with strangers. This breed is lively and alert by nature, but it is unlikely to be an effective guard dog, since it rarely barks.

Health and care The Japanese Chin is generally a very healthy breed, although those that were first kept in the West had a reputation for being delicate. As a result of their face shape they may sometimes be inclined to snore. Be prepared to groom the luxuriant coat of this breed daily. Although the puppy coat is noticeably shorter than that of adult dogs, it is advisable to accustom them to grooming from an early age.

As an owner This breed is ideal if you live in a flat, because it is one of the few dogs that is content in these surroundings, provided that it can be taken out as necessary during the day. Training this breed is straightforward, because the Japanese Chin is keen to please. Its intelligence means that it learns quickly, although members of the breed will sometimes reveal a stubborn side. Scolding under these circumstances can be counterproductive.

Also consider If you like the facial shape of the Japanese Chin but are looking for a shorter dog, consider the Pekingese (*see pages 198–199*). If you want a smooth-coated breed, a Pug may be a good choice (*see pages 202–203*). It has more of a wrinkled face and is somewhat larger.

Tech Spec

Features

A *Head:* Large, yet proportionate; rounded, not domed

B *Eyes:* Well-spaced, large and dark; ideally showing some white near the nose

C *Ears:* Widely spaced, set high, small and V-shaped; held slightly forwards

D *Chest:* Wide, contributing to its stocky appearance

E *Tail:* Set high; twisted either right or left from the base or carried over the back, flowing to the other side

F *Bite:* Level bite

G *Height at shoulder:* 23cm (9 in)

H *Weight:* 1.75–3kg (4–7 lb)

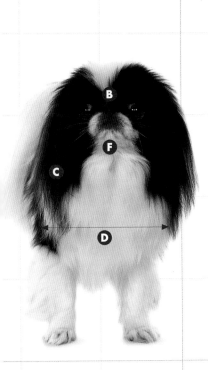

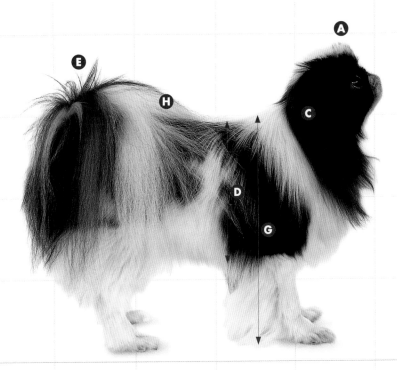

Maltese

Overview

Recognition
North America, Britain and
FCI member countries

Life expectancy
11–13 years

Colour
Must be white, although
slight lemon or light tan on
the ears may be permitted

Grooming

Feeding

Child friendliness

Exercise
Short walks in the park will
be sufficient

A breed that may be the oldest of all today's toy dogs, the Maltese was so highly valued in ancient times as a companion that it was described as the 'lady's jewel'. These dogs feature prominently in writings and on artefacts from Classical times, and they are thought of just as highly today, both as pets and in the show ring.

Origin As their name suggests, these dogs have become inextricably linked with the Mediterranean island of Malta, where they may have been introduced by the Phoenicians, who traded widely in the region. The modern type of the Maltese was established by the early 19th century, at a time when the dogs were actually becoming scarcer on their native island. The breed was exhibited at some of the earliest dog shows, including the first Westminster show in North America, which took place in 1877.

Appearance The long flowing coat lies flat and consists of a single layer, reaching almost to the ground around the sides of the body. The hair on the head is often tied up to form a characteristic topknot. Maltese are always white, with a black nose and black pads on the feet. In this breed, the top of the head is slightly rounded, and the hanging ears are set low.

Personality Do not be fooled by its small size – the Maltese is a fearless as well as a friendly breed. These dogs have highly affectionate and gentle natures, and they will happily spend much of the day in the company of their owner in the home.

Health and care A particular health problem that afflicts some Maltese, and that is probably an inherited weakness, is abnormalities of the eyelashes. The hairs rub against the surface of the eye, causing intense irritation and resulting in excessive tear production. Watch for tear staining at the corners of the eye nearest the nose. Surgical correction may be necessary in some cases.

As an owner Regular grooming is a vital part of this small dog's care, although the lack of a dense undercoat makes the task quite easy. While grooming, check that the ears are clean – with such a lot of hair they are susceptible to infection. The corners of the eyes may need to be to be wiped occasionally, too.

Also consider Other breeds of Bichon origin share some of the same characteristics, and they are also probably descended from the Maltese. These include the Bichon Frise (see pages 174–175), the Bolognese and the Havanese. All are white in colour, with a similar type of coat, and have the same compact muzzle shape.

Tech Spec

Features

A *Head:* Balanced head, from the stop to the top of the skull and down to the tip of the nose

B *Eyes:* Black eye rims, dark brown in colour; located centrally and without bulging

C *Ears:* Long, with good feathering and merging into the sides of the head

D *Chest:* Balanced in proportion to the body

E *Tail:* Carried over the back, lying to one side over the hindquarters

F *Bite:* Scissors or level bite

G *Height at shoulder:* 25.5cm (10 in)

H *Weight:* 1.75–2.75kg (4–6 lb) preferred, but up to 3kg (7 lb) acceptable

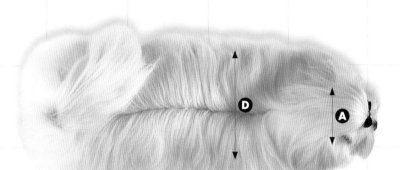

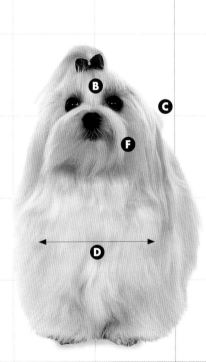

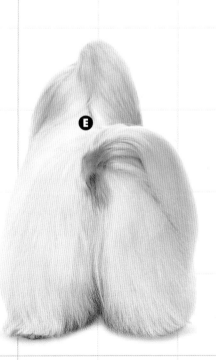

Overview

Recognition
North America, Britain and
FCI member countries

Life expectancy
10–12 years

Colour
Black and tan, with the
colours clearly separated
in the coat

Grooming

Feeding

Child friendliness

Exercise
Requires a good daily walk
in the park, ideally with the
opportunity to explore off
the leash

The Manchester Terrier exists in two sizes, with the smaller form better known in Britain as the English Toy Terrier. Early on, these terriers were exhibited together but today they are grouped separately. The toy form differs from its larger relative not just in size but also by its erect ears which are described as 'candle-flamed'.

Origin The hometown of the breed is the city of Manchester, where it became popular during the 19th century. A fashion to breed smaller versions of the Manchester terrier grew. These small dogs were skilled ratters, and ratting contests were used to attract gambling. The most famous ratter of this early period was called Tiny the Wonder, and he was renowned for killing 300 rats in just three hours in 1848, despite weighing only 2.5kg (5 lb).

Appearance Apart from the fact that the Toy form is smaller, there is one other significant difference in type between the forms of this breed. In the case of the Toy, only naturally erect ears are acceptable, whereas in the Standard they may be folded down – creating what is known as a button ear. Both forms can only be black and tan in colour.

Personality Lively and loyal, with a true terrier personality, the Toy form of the Manchester Terrier is not a dog that is easily overlooked in the home, in spite of its diminutive size. It usually gets along well with other breeds, even if they are much larger.

Health and care The trend towards miniaturization that began in 19th-century Britain led to an overall breed weakness – the natural consequence of persistently breeding weaker, smaller dogs from Manchester Terrier litters together – and this helps to explain why the Toy form had become scarce by the early 20th century. Since then, however, great efforts have been made to ensure the breed is generally strong and healthy. When individual dogs have health problems today, these are most likely to be skin and eye conditions.

As an owner This is an ideal choice if you do not want to spend much time on grooming. Manchester Terriers have short dense coats, with a glossy appearance.

Also consider The Toy Fox Terrier (*see page 211*), also known as the American Fox Terrier, to which this breed has contributed, may be an alternative. The Miniature Pinscher (*see pages 194–195*) is another possibility, with the same black-and-tan colouring as the English Toy Terrier. If you are looking for a much larger dog, consider the Dobermann (*see pages 224–225*).

Tech Spec

Features

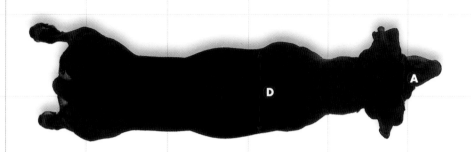

A *Head:* Long and narrow, appearing as a blunt wedge both in profile and from the front, with the length of the skull corresponding to that of the muzzle

B *Eyes:* Almond-shaped, virtually black, and bright

C *Ears:* Wide at the base, tapering to points and set high; can be erect or button-shaped

D *Chest:* Brisket is close to the elbows

E *Tail:* Tapered to a point; carried in a slightly upward curve, but not extending over the back

F *Bite:* Scissors or level bite

G *Height at shoulder:* 38cm (15 in)

H *Weight:* 4.5–10kg (12–22 lb)

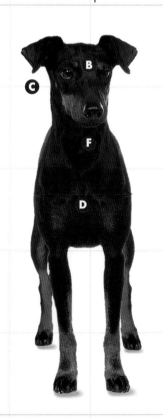

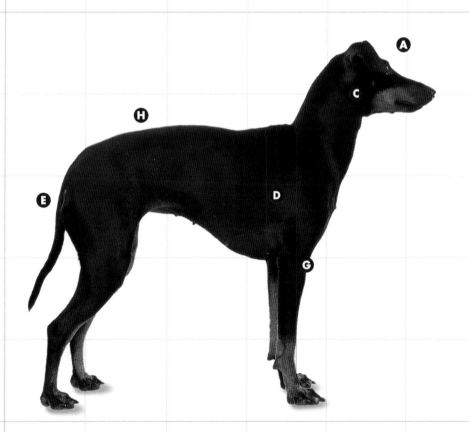

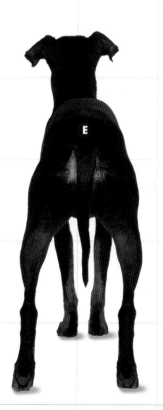

Overview

Recognition
North America, Britain and
FCI member countries

Life expectancy
11–13 years

Colour
Solid red; chocolate and
red; black and red. When
dogs are bicoloured, the
colours must be well-
defined and separate

Grooming

Feeding

Child friendliness

Exercise
Regular daily walks in the
park are required, and this
breed needs to be carefully
socialized with other dogs

Sometimes also known as the MinPin, this breed has a most distinctive high-stepping gait, somewhat like that of a hackney horse. Miniature Pinschers literally prance around the show ring, holding a front leg out straight and then bending it at the joint before putting it down again.

Origin In common with other Pinschers, this breed hails from Germany, where it is known as the Zwergpinscher. Its origins there may extend back as far as the 18th century. The MinPin was originally kept to hunt vermin, and the designation 'pinscher' is now synonymous with 'terrier'. In earlier times it was larger than it is today. It began to become known in North America during the early 1920s, and a breed club was established in 1929. In its homeland, the Miniature Pinscher was recognized for show purposes in 1895.

Appearance A well-muscled athletic profile is characteristic of this breed and is emphasized by its short glossy coat. The Miniature Pinscher has a slightly curved neck and erect ears set high on the head. The skull tapers to the muzzle, and the teeth have a scissor bite. The feet are catlike in appearance, with strong pads and broad, blunt claws. The tail is set high on the back.

Personality This is a breed that has no concept of its small size – the MinPin is bold by nature and individuals are usually willing not only to stand their ground, but also to challenge much larger dogs if threatened. It also excels as a guard dog.

Health and care The only inherited breed weakness that may be seen occasionally in the Miniature Pinscher is a tendency to dislocate its shoulder. If this occurs, you need to seek veterinary advice to prevent any recurrence in the future, and this may entail surgery. Otherwise, in spite of its delicate appearance, the MinPin is a robust breed.

As an owner You need to train your pet carefully to avoid potential conflicts when you are out walking and to ensure that your dog returns to you readily on command. Intelligent by nature, this is a breed that also learns quickly. Coat care is straightforward for the MinPin: occasional brushing is all that is needed to maintain the breed's sleek and attractive appearance.

Also consider Similar German breeds include the German or Standard Pinscher. It is larger, standing up to 51cm (20 in) tall, and a hackney gait is considered a fault in this bigger Pinscher. If you are interested in an even bigger dog of this type, consider the Dobermann (*see pages 224–225*); at the other end of the scale, the feisty Manchester Terrier is an option (*see pages 192–193*).

Tech Spec

Features

A *Head:* Elongated rather than round, with no cheek bulges; appears flat from the front

B *Eyes:* Slightly oval, dark, almost round

C *Ears:* Small in size, set high and erect

D *Chest:* Full, relatively broad, and contributes to the distinctive action

E *Tail:* Set relatively high, continuing the top line

F *Bite:* Scissors bite

G *Height at shoulder:* 25.5–31.5cm (10–12½ in)

H *Weight:* 5.5kg (12 lb)

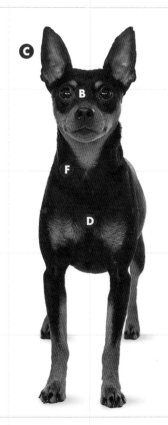

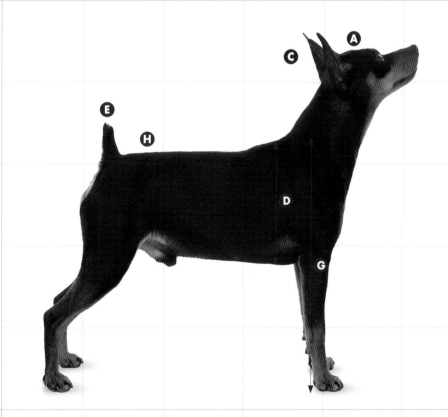

Group **Toy**

Overview

Recognition
North America, Britain and
FCI member countries

Life expectancy
11–13 years

Colour
Chestnut and white; red
and white; black and
white; tricolour–black,
tan and white

Grooming

Feeding

Child friendliness

Exercise
This dog will enjoy the
opportunity to explore in
the park or country

Few breeds have proved such an inspiration to artists as this continental toy spaniel – the Papillon appears in works by artists including Titian, Goya, Rubens and Rembrandt. However, the Papillon is much more than just a decorative companion breed; it is a highly effective ratter as well.

Origin This breed originated in mainland Europe over 500 years ago, and it became a fashionable lap dog among ladies of the royal courts. Papillons were particularly popular at the court of Louis XIV of France. It was imported into France from its breeding centre, Bologna in Italy, travelling overland by mule. Despite its popularity in Europe, the Papillon was apparently not introduced to Britain until 1901, and it did not have its own breed club in North America until 1935.

Appearance Papillon in French means 'butterfly', and the name refers to the large raised ears of the breed, which are said to look like a butterfly's spread wings. They are set far back and slightly to the sides of the head and are fringed with hair. A characteristic of the breed is that the coloured areas of fur must not only cover the ears entirely, but must also extend from the ears to the eyes.

Personality A cheerful disposition characterizes the Papillon, and it is also a highly affectionate breed. It has a peaceful and adaptable nature, is at home in either the country or the city, and is just as happy trotting gracefully about in open fields as in an urban park.

Health and care Despite their delicate looks, these continental toy spaniels are hardy but, as with other toy dogs, they can develop a weakness that afflicts the kneecaps. They are also known as Squirrel Dogs because of the bushy plume of fur on their tails, which are carried high. Grooming this dog is straightforward, in spite of the long coat, because the Papillon's fur does not have a thick undercoat.

As an owner If you choose a Papillon you are guaranteed a companion that is sufficiently flexible to adjust to changes in your life without problems. It is an ideal choice both for people living on their own and for those with families. The Papillon can be recommended for obedience competitions because this breed learns quickly and is very responsive.

Also consider A form of the continental toy spaniel known as the Phalene, which is very closely related to the Papillon, is bred in the same range of colours. It looks identical to the Papillon, apart from the fact that it has drop ears. Another solid-coloured dog is the Volpino, although it lacks the long hair on the ears.

Tech Spec

Features

A *Head:* Slightly rounded top to the skull between the ears, with a delicately pointed muzzle

B *Eyes:* Round, dark, and set low on the skull

C *Ears:* Large, set towards the back of the head, and with rounded tips; carried erect

D *Chest:* Relatively deep, separating straight, fine-boned front legs

E *Tail:* Long and carried high over the back, creating a plume

F *Bite:* Scissors bite

G *Height at shoulder:* Up to 30.5cm (12 in)

H *Weight:* 4.5kg (10 lb)

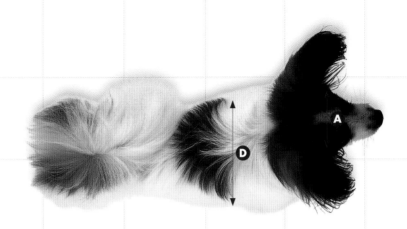

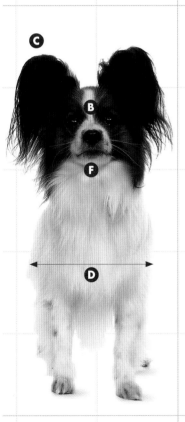

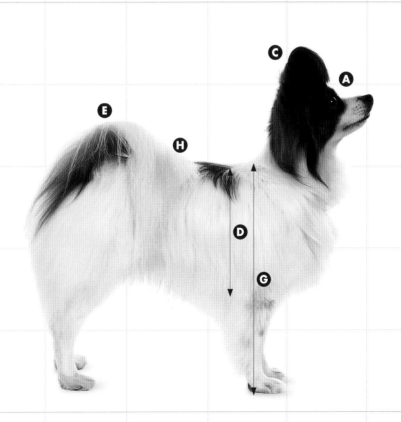

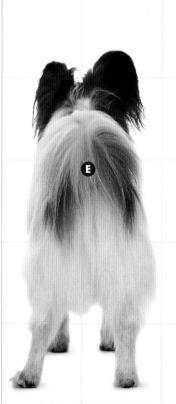

Pekingese

Recognition
North America, Britain and
FCI member countries

Life expectancy
10–12 years

Colour
Any colour or pattern; the
most commonly found coat
is golden-red, and dogs
with this colouring are often
described as Sun Dogs

Grooming

Feeding

Child friendliness

Exercise
A good daily walk in the
park will suffice

Named after Peking, the former name for the Chinese capital Beijing, few dogs have enjoyed a more pampered early existence than the Pekingese. Ownership of these very individual dogs was restricted to the Emperor of China. They were cared for by eunuchs, and stealing or selling a Pekingese was punishable by death.

Origin When it first became known in the West in the 1860s, the Pekingese was much more like the Tibetan Spaniel (*see pages 94–95*) in appearance, and the breeds may share a common ancestry. In early times Pekingese were even more diminutive than they are today and were known as Sleeve Dogs, because of the way in which they could be carried in the sleeves of the flowing robes of Chinese courtiers. Queen Victoria, a great dog lover, was presented with the first Pekingese seen outside China in the 19th century.

Appearance Today's Pekingese have compact faces with very prominent eyes. The coat is also more profuse than in the past, trailing to the ground, and their legs are shorter than those of their ancestors. They retain a long area of hair, resembling a mane, around the neck, which led to another of their old names – the Lion Dog.

Personality Loyal yet stubborn best describes the Pekingese's personality. This is a breed with a confident and independent nature. Pekes are also courageous little dogs.

Health and care The profuse coat of the breed needs daily grooming. Its prominent eyes are susceptible to injury, and the compacted shape of the Peke's face makes these dogs prone to tearstaining at the corner of the eye nearest the nose. In some cases the opening to the tear ducts is absent, and this will require surgical correction. The long body shape also means that the breed can be at risk from slipped discs, so Pekes should not be encouraged to jump or to climb too many stairs.

As an owner Do not be fooled by the appearance of the Pekingese. Its origins are believed to go back to much larger mastiff dogs, and it is self-assured, active and playful. It has good stamina, but in hot weather you should avoid exercising a Pekingese in the middle of the day, because they are vulnerable to heatstroke.

Also consider The Tibetan Spaniel (*see pages 94–95*) is a possible alternative, although it has a relatively short coat. You might also be interested in the Tibetan Terrier (*see pages 96–97*), which originates from the same part of the world. The Tibetan Terrier is a taller, heavier dog, but with a coat that is more like that of the Pekingese. However, in many ways, the Pekingese is unique.

Tech Spec

Features

A *Head:* Massive, broad skull that is flat between the ears; deep stop and short nose

B *Eyes:* Large, prominent and dark

C *Ears:* Heart-shaped, level with the top of the skull and lying close to the head

D *Chest:* Broad, with well-sprung ribs

E *Tail:* Set high on the back and slightly curved over it

F *Bite:* Level bite

G *Height at shoulder:* Up to 23cm (9 in)

H *Weight:* Up to 6.5kg (14 lb)

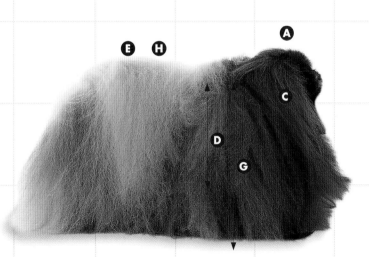

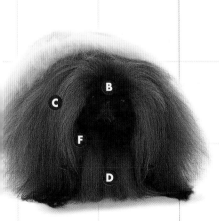

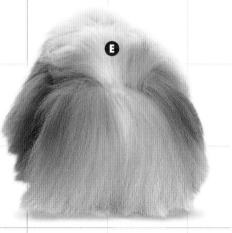

Pomeranian

Overview

Recognition
North America, Britain and
FCI member countries

Life expectancy
11–13 years

Colours
There are no restrictions on
colours or patterns

Grooming

Feeding

Child friendliness

Exercise
A good walk every day
in a park is essential

In spite of its diminutive size, this breed is in many ways a typical member of the spitz group. The group's origins lie in northerly latitudes, and they are clearly identifiable by their erect ears, foxlike faces and a tail that curls forwards over the back. But while larger spitz breeds pull sleds, the Pom is kept as a companion.

Origin Named after the German province of Pomerania, this breed was created in Britain in the 19th century by down-scaling a dog known as the Mittel Spitz through selective breeding. Towards the end of the century, Queen Victoria's interest in the breed led to a surge in its popularity. The Pomeranian was being shown as early as 1892 in North America, and breeding through the 20th century led to a further reduction in the Pomeranian's size and an increase in the length of its coat.

Appearance The original ancestors of the Pomeranian were white, but today the breed has more than a dozen colour variations. The Pomeranian is sometimes described as the Puffball, because of its thick, erect coat, which arises from the combination of a soft, dense undercoat and a long, straight, harsh-textured topcoat. There is a distinct frill on the chest, extending around to the shoulders on each side of the body.

Personality Lively and energetic, the Pomeranian retains attributes seen in its larger relatives, but it settles well as a household pet, even in relatively confined surroundings. Alert by nature, a Pom is an excellent watchdog.

Health and care Unfortunately, Pomeranians are susceptible to a number of the congenital problems often found in small dogs. These include patellar luxation, where affected puppies typically develop signs of lameness at between 4 and 6 months. This weakness can cause dislocation of the kneecap, affecting one or both hind legs, and is likely to require surgical correction. Subsequently, dogs generally recover well.

As an owner If you choose a Pomeranian you must be prepared to groom your pet daily to prevent the coat from becoming matted. Wipe the corners of the eyes with damp cotton wool, too, if tearstaining is evident, as it sometimes is in cold weather.

Also consider Related spitz breeds that have been developed as companion dogs are worth consideration, notably the German Spitz, from which the Pomeranian is descended. The nearest equivalent to the Pomeranian is the 'Klein', or small, form, also known as the German Toy Spitz. The largest member of this particular group, the Giant German Spitz, stands 40.5cm (16 in) tall and weighs around 18kg (40 lb).

Tech Spec

Features

A *Head:* Skull flat and large compared with the muzzle, with an overall foxlike appearance

B *Eyes:* Slightly oval in shape, medium-sized and dark; relatively close together

C *Ears:* Small and erect, set reasonably high

D *Chest:* Relatively deep, but not too wide

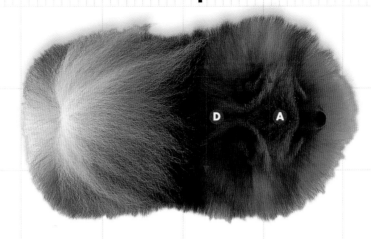

E *Tail:* Turned over the back, carried flat and straight

F *Bite:* Scissors bite

G *Height at shoulder:* 28cm (11 in)

H *Weight:* Dogs 1.75–2kg (4–4½ lb); bitches 2–2.5kg (4½–5½ lb)

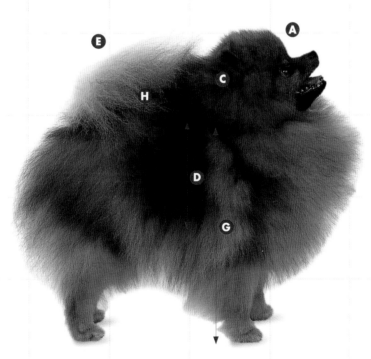

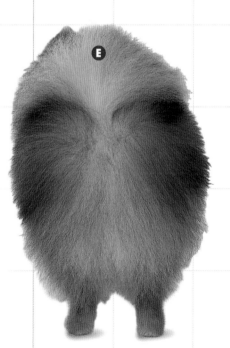

Group **Toy**

Pug

Overview

Recognition
North America, Britain and
FCI member countries

Life expectancy
13–15 years

Colour
Silver or apricot-fawn with
black markings; solid black

Grooming

Feeding

Child friendliness

Exercise
A daily walk in the park
will be essential

This breed was originally known as the Pug Dog, which means 'monkey-faced dog'. It got its name because it became popular as a pet in Britain at the same time as marmoset monkeys, which have a similar face shape. In Germany the Pug was known as the Mops – a slang term also used in Britain for marmoset monkeys.

Origin Pugs probably originated in China nearly 2,000 years ago. Merchants brought the breed to Europe, where it first became popular in the Netherlands. It was introduced to Britain by William and Mary of Orange when they ascended the throne in 1688. Pugs were originally fawn in colour, with a black mask and saddle marking. By the 1850s, both the lighter-coloured Willoughby strain and the more golden-apricot Morrison bloodline existed. Black pugs were first bred in the late 1870s.

Appearance The Pug is generally considered to be the biggest of the toy breeds, and it can be recognized by its stocky build and thick, powerful legs. It has a large rounded head with a flat, wrinkled face and large prominent eyes. The ears hang down over the sides of the head and the tail curls forwards low over the back. The Pug's body has a square-shaped profile and its fur has a fine, soft texture.

Personality Pugs make excellent pets for any age of owner, thanks to their tolerant natures. They are patient dogs and will not yap to gain attention, although they are effective watchdogs and have been known to defend their owners against attack.

Health and care The Pug's prominent eyes can be prone to injury, and they sometimes have ingrowing eyelashes, which inflame the eyeballs and need to be removed surgically. The wrinkling on the Pug's face is occasionally the site of localized skin infections, but this is not common. This breed's grooming needs are minimal, thanks to their short coats. Avoid exercising a Pug in hot weather, because they can succumb to heatstroke.

As an owner If you own a Pug, you must make sure that your pet does not become overweight, because this is a problem to which the breed is especially susceptible. Carefully measure out the amount of food required for your Pug and only offer healthy treats, such as pieces of raw carrot or apple. Regular periods of exercise are also essential for a Pug.

Also consider If you like the Pug's thick-set appearance, a Bulldog (*see pages 74–75*) might be worth considering, although these dogs are larger and significantly heavier, as well as being less agile. There is no close relative to the Pug within the Toy group, although if you are happy to undertake the necessary grooming, a Pekingese (*see pages 198–199*) might be another possible choice.

Tech Spec

Features

A *Head:* Massive and round, relative to the size of the body, with a short square muzzle

B *Eyes:* Prominent, dark and large

C *Ears:* Thin, small, and either the preferred button shape or roselike

D *Chest:* Broad

E *Tail:* Twisted tightly over the hip, with a double curl being ideal

F *Bite:* Slightly undershot bite

G *Height at shoulder:* 28cm (11 in)

H *Weight:* 6.5–8kg (14–18 lb)

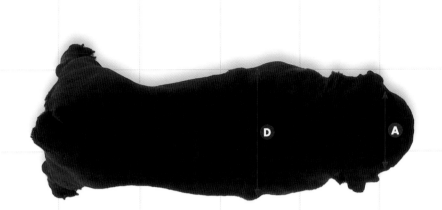

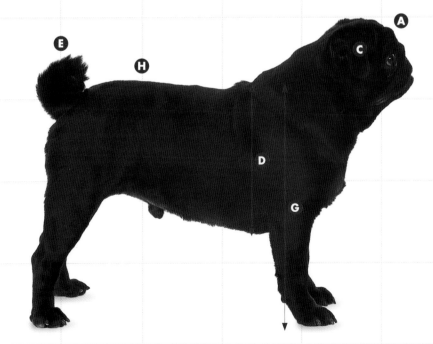

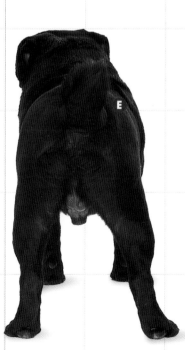

Shih Tzu

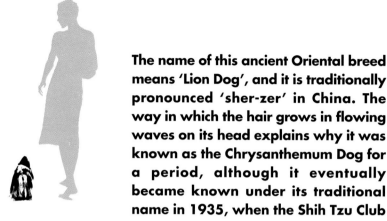

Overview

Recognition
North America, Britain and
FCI member countries

Life expectancy
11–13 years

Colour
There are no restrictions on
either colour or markings

Grooming

Feeding

Child friendliness

Exercise
Provide a daily walk in a
local park

The name of this ancient Oriental breed means 'Lion Dog', and it is traditionally pronounced 'sher-zer' in China. The way in which the hair grows in flowing waves on its head explains why it was known as the Chrysanthemum Dog for a period, although it eventually became known under its traditional name in 1935, when the Shih Tzu Club of England was founded.

Origin The Shih Tzu is the result of crossbreeding between Lhasa Apso and Pekingese at the Imperial Palace in what is now Beijing. The Lhasa Apsos were gifts to the Chinese Emperors from the Dalai Lama, who ruled Tibet. The origins of the Shih Tzu may date back over 300 years, but it remained unknown in the West until the 1930s, when a few examples were seen in Europe for the first time. The Shih Tzu reached North America in the 1960s.

Appearance The head shape of the Shih Tzu reflects both of its ancestral breeds. It has a more rounded skull than the Lhasa Apso, but a longer, more prominent muzzle than the Pekingese, and its eyes are clearly visible. In China, golden-coloured Shih Tzus were the most highly regarded. An unusual characteristic is the way in which the hair on the nose grows up towards the forehead.

Personality The Shih Tzu has inherited a playful side to its nature from its Pekingese forebears, but shares their dignified temperament, too. These dogs make friendly, affectionate companions.

Health and care A hereditary malformation of the kidneys can sometimes afflict the Shih Tzu, but symptoms will not become apparent until young dogs are at least a year old. Another hereditary problem in the breed is various abnormalities affecting the blood clotting system. The first visible symptom of this can be the presence of blood blisters, which may become large, under the skin.

As an owner The Shih Tzu demands considerable grooming time because of its long, dense, double-layered coat. The hair extending up from the nose is usually tied up on the head in a topknot. This is a suitable breed for a flat dweller, because it is content living in a fairly limited space, provided that it can be taken out through the day as required.

Also consider Both the Lhasa Apso (*see pages 86–87*) and the Pekingese (*see pages 198–199*), from which the Shih Tzu is jointly descended, are worth considering, depending on which aspect of the Shih Tzu's appearance and character most appeals to you. If the grooming involved in caring for these breeds seems daunting, think about the Tibetan Spaniel (*see pages 94–95*), which is a relative of the Pekingese but has a much shorter coat.

Tech Spec

Features

A *Head:* Broad and round in shape, and wide between the eyes

B *Eyes:* Well-spaced, positioned directly ahead and dark in colour

C *Ears:* Large, set just below the level of the crown

D *Chest:* Deep and broad, with rib cage extending to a point just below the level of the elbow

E *Tail:* Set high and curved forwards over the back

F *Bite:* Undershot bite

G *Height at shoulder:* 20–28cm (8–11 in), but 23–26.5cm (9–10½ in) preferred

H *Weight:* 4–7kg (9–16 lb)

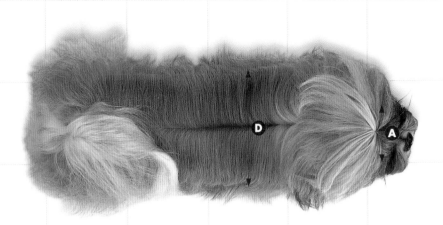

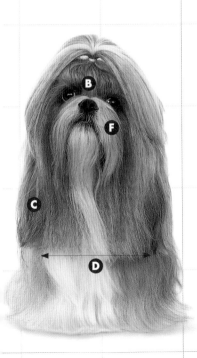

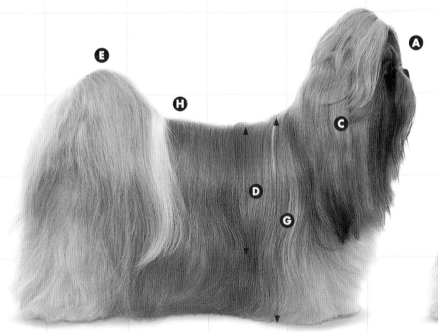

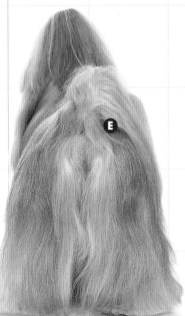

Silky Terrier

Recognition
North America, Britain and
FCI member countries

Life expectancy
11–13 years

Colour
Blue and tan, with a lighter
silvery or fawn topknot on
the head

Grooming

Feeding

Child friendliness

Exercise
A breed that likes to
explore off the leash
on its daily walks

Unlike other breeds originating from Australia, the Silky Terrier was created as a companion rather than as a working dog. Today it has established a worldwide following. In its homeland it was originally called the Sydney Silky Terrier, but is now known as the Australian Silky Terrier.

Origin The Silky was created in the late 19th century. Its development was centred in the southeastern states of Victoria and New South Wales, particularly in the vicinity of Sydney. It was bred from a combination of Yorkshire Terrier and Australian Terrier crosses, which were originally carried out to improve the colouring of the latter's blue and tan coat. Skye Terriers may also have played a part in the mix and were probably responsible for the pricked ears, which are a feature of the breed today.

Appearance The crosses carried out in its breeding has led to the Silky Terrier being developed into a true toy breed, as reflected in its size. The breed's coat is a particularly distinctive feature – it has a silky texture and is parted down the midline of the body. These terriers have a fine-boned appearance, but they are not delicate. Silky Terriers are always blue and tan in colour, but the depth of the blue colouring varies from a silvery shade to a dark slate blue.

Personality Silky Terriers possess the character typical of a larger terrier; they are lively and alert, and they are good guard dogs, despite their size. They are also friendly and trusting with their owners.

Health and care The Silky Terrier is a robust breed, in spite of its reduction in size. The original judging standard in Victoria allowed drop as well as prick ears. This was later superseded, but the drop-ear trait reemerges in puppies occasionally today. Drop ears prevent a dog from being exhibited, but they have no effect on its suitability as a pet. Silky Terriers must also have dark nails according to the breed standard – pale nails are a fault.

As an owner Although popular in its homeland, the Silky Terrier is not frequently seen elsewhere. It is particularly uncommon in Britain, where Yorkshire Terriers have retained their popularity. One of the advantages of the Silky Terrier is that it does not moult. As the dog's name suggests, the coat has a wonderful silky texture, which is most profuse in adult dogs.

Also consider Alternative breeds to consider are the Yorkshire Terrier (*see pages 208–209*) and the Australian Terrier (*see pages 138–139*). Both are slightly larger than the Silky Terrier. Other terriers that may appeal as alternatives include the Cairn (*see pages 142–143*) and the Skye Terrier (*see page 173*). The coats of these dogs do not, however, share the Silky's luxurious texture.

Tech Spec

Features

A *Head:* Medium-length, with flat top to the skull; wide between the ears

B *Eyes:* Round, small and dark in colour

C *Ears:* Small, V-shaped pricked ears; set high

D *Chest:* Medium both in depth and breadth

E *Tail:* Held erect and so clearly visible

F *Bite:* Scissors bite

G *Height at shoulder:* 23cm (9 in)

H *Weight:* 3.5–4.5kg (8–10 lb)

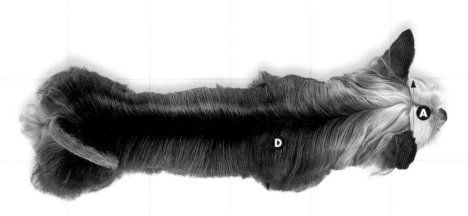

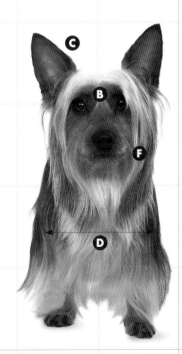

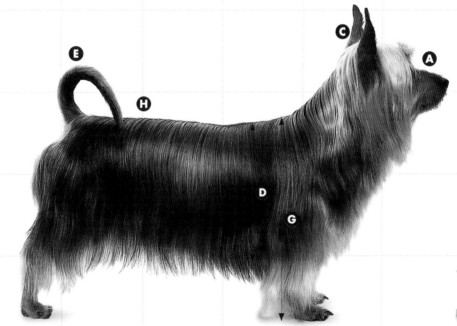

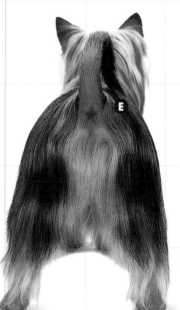

Group **Toy**

Overview

Recognition
North America, Britain and
FCI member countries

Life expectancy
11–13 years

Colour
Blue and tan

Grooming

Feeding

Child friendliness

Exercise
A trot around the local park
each day will be sufficient

This terrier has attracted a strong worldwide following today. In spite of its working origins, it is now kept exclusively as a companion breed and for show purposes, and it has been very popular in both these roles for well over a century. This is also a breed that is well-suited to urban living; it does not need a great deal of space.

Origin The Yorkshire Terrier's history goes back to the mill towns of Yorkshire in northern England, where its ancestors were used to hunt rats and mice. It is unclear which particular breeds played a part in its ancestry, but they probably included the Manchester Terrier and the now-extinct Leeds Terrier. Both the Skye Terrier (*see page 173*) and the Dandie Dinmont (*see pages 144–145*) may have played some part in the Yorkshire's development.

Appearance The coat of the Yorkshire Terrier makes a major contribution to its appearance. It has a fine texture with an attractive gloss and should extend down each side of the body to ground level. The hair on the head is often tied in the centre with a bow, or parted to the sides and held in place with two bows. Hair on the tips of the ears is trimmed short.

Personality A dog with a large personality in spite of its diminutive size, the Yorkshire Terrier has a bossy yet bold nature. It is also fearless and, in spite of its pampered appearance, it has not forgotten its rodent-killing past.

Health and care Unfortunately, an inherited weakness of the kneecaps, known as patellar luxation, is relatively common in this terrier and will need surgical correction. Signs of lameness will become apparent in puppies when they are between 4 and 6 months old. Affected individuals should not be used for breeding. It is normal for puppies to have black areas on the coat; these will turn to the characteristic steel blue as the dogs mature.

As an owner You need to invest considerable time in grooming a Yorkshire Terrier. If the dog gets muddy, it is easiest to allow the mud to dry and then comb it out of the coat. The area around the mouth needs to be kept clear of food and combed and cleaned regularly.

Also consider The Australian Silky Terrier (*see pages 206–207*) is a direct descendent of the Yorkie. The Australian Terrier (*see pages 138–139*) represents another possibility, with a significantly shorter and harder coat than that of the Yorkshire Terrier. The perky Norwich Terrier (*see pages 154–155*) may also appeal.

Tech Spec

Features

A *Head:* Relatively small and flat above, with a muzzle of proportionate length

B *Eyes:* Medium-sized, dark in colour and directed forwards

C *Ears:* Small, V-shaped and erect or semi-erect, with relatively little space between them

D *Chest:* Moderate, separating straight front legs

E *Tail:* Carried above the level of the back

F *Bite:* Scissors or level bite

G *Height at shoulder:* 23cm (9 in)

H *Weight:* 3kg (7 lb)

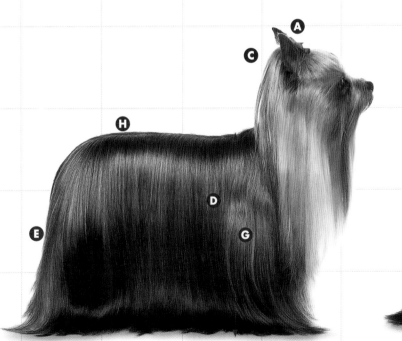

Pet Spec
Affenpinscher

This dog's name literally means 'monkey terrier' in German, reflecting both its appearance and ancestry. Its origins date back to the 18th century, when the Affenpinscher was created in southern Germany, in the area around Munich, from scaled-down terrier stock. The breed retained its hunting instincts, but the Affenpinscher's miniature size indicates that it was more likely bred to catch mice than rats.

Appearance A broad, moustachioed face is a key characteristic of this breed. Its coat is dense and rough, and is shorter on the rear of the body and the tail. Affenpinschers exist in a wide range of colours, from beige and silver to red and grey to black (which is especially popular). The colours are sometimes mixed, and there is a black and tan variety.

Breed care and health The Affenpinscher's rough coat does not need much grooming. Its gait is considered very important: the legs trot along in parallel, creating a confident impression. The lower jaw is broad, with no overcrowding of the teeth.

As an owner This breed is generally quiet, but it can become excitable and noisy if roused. The hair on the ears is usually cut short, contrasting with its long eyebrows and emphasizing the Affenpinscher's comic, monkeylike appearance.

Also consider The Affenpinscher has made a major contribution to the development of the Griffon Bruxellois (*see pages 176– 177*), another wire-coated breed, but with a shorter coat. You may also consider the Petit Brabancon, which has a smooth, short coat – it may have been created from crossbreeding with pugs. In spite of their compact facial shape, none of these dogs is prone to snoring.

Pet Spec
Bolognese

This rare toy breed is of Italian origin. As its name suggests, it was first bred in the area around the city of Bologna. It is descended from Bichon stock, which appears to have been widely distributed through the Mediterranean region as long ago as the 13th century. The Bolognese was originally kept as a ladies' companion among the nobility, but it has now become much rarer. It makes an excellent pet.

Appearance The Bolognese shares a tousled, fair appearance with other related breeds. Although breeders favour a pure white coat, it often has a slight blond tone. The coat grows in tufts and has a distinctive cottonlike texture. There is no undercoat. The nose is black.

Breed care and health This breed is both robust and long-lived, but its small size and lack of undercoat mean that it should be protected from cold wet weather to avoid chills.

As an owner Obtaining a Bolognese may take patience. In spite of their long history in Europe, they were only introduced in North America in the 1980s. This breed forms a strong bond with its immediate family.

Also consider There are several other breeds of Bichon stock, including the Maltese (*see pages 190–191*), which is much easier to find in North America than the Bolognese. It has a much more profuse coat than the Bolognese, so it requires more dedicated grooming. The Bichon Frise (*see pages 174–175*) has a shorter, fluffier coat. The rare Havanese is another option.

Pet Spec
King Charles Spaniel

This breed is better-known in America as the English Toy Spaniel. It became popular in Britain during the latter part of the 1600s, after Charles II was restored to the throne. Its origins are obscure however, and its ancestors may originally have been brought over from France during the previous century, or even from Spain. This breed is an attractive and affectionate companion.

Appearance This breed now has a much more compact facial shape than in the past – a trend that first became apparent in the 1800s. The traditional colour used to be black and tan, but the strain originally developed at Blenheim Palace in the 1700s, which is chestnut red and white, is now often seen. The other varieties are the tri-coloured Prince Charles and the mahogany red Ruby form, with its attractive glossy coat.

Breed care and health The short nasal chambers of these spaniels mean they are prone to snoring. They should not be exercised when the weather is at its hottest, as this feature also predisposes them to heatstroke. The breed can display a tendency to obesity too, so watch your pet's weight closely.

As an owner You need to be prepared to groom your pet regularly, and to keep a close watch for ear infections, which will be manifested by the dog scratching repeatedly at its ears. This requires prompt veterinary attention to minimize the risk of any recurrence.

Also consider The Cavalier King Charles Spaniel (*see pages 178–179*) is a choice. Both breeds are descended from exactly the same ancestral stock and are essentially identical, apart from the fact that the Cavalier has a longer nose. The continental toy spaniels, known as the Papillon (*see pages 196–197*) and Phalene are another option.

Height 24–29cm (9¹/₂–11¹/₂ in)
Weight 3–3.5kg (7–8 lb)
Exercise Curious by nature, these dogs like to explore when out for a walk

Height 25.5–30.5cm (10–12 in)
Weight 3–4kg (5¹/₂–9 lb)
Exercise Although playful, this is not a breed that requires long walks

Height 43–51cm (17–20 in)
Weight 13.5–16kg (30–35 lb)
Exercise With an abundance of energy and stamina, these dogs need good long walks

German Spitz

The German Spitz exists in several different sizes. As the breed began to be kept as a pet, it also became smaller, in contrast to its larger working relatives. The classification is based on size, and the breed description may include the Giant and Standard (Mittel), as well as the Miniature (Klein) and Toy (also Klein).

Appearance The spitz group has a foxlike facial shape, with upright ears and a tail that curls forwards over the back. The appearance of the different forms is similar, irrespective of their size. The hair on the face is significantly shorter than that on the rest of the body. They are bred in various colours, including the grey variety, which is described as 'wolf spitz'.

Breed care and health Regular grooming is an important part of keeping these lively dogs. They are not prone to any particular weaknesses, although the Toy is more susceptible to a weakness of the kneecaps than the larger forms.

As an owner You must decide which variety would be most appropriate for you. The smallest Toy examples are about half the size of the Giant German Spitz. They are bred in a wide range of colours, both solid and mixed.

Also consider The Pomeranian (*see pages 200–201*) is very similar to the German Toy Spitz, and may be grouped with it in some cases. While the Pom is especially popular in Europe, in North America the Toy American Eskimo, with its distinctive white coat, still clearly reflects its German Spitz ancestry. If you want a different but significantly larger spitz breed, a Keeshond (*see pages 84–85*) would be a good choice.

Height 20–40.5cm (8–16 in)
Weight 2–18kg (4–40 lb)
Exercise The larger German Spitz varieties will require the most exercise

Toy Fox Terrier

This small breed is the result of matings between Smooth Fox Terriers and Chihuahuas, with some input from English Toy Terriers. This means they are lively, feisty little dogs, with great character. They are sometimes also known as American Fox Terriers and Amertoys. As these names suggest, the Toy Fox Terrier was created in the US, being first registered during 1936, but only obtained full AKC recognition in 2003.

Appearance The body shape of these terriers is relatively square, with straight front legs. Their facial appearance reflects the influence of the Chihuahua and is much more rounded and domed than that of the Smooth Fox Terrier. The tricoloured variety is most common, with a predominantly white coat, even in bicolours. They often have a white blaze, which extends down between the eyes.

Breed care and health This breed is quite sturdy by nature, while their smooth, short coat needs relatively little grooming to look immaculate. As with other breeds, it will help to brush their teeth regularly, using a special canine toothpaste, to prevent any build-up of tartar.

As an owner Toy terriers are loyal, very responsive and easily-trained, with a very playful side to their natures. They can be quite fearless as well, so you must ensure that your pet does not become embroiled in conflicts with larger dogs.

Also consider You could always opt for a Smooth Fox Terrier (*see pages 160–161*) or even its wirehaired relative (*see pages 170–171*), although these breeds are definitely not as well-suited to urban living, as well as being slightly larger. The Chihuahua (*see pages 180–181*) is another possibility, as it is smaller, as well as available in a much wider range of colours, while the English Toy Terrier is another option.

Height 21.5–29cm (8½–11½ in)
Weight 2.25–3kg (5–7 lb)
Exercise These toy terriers like the opportunity to explore when out for a walk

Toy Poodle

The Toy Poodle is a scaled-down version of the Standard Poodle – another instance of a Toy being derived from a working dog. It is the smallest of the three Poodle breeds; the Miniature Poodle is larger than the Toy, but still substantially smaller than the Standard. The origins of the Toy Poodle date back at least as far as the 16th century, when it was fashionable to create small dogs by selective breeding.

Appearance The styling of the poodle's coat has a dramatic impact on its appearance, and there is a variety of professional trims available. The lamb trim is the most straightforward. The coat itself is dense and water-resistant, as befits a breed whose ancestor was originally bred to retrieve waterfowl. Toy Poodles are bred in a wide range of solid colours, with apricot being the most popular. Individuals sometimes show slight colour shading.

Breed care and health Teach your Toy Poodle puppy to allow you to brush its teeth from an early age, using a special canine toothpaste and brush. These small poodles are particularly vulnerable to dental decay, and preventing the buildup of plaque on their teeth is important.

As an owner These dogs do not moult, so you must be prepared to have the coat trimmed and clipped every six to eight weeks. The advantage is that Toy Poodles, like their larger relatives, will not shed hair around the home.

Also consider The obvious choices if you want a similar but larger dog are either a Miniature or a Standard Poodle (*see pages 92–93*). They have a highly distinctive appearance, emphasized by the styling of their coats. There are no similar breeds of toy to choose from, although there are other possibilities more in keeping with the size of the Standard Poodle, such as the Irish Water Spaniel (*see page 134*).

Height Up to 25.5cm (10 in)
Weight 7kg (15 lb)
Exercise A lively trot around the park should be adequate for these small dogs

Japanese Akita Inu

Overview

Recognition
North America, Britain and
FCI member countries

Life expectancy
10–12 years

Colour
There are no breed
restrictions on colour

Grooming

Feeding

Child friendliness

Exercise
A daily opportunity
to run is vital

These large, powerful dogs are a national symbol in their Japanese homeland. Akita Inus need plenty of space, and this is certainly not a breed to contemplate unless you have a large back garden and the time and energy to take your dog for long, strenuous walks.

Origin This breed was originally developed in the 17th century for hunting bears in the province after which it is named, on the island of Honshu. Akita Inus are versatile working dogs – they have acted as retrievers, and it is even said they have helped fishermen by diving into the water and driving shoals of fish into the nets. The breed attracted international attention with the widely published story of the devotion of an Akita Inu named Hachiko. This dog had accompanied his owner to and from the train station every day but, sadly, the man died at work, and for the rest of Hachiko's life, the dog went to meet the train in the vain hope that he would return.

Appearance The Akita Inu is large and strongly built, with pricked ears that give it an alert expression. The neck is thick and muscular, and the shoulders are powerful. The dog is protected against the cold by a double-layered coat, which includes a thicker, soft undercoat. The outer layer is harsh and is longest over the withers and rump.

Personality The Akita Inu is an immensely loyal breed and can display a strong, protective nature – traditionally these dogs were even left to guard young children in their mother's absence. Intelligent and versatile, they are brave and not easily intimidated.

Health and care Because of their great strength, Akita Inus need to be well trained from puppyhood. If they are not obedient they can be a liability, even on a leash. Although they need more grooming in the spring, when they shed their winter coat, this is not a breed that is demanding to care for. Be cautious of Akita Inus when meeting other dogs, especially dominant breeds – if challenged, they are unlikely to back away from a fight.

As an owner Bear in mind that the Akita Inu is a big dog, with a correspondingly large appetite. It is a very territorial breed by nature and must be trained to accept visitors without proving a nuisance. Akita Inus are often not especially well-disposed to other dogs, so early socialization and training in this regard are essential, to prevent conflicts as your puppy grows older. If your dog is troublesome, keep him muzzled when out walking.

Also consider If you like the Akita Inu, but are looking for a smaller dog, some members of the spitz group may be possibilities. The Shiba Inu (see pages 90–91), whose name means 'little dog', is another Japanese breed that may be descended from the same ancestral line as the Akita Inu. Other spitz-type breeds, such as the Norwegian Buhund (see pages 36–37), may appeal, while another breed of similar appearance and size to the Akita Inu, but with a different background, is the Alaskan Malamute (see pages 214–215).

Tech Spec

Features

A *Head:* Large, flat between the ears, with a well-defined stop and square, powerful jaws

B *Eyes:* Small, dark brown and triangular; set deep

C *Ears:* Small, triangular and rounded at the tips; set high

D *Chest:* Deep and wide

E *Tail:* Large, set high and carried either over the back or to the side in a curl

F *Bite:* Scissors bite preferred; level acceptable

G *Height at shoulder:* Dogs 66–71cm (26–28 in); bitches 61–66cm (24–26 in)

H *Weight:* 34–50kg (75–110 lb)

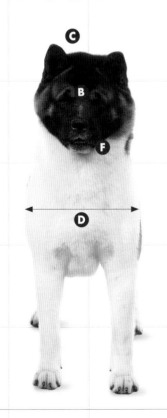

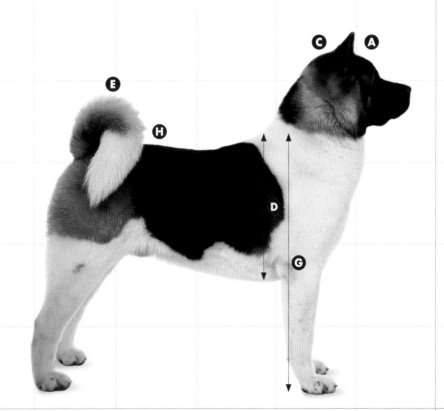

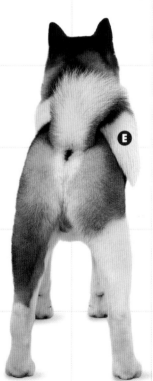

Overview

Recognition
North America, Britain and
FCI member countries

Life expectancy
10–12 years

Colour
Solid white, or a shaded
appearance ranging from
grey to black and from
sable to red

Grooming

Feeding

Child friendliness

Exercise
An active breed that
needs plenty of exercise

These powerful sled dogs tend to have dominant natures. Because of this, they are only recommended for experienced owners. Like other breeds from the far north, Alaskan Malamutes usually communicate by howling rather than by barking.

Origin Originally bred by the Mahlemuts, an Inuit tribe living in the vicinity of Kotzebue Sound in northwest Alaska, Malamutes are thought to be one of the oldest ancestral breeds of this type. Long before the advent of motorized vehicles, they provided a vital means of transport in the frozen wastelands of this region. As sled racing became an increasingly popular sport, so the breed grew in international popularity. It was accorded show recognition by the American Kennel Club for the first time in 1935.

Appearance A powerful body with strong shoulders, for pulling the sled, and a deep chest with plenty of lung capacity characterize this breed. Alaskan Malamutes have sturdy legs and tight, deep paws, which enable them to move across the snow without sinking into it. The breed is also protected against the elements by its woolly undercoat, which can be up to 5cm (2 in) long, and provides good insulation. The outer coat is thick, with a coarse texture, and is longest on the back of the body.

Personality Strong-willed and determined, Alaskan Malamutes are trained to work in teams, but they form a distinct hierarchy within the group, as occurs in a wolf pack. The result is that males in particular can often be aggressive towards other dogs.

Health and care This breed can develop a number of inherited conditions, including a form of hereditary dwarfism, which causes puppies to be born with short legs. Other genetic problems include a susceptibility to kidney disease and hemeralopia, an eye condition that results in dogs being blinded by bright light. Check the health of the breeding stock with the breeder before acquiring a puppy.

As an owner Malamute puppies must be trained firmly from an early age, or they will be increasingly challenging as they mature. You will need to assert your authority from the beginning so that your dog learns its place in the family hierarchy, rather than seeking to displace you. Male dogs may display aggressive tendencies, and neutering should be seriously considered.

Also consider Smaller sled breeds, such as the Samoyed (*see pages 244–245*) or the Siberian Husky (*see pages 246–247*) tend to be more easily managed, partly because of their size. Other multipurpose breeds from the far north, such as the Norwegian Elkhound (*see pages 64–65*) have been bred to work more closely with their owners, and are often easier to train in consequence.

Tech Spec

Features

A *Head:* Broad skull, slightly rounded between the ears, with a large, powerful muzzle

B *Eyes:* Medium-sized, brown and almond-shaped

C *Ears:* Well-spaced towards the back of the skull, rounded at the tips and usually erect

D *Chest:* Deep and powerful

E *Tail:* Resembles a plume, with plenty of fur, and carried forwards at rest

F *Bite:* Scissors bite

G *Height at shoulder:* Dogs 63.5cm (25 in); bitches 58.5cm (23 in)

H *Weight:* Dogs 38.5kg (85 lb); bitches 34kg (75 lb)

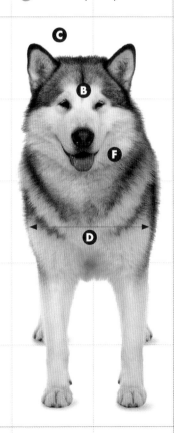

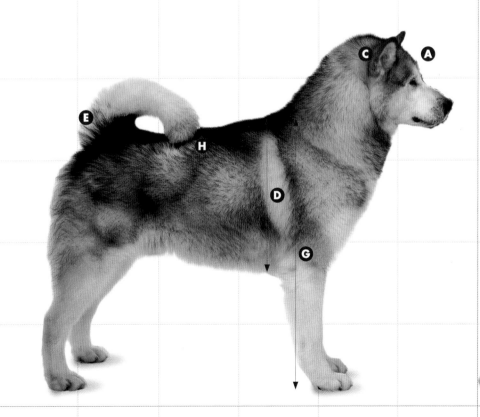

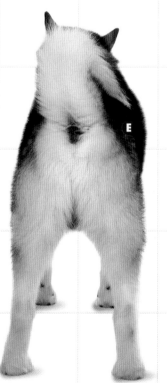

215

Bernese Mountain Dog

Overview

Recognition
North America, Britain and
FCI member countries

Life expectancy
10–12 years

Colour
Distinctive tricoloured
appearance: white,
black and rust in a
consistent coat pattern

Grooming

Feeding

Child friendliness

Exercise
A good opportunity
to exercise every day
is essential

Combined with its appealing personality, the beautiful colouring of the Bernese Mountain Dog makes this breed a popular choice as a companion, particularly as it has been developed to work closely alongside people. Although trustworthy, it is alert by nature and will protect by instinct if confronted by strangers.

Origin The Bernese Mountain Dog has been associated with the area of Berne in the Swiss Alps for centuries. The breed is the result of crossing between flock guardians and mastiff stock. These dogs are versatile working companions, and they were often used to pull carts carrying agricultural produce, such as milk, for the cheese-making industry of the region. They also worked with livestock. By the 1890s, however, their numbers had fallen, and it is only thanks to a few dedicated enthusiasts that the breed has survived.

Appearance The Bernese Mountain Dog can be distinguished from related Swiss breeds by its long and slightly wavy coat. It is also larger in size. The markings of these dogs are distinctive, with rust-coloured patches over the eyes and a white blaze extending down from the forehead to the muzzle. The feet and the chest must also be white, forming a broad and crosslike chest marking.

Personality A patient, tolerant breed, and a dutiful worker, the Bernese Mountain Dog makes an excellent family pet. It gets along well with children and often displays considerable patience with them. It is also an easy breed to train

Health and care Occasionally, Bernese Mountain Dogs are born with blue eyes. This is regarded as a major flaw, and such dogs should not be used for breeding, although they will make perfectly satisfactory pets. Another occasional genetic problem is a cleft palate or lip, although either problem is easily identifiable even in a very young puppy.

As an owner The Bernese Mountain Dog needs plenty of exercise, because this is a breed with recent working roots, which has always been actively involved in agricultural work. The natural gait is a trot rather than a walk. Some owners even train these dogs to pull carts, in the traditional manner. Grooming is relatively straightforward, in spite of the length of the coat, and will help to maintain its characteristic glossy sheen.

Also consider The three other indigenous breeds of Swiss mountain dog, all of which are smooth-coated, may be worthwhile options. The Entelbuch Mountain Dog typically stands about 51cm (20 in) high; there is also the Appenzell Mountain Dog, measuring up to 58.5cm (23 in), with a tail that curls forwards over its back, and the smooth-coated Greater Swiss Mountain Dog with a height of up to 72cm (28½ in).

Tech Spec

Features

A *Head:* Flat, broad, furrowed skull, with a well-defined stop and a strong, straight muzzle

B *Eyes:* Oval and dark brown

C *Ears:* Triangular and rounded at the tips; they hang down the sides of the head at rest

D *Chest:* Deep, with the brisket reaching to the elbows

E *Tail:* Bushy; carried low and never over the back

F *Bite:* Scissors bite

G *Height at shoulder:* Dogs 63.5–70cm (25–27½ in); bitches 58.5–66cm (23–26 in)

H *Weight:* 38.5–41kg (85–90 lb)

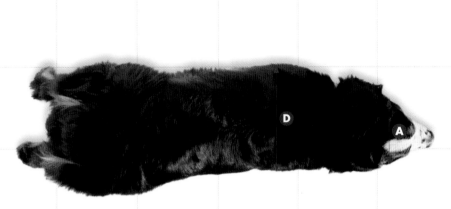

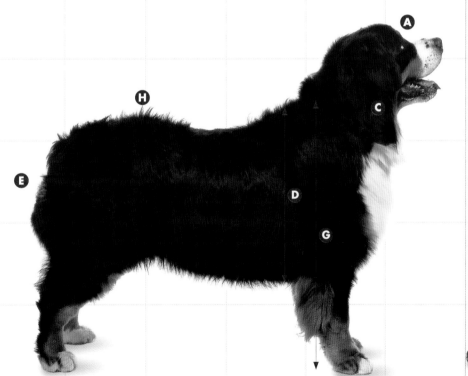

Overview

Recognition
North America, Britain and
FCI member countries

Life expectancy
10–13 years

Colour
Solid black

Grooming

Feeding

Child friendliness

Exercise
A good daily walk
will be essential

Although originally classified in the terrier group, this breed is now considered to be a working dog. This is a reflection of its original use, which was as a guard dog rather than a hunting dog – and this is, in turn, reflected in its personality. The Russian Black Terrier does not take readily to strangers, but it is friendly towards people it knows well.

Origin As its name suggests, the Russian Black Terrier was first bred in the former Soviet Union. It was part of a breeding programme created during the 1940s at the Central School of Cynology Specialists, located just outside Moscow. The breed was developed from, amongst others, the Giant Schnauzer, the Rottweiler and the Airedale Terrier. Great emphasis throughout its development was placed on soundness. This breed was added to the American Kennel Club's Working Group in 2004.

Appearance The Russian Black Terrier is a powerful breed, notable for its solid black colouring and its tousled, wiry coat. Its overall appearance suggests that the Giant Schnauzer was the dominant influence in its development. The outer coat layer is up to 10cm (4 in) long. The nose and lips are also black, and there is sometimes a black mark on the tongue.

Personality A determined guard dog with a steadfast nature, the Russian Black Terrier is responsive to training, and, once trained, it is easy to control. Intelligent and with a dependable temperament, it makes a loyal companion.

Health and care Confident by nature, the Russian Black Terrier is a breed that learns quickly what is expected and thrives on an established routine. As with many larger working breeds, there is a natural variance in size and appearance between male dogs and bitches. The breed needs to be trimmed slightly for show purposes, but the overall effect must remain natural. It has the benefit of enabling judges to study the physique more easily.

As an owner The breed has been developed to work closely with people, and with careful training you can be certain of having an attractive and reliable pet. Bear in mind that Russian Black Terriers can be strong-minded dogs, and if not properly trained they may become a liability. If you encounter difficulties in training, do not delay in seeking expert advice.

Also consider If you like the appearance of the Russian Black Terrier, the Schnauzer breeds, which are similar in appearance, may present an alternative. These are bred in three sizes – Miniature (*see pages 152–153*), Standard (*see pages 248–249*) and Giant (*see pages 226–227*) forms, all of which are bred in pepper-and-salt mixes as well as black. Another possibility that may appeal, although its colouring is different, is the Airedale Terrier (*see pages 136–137*).

Tech Spec

Features

A *Head:* Broad skull and flat forehead with an evident stop; the muzzle is slightly shorter

B *Eyes:* Oval, medium-sized and dark

C *Ears:* Set high, small and triangular

D *Chest:* Wide and deep

E *Tail:* Thick, set high and carried above the vertical

F *Bite:* Scissors bite

G *Height at shoulder:* Dogs 68.5–76cm (27–30 in); bitches 66–73.5cm (26–29 in)

H *Weight:* 38.5–63.5kg (85–140 lb)

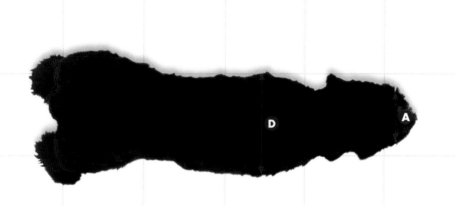

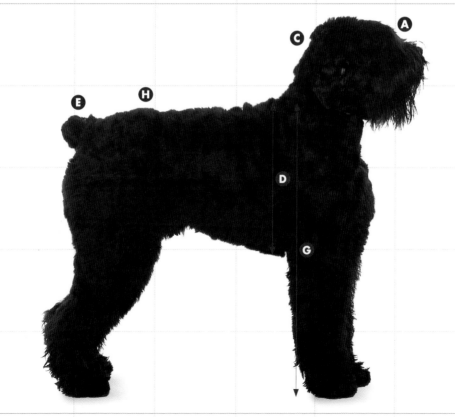

Overview

Recognition
North America, Britain and
FCI member countries

Life expectancy
9–11 years

Colour
Either fawn or brindle, with
or without white markings;
white Boxers exist, but are
not accepted under the
breed standard

Grooming

Feeding

Child friendliness

Exercise
Must be given a good
opportunity to run
every day

There are few dogs with a more playful nature than the Boxer. Its name is thought to come from the way in which these dogs use their forelegs when leaping up to greet their owners or wrestling good-naturedly with one another. However, this is a boisterous breed, so may be better suited to a home with teenagers than family life with young children.

Origin The Boxer was created in Germany in the mid-19th century from crossings between a hunting dog known as the Bullenbeisser and the English Bulldog. The emerging breed was scaled down in size, and it was known as the Brabanter for a period before its current name was established. The breed was used as a messenger in World War I, and it subsequently started to become a popular pet. It was first seen in North America in around 1904, and it is used today for work as varied as herding cattle and acting as a guide dog for the blind.

Appearance The Boxer's powerful head is a reminder of its sporting ancestry. It has a distinctive sloping stance, with the hind legs angled back considerably beyond the point of emergence of the tail. The patterning of bicoloured Boxers is relatively consistent, with white areas on the muzzle and chest, and often the lower parts of the legs. To meet with the standard, no more than one-third of the coat should be white.

Personality Highly exuberant, the Boxer is a genuinely good-natured dog, and it is remarkably agile as well. Its active nature means that it is not suited to the confined living conditions in a flat – it needs plenty of space to run and exercise.

Health and care Boxer puppies can develop a number of heart and circulatory defects, and it is especially important that they are checked thoroughly by a vet at an early age. Unfortunately, the breed is also highly vulnerable to cancers of many types, so be alert to any possible indicators, such as unexplained swellings on the body or behavioural changes. Early diagnosis can dramatically increase the likelihood of successful treatment.

As an owner Like many short-nosed breeds, Boxers are susceptible to heatstroke and should not be exercised in the middle of the day when the sun is at its hottest. Nor should they be encouraged to remain in the sun for long periods, because of the risk of skin cancer. White Boxers are particularly vulnerable to this, and they often also suffer from congenital deafness.

Also consider Consider the Boston Terrier (*see pages 72–73*) or the French Bulldog (*see pages 82–83*) if you are looking for a smaller companion. The Bulldog (*see pages 74–75*) may be another breed that appeals, although it is also significantly shorter in stature than the Boxer. On the other hand, the Dogue de Bordeaux (*see page 98*) may grow slightly taller.

Tech Spec

Features

A *Head:* Broad, with a slight indentation between the eyes; the muzzle is higher at the nose than the base

B *Eyes:* Large, not protruding and dark brown

C *Ears:* Set high on the skull, medium-sized and lying over the cheeks at rest

D *Chest:* Wide, with a deep brisket

E *Tail:* Broad at the base, often held away behind the body

F *Bite:* Undershot bite

G *Height at shoulder:* Dogs 58.5–63.5cm (23–25 in); bitches 54.5–59.75cm (21½–23½ in)

H *Weight:* 27–32kg (66–70 lb)

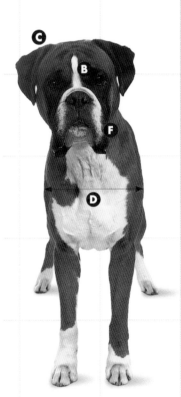

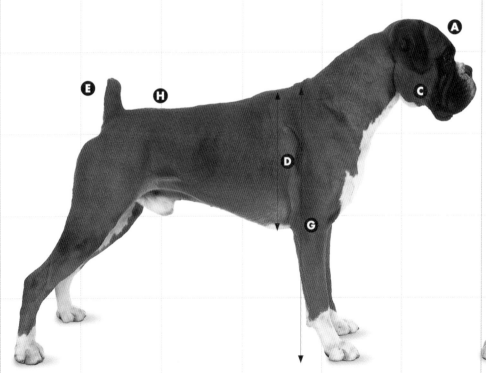

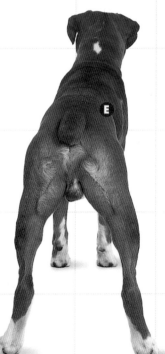

Overview

Recognition
North America, Britain and
FCI member countries

Life expectancy
9–11 years

Colour
Fawn, red or brindle; any
white should be restricted
to a small area on the chest

Grooming

Feeding

Child friendliness

Exercise
Plenty of opportunity
for exercise is vital

Massive, immensely powerful and with a fierce reputation, the Bullmastiff is not suited to living in urban surroundings. Although the breed is more placid now than in the past, it will use its physical strength if it feels threatened. Adequate early training is important to suppress any underlying aggressive instincts.

Origin The Bullmastiff was developed on the large country estates of England in the 19th century, at a period when gamekeepers were often attacked by poachers. It was created by crossings between the Mastiff and old-style English Bulldog, which was then a much more formidable guard dog than today's breed. The Bulldog contributed extra pace to the Mastiff's strength. Bullmastiffs are more than capable of overpowering an intruder, even if strongly resisted.

Appearance Strong jaws are a feature of this breed, and the characteristic black colouration on the muzzle, extending up around the eyes, enhances the formidable appearance of this dog. The coat is short and hard in texture, lying close against the body. Lighter fawn colouring is often preferred today, although the darker brindle shades were originally favoured for the breed's working role, because they provided better camouflage at night.

Personality Today's Bullmastiffs retain a fearless streak in their nature, and they are loyal to those in their immediate circle. Equally, they are much more kindly disposed to strangers than in the past, especially those they meet outside their home territory.

Health and care Possibly because they were bred at a time when the Bulldog was a more robust breed than it subsequently became, Bullmastiffs are largely free of inherited weaknesses. They may sometimes have an extra incisor tooth in their jaws at the front of the mouth, and they may also develop entropion, a condition of the eyes that requires correction by minor surgery.

As an owner Remain aware and respectful of the immense power of these dogs. They must be trained to walk properly on the leash, so they cannot pull you over, and they are certainly too strong for children to control adequately. This is a breed that will benefit from play while young. Games will help it to improve its coordination – like many larger breeds, Bullmastiff puppies are rather clumsy.

Also consider The Mastiff (*see pages 234–235*) is a possible alternative, with many of the same traits. There are also some other mastiff breeds you may find appealing. The Neapolitan Mastiff (*see pages 236–237*) has become more popular in recent years, while flock guardians such as the Pyrenean Mountain Dog (*see pages 230–231*) or Pyrenean Mountain Dog, or the Tibetan Mastiff, are alternatives.

Tech Spec

Features

A *Head:* Large and broad with a flat forehead, a moderate stop and a broad, deep muzzle

B *Eyes:* Medium-sized and dark

C *Ears:* Set high, widely spaced, and V-shaped, lying close to the cheeks

D *Chest:* Deep and wide

E *Tail:* Broad at the base, tapered along its length and set high, reaching the hocks

F *Bite:* Level or slightly undershot bite

G *Height at shoulder:* Dogs 63.5–68.5cm (25–27 in); bitches 61–66cm (24–26 in)

H *Weight:* Dogs 50–59kg (110–130 lb); bitches 45.5–54.5kg (100–120 lb)

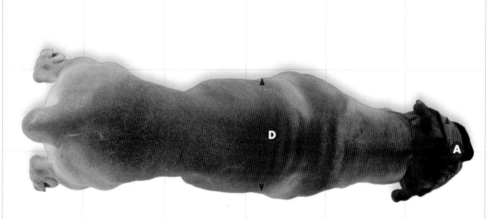

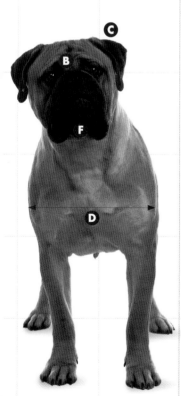

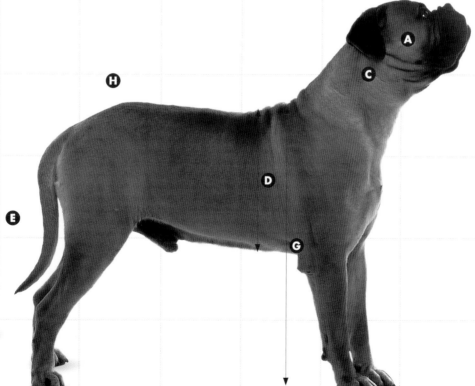

Dobermann

Overview

Recognition
North America, Britain and
FCI member countries

Life expectancy
10–12 years

Colour
Black, red, blue or fawn
(also called the Isabella
type), all with characteristic
rust markings

Grooming

Feeding

Child friendliness

Exercise
Must have an energetic
daily run

The Dobermann's elegant looks and strong character make it a good choice for someone with the application and energy to train it carefully and form a relationship with it. This breed is less suitable as a family pet, especially alongside young children, because it can sometimes be short-tempered. Dobermanns can form a close bond on a one-to-one basis, and they are used successfully as police and military dogs because of the relationships they form with their handlers.

Origin This breed was created at the end of the 19th century by a German tax collector, Louis Dobermann, to protect him when he was working. He also ran the local dog shelter, so he was well positioned to experiment with different crosses for this purpose. There is no true record of the Dobermann's roots. All that is known with certainty is that German Pinschers played a part, alongside a variety of different dogs of uncertain parentage. It is possible that Rottweilers may have been used as well.

Appearance A fit and muscular breed, the Dobermann has a sleek, tight-fitting coat. Bred in a variety of colours, it is characterized by rust-coloured markings above each eye. There are also patches of rust on the muzzle and upper chest, extending to the legs and feet and below the tail. This pattern is a key part of the breed standard.

Personality Bold, determined, fearless and loyal to its owner, the Dobermann is a breed that has become much friendlier since its early working days, when it was used to intimidate reluctant payers and would-be thieves.

Health and care The Dobermann is vulnerable to skin problems, which often result in inflammation and irritation. These may develop as a reaction to allergies or intolerances. An allergic reaction to fleabites is not unusual, so your dog should be treated regularly against parasites. If you suspect that diet may be the cause, switching to a hypoallergenic diet may help, although this should only be done under veterinary supervision.

As an owner Buy a Dobermann puppy only from a reputable breeder, and train it carefully. Be wary of taking on an adult Dobermann that needs rehoming for any reason – its temperament may be a problem, even if it initially seems friendly. Overpossessiveness – with toys, for example – can be a problem with this breed, often because of inadequate training in puppyhood.

Also consider The Rottweiler (see pages 240–241) shares the German ancestry of the Dobermann, and it is similar in colouration and coat type. It has a much broader head, and a heavier build. If you are looking for a smaller dog the German Pinscher (see page 250), or even the Miniature Pinscher (see pages 194–195) may be possibilities worthwhile considering.

Tech Spec

Features

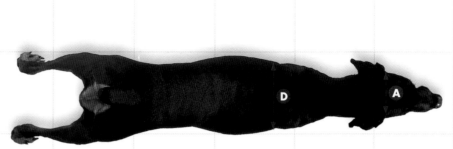

A *Head:* Long, resembling a blunt wedge in profile, with a flat top to the skull and a slight stop

B *Eyes:* Almond-shaped and set deep, with colouration matching that of the coat

C *Ears:* Small and set high

D *Chest:* Broad, with an evident fore chest

E *Tail:* Forms a continuation of the back, carried slightly above the horizontal

F *Bite:* Scissors bite

G *Height at shoulder:* Dogs 66–71cm (26–28 in); bitches 61–66cm (24–26 in)

H *Weight:* 30–40kg (66–88 lb)

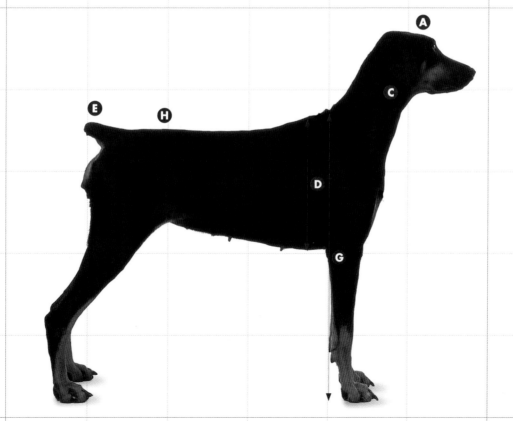

Giant Schnauzer

Overview

Recognition
North America, Britain and
FCI member countries

Life expectancy
10–12 years

Colour
Black or pepper and salt

Grooming

Feeding

Child friendliness

Exercise
Good walks are essential,
both for exercise and to
prevent boredom

Large and impressive in build, the Giant Schnauzer is every bit as solid and dependable as its physique suggests. This is not a breed that is highly strung in any way, and it makes an excellent pet. Alert by nature, it is a good guard dog, and its sheer size is likely to deter intruders.

Origin This breed was developed in Germany from the Schnauzer (*see pages 248–249*), an unusual case of a breed increasing in size as a result of selective breeding, rather than becoming smaller. Great Danes and Rottweilers were both also used in the breeding mix. Giant Schnauzers originally worked as cattle drovers in the area around Munich in southern Germany, until this role disappeared, replaced with the increased use of rail transport. Subsequently, these dogs were used by the police, and for guarding property, and they have adapted well to these new roles.

Appearance This is a powerfully built dog, with longer hair on its head and a characteristic beard. There are two acceptable colours in the breed standard – solid black and a mix described as 'pepper and salt'. The hairs in the latter case are banded in black and white along their length, creating a grey impression. A medium shade is preferred, although pepper-and-salt dogs vary from dark iron-grey to a silvery colour.

Personality Intelligent and adaptable, as well as being easy to train, the Giant Schnauzer makes a reliable, good-tempered companion. Spirited and powerful, these dogs display good stamina and are keen to exercise outdoors in all types of weather.

Health and care This breed has a high incidence of hip dysplasia. This is an inherited weakness of the back legs in which the cup-shaped part of the hip joint is too shallow to allow the rounded head of the femur to fit properly into the socket. The screening of breeding stock is helping to reduce the problem. If you are buying a puppy, check with the breeder that their stock has been screened.

As an owner This breed does not shed conventionally, and your dog will need stripping every six months to remove unwanted hair from the coat. This job is best done by a professional dog groomer. Be careful with a Giant Schnauzer around cattle in case its dormant herding instincts re-emerge.

Also consider If you want a smaller dog of the same appearance, either the smaller Schnauzer (*see pages 248–249*), or even the Miniature Schnauzer (*see pages 152–153*), may appeal to you. The latter is classed as a terrier, because it was originally kept for hunting rodents. Other terriers with similar long, broad faces include the Irish Terrier (*see page 172*) and the Wire Fox Terrier (*see pages 170–171*).

Tech Spec

Features

A *Head:* Rectangular and elongated, with a slight stop; a strong muzzle, matching the skull in length

B *Eyes:* Oval, dark brown and medium-sized; set deep

C *Ears:* Set high, V-shaped and medium-length; carried close to the head

D *Chest:* Medium-width; deep brisket

E *Tail:* Set high; carried high when the dog is alert

F *Bite:* Scissors bite

G *Height at shoulder:* Dogs 64.75–70cm (25½–27½ in); bitches 59.75–64.75cm (23½–25½ in)

H *Weight:* 32–35kg (70–77 lb)

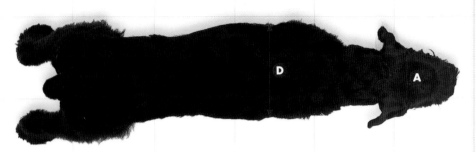

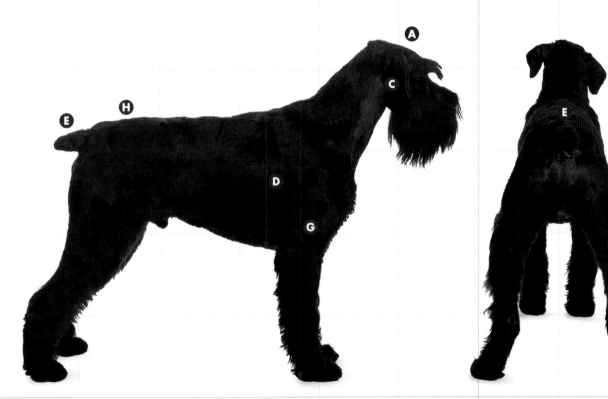

Great Dane

Overview

Recognition
North America, Britain and
FCI member countries

Life expectancy
8–11 years

Colour
Fawn, blue, black,
Harlequin and Mantle

Grooming

Feeding

Child friendliness

Exercise
A daily opportunity to
exercise off the leash
is important

This is one of the tallest breeds in the world, measuring over 101.5cm (40 in) at the shoulder – literally as large as a small pony. Their sheer size precludes Great Danes from being kept in cramped surroundings, or without a reasonably large garden. If you have the space both outdoors and in your home, however, a Great Dane can make a wonderful pet.

Origin Giant dogs of the type from which the Great Dane is descended have been known for hundreds of years. Their ancestors were highly prized as hunting dogs, and they were heavier in build and more aggressive than the modern breed. During the late 19th century, the first steps to standardize these dogs were taken in Germany, and the breed was declared the country's national dog in 1876. The Great Dane made a smooth transition into the show ring, where great emphasis was placed on its friendly temperament.

Appearance Its huge size alone distinguishes this breed. The smooth coat comes in a wide variety of colours and patterns, including a striking white type with irregular black patches on the head and body, although not the neck, known as the Harlequin A modified form of the Harlequin also exists. Called the Mantle, it has a black area, resembling a coat, covering the body.

Personality Docile and gentle despite their huge size, Great Danes have friendly, approachable natures and an enthusiastic, playful approach to life.

Health and care The breed can develop a number of inherited problems, including spondylomyelopathy, also known as 'Wobbler Syndrome'. This affects the cervical vertebrae in the neck, through which the spinal cord runs. The symptoms can range from a mild weakness of the hind legs to paralysis, and the condition may require corrective surgery. As a breed, Great Danes are relatively short-lived, and they are vulnerable to arthritis and bone cancer as they age.

As an owner Great Dane puppies develop slowly and, as with other giant breeds, it is important not to over exercise them, because this can lead to joint weaknesses in later life. Great Danes can also develop bloat, a buildup of gas caused by a twisted stomach, and they should not be allowed to exercise too soon after being fed because this increases their susceptibility.

Also consider If you are looking for a giant breed, the rough-coated Irish Wolfhound (*see pages 62–63*) may be a possibility. No smaller breed resembles the Great Dane, although if the Harlequin patterning appeals to you, a Dalmatian (*see pages 80–81*), with its spotted appearance and smooth coat may be worth considering. However, both its personality and its breed background are different.

Tech Spec

Features

A *Head:* Long and rectangular; the length of the muzzle corresponds to that of the skull

B *Eyes:* Set deep, almond-shaped, medium-sized and dark

C *Ears:* Set high and medium-sized, with the ear fold level with the top of the skull

D *Chest:* Broad, deep and muscular

E *Tail:* Broad and tapered along its length to the level of the hocks; not carried above the level of the back

F *Bite:* Scissors bite

G *Height at shoulder:* Dogs 76–81cm (30–32 in) or more; bitches 71–76cm (28–30 in) or more

H *Weight:* 45.5–54.5kg (100–120 lb)

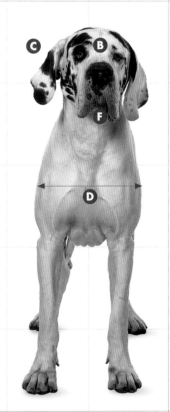

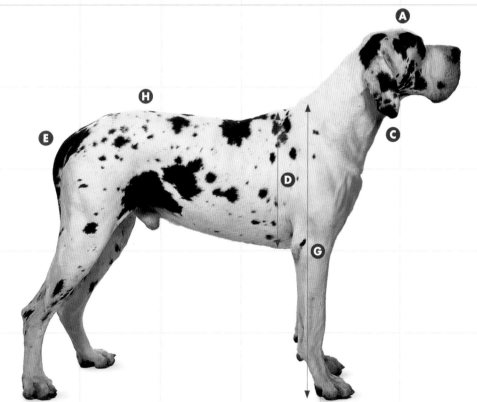

Overview

Recognition
North America, Britain and
FCI member countries

Life expectancy
10–12 years

Colour
Solid white, or white with
markings in shades of
grey, badger, reddish
brown or tan

Grooming

Feeding

Child friendliness

Exercise
A long daily walk
is essential

Also known as the Great Pyrenees, this ancient mastiff breed has an impressive appearance, but it is also an amiable companion. The breed was accorded the title of the Royal Dog of France by Louis XIV in the 17th century, and it has attracted many devotees since then, partly as the result of numerous recent film appearances.

Origin These huge dogs were originally used to guard flocks in the Pyrenean mountains between France and Spain Traditionally, they wore ferocious spiked collars to protect them from the wolves that were then numerous in the area. Wolves had been hunted to near extinction by the early 19th century, and the breed began to decline in number. However, it gradually built a new popularity in the show ring, ensuring a secure future. These dogs still sometimes have a working role, accompanying skiing groups in the mountains.

Appearance Massive and unmistakable, the Pyrenean Mountain Dog is predominantly white, sometimes broken by darker markings of various colours. The breed is well protected by a double coat – the outer layer is flat and thick, while the undercoat is fine and dense. Unusually the Pyrenean has double dew claws on its hind legs, although they do not serve a practical function.

Personality Affectionate and devoted to its family, the Pyrenean remains watchful and is often reserved with strangers. The breed has a somewhat independent streak, and is both intelligent and resourceful.

Health and care The double dew claws are disallowed in show dogs and must be removed. Even in a pet, they should be trimmed back regularly so that they do not curl around into the supporting fleshy pad. Special strong clippers will be needed for this purpose.

As an owner These dogs need plenty of indoor space. Provide a clear floor area, and remove objects that could be swept off low surfaces by your dog's tail. Invest in a large-size beanbag, for your dog to stretch out on and sleep. Conventional dog beds are often not very comfortable for large dogs in general.

Also consider The Newfoundland (*see pages 238–239*) is descended from Pyrenean Mountain Dog stock and may be an alternative option. The more rare white Maremma Sheepdog, originating in Italy and also possibly related to the Pyrenean Mountain Dog, is another possibility. The Tatra Mountain Sheepdog from Poland, which has similar colouring, may also appeal.

Tech Spec

Features

A *Head:* Wedge-shaped, with the muzzle and back skull being equivalent in length and blending together

B *Eyes:* Almond-shaped, rich dark brown and medium-sized; set obliquely

C *Ears:* V-shaped, small to medium with rounded tips; usually carried low and flat

D *Chest:* Broad

E *Tail:* Well-plumed; can extend down to the hocks; may be carried above the back

F *Bite:* Scissors bite preferred, level bite accepted

G *Height at shoulder:* Dogs 68.5–81cm (27–32 in); bitches 63.5–73.5cm (25–29 in)

H *Weight:* Dogs 45.5kg (100 lb); bitches 38.5kg (85 lb)

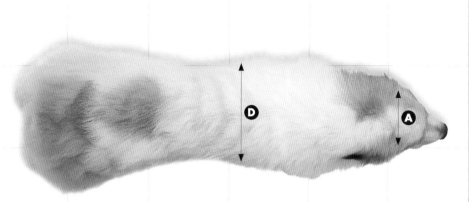

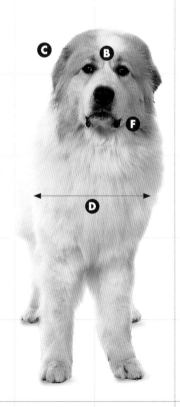

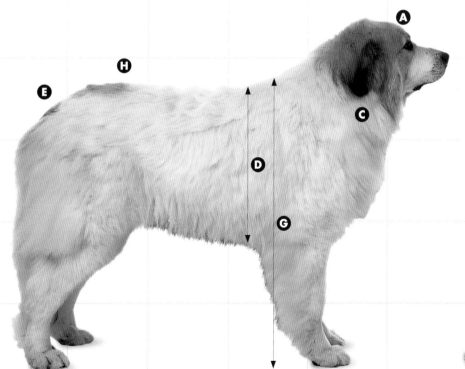

231

Overview

Recognition
FCI member countries

Life expectancy
10–12 years

Colour
Black, blond, or black
and gold

Grooming

Feeding

Child friendliness

Exercise
Must have the opportunity
to run off the leash
every day

The name of this breed is pronounced 'hoffavart', and it means 'farm guardian.' Since being introduced to North America in the 1980s, this is a breed that is now seen more frequently internationally. It is becoming popular as a family companion, because it is both loyal and a good guard dog.

Origin The existence of this ancient breed was first recorded in the 13th century, and it used to be a common sight working on farms in Germany. By the early 20th century, however, it was virtually extinct. A number of breeders set out to re-create it, using farm dogs that resembled the Hovawart in appearance, and mating these with other breeds, such as the Leonberger and the German Shepherd Dog. Today's breed is therefore a modern creation, rather than a descendant of the traditional breeding stock.

Appearance The Hovawart looks more like a gundog than a working breed, bearing some resemblance to the Flat Coated Retriever (see pages 112–113). The topcoat is long and the undercoat may be slightly wavy. There is distinctive feathering on the backs of the front legs.

Personality Affectionate and loyal, today's Hovawart tends to be kept more as a companion than used as a working breed, although it retains its protective instincts. It can be trained easily, and it has a surprisingly playful side, often settling in well with children.

Health and care Unexplained weight gain and a loss of energy in the dog may be symptoms of hyperthyroidism – an underactive thyroid gland – a condition to which this breed is susceptible. It can usually be treated with prescribed drugs. The Hovawart should be groomed regularly and inspected for ticks after country walks. If you find any of these parasites, they should be removed because they can cause infections.

As an owner With this dog you are committing yourself to an active breed that needs plenty of exercise. Do not be tempted by a Hovawart if you are living in a city environment where there is relatively little space to exercise your pet. These dogs will thrive, however, if they can have regular country walks. They sometimes display surprisingly good scenting skills.

Also consider If you like the appearance of the Hovawart, you might want to consider one of the gundog breeds, although they are slightly different temperamentally. Breeds that contributed to the Hovawart's development, such as the larger Kuvasz (see page 251) may also be of interest. The Dobermann (see pages 224–225) is another option – the black-and-tan patterning of the two breeds is similar, although the coat of the Dobermann is shorter and sleeker.

Tech Spec

Features

A *Head:* Strong, with a moderate stop and a relatively broad muzzle; the length of the head corresponds to that of the muzzle

B *Eyes:* Oval-shaped, medium-sized, not prominent and dark in colour

C *Ears:* Pendulous, triangular, and set medium-to-high towards the back of the head

D *Chest:* Deep and powerful

E *Tail:* Set just below the topline, reaching down to below the hocks, well-feathered and carried up when alert

F *Bite:* Scissors bite

G *Height at shoulder:* Dogs 63.5–70cm (25–27½ in); bitches 58.5–64.75cm (23–25½ in)

H *Weight:* Dogs 30–40kg (66–88 lb); bitches 25–35kg (55–77 lb)

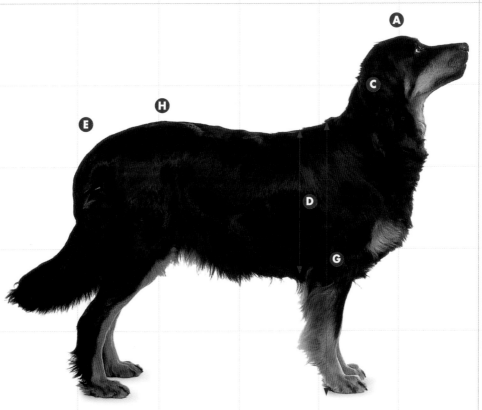

Overview

Recognition
North America, Britain and
FCI member countries

Life expectancy
10–12 years

Colour
Apricot or fawn, or
brindled with either
apricot or fawn

Grooming

Feeding

Child friendliness

Exercise
This dog particularly likes
walks in wooded areas, as
it enjoys exploring

Also known as the Old English Mastiff, this ancient breed was kept as a fighting dog for a long period. The breed is still immensely strong, and firm, responsible training from an early age is essential.

Origin The ancestors of these dogs were already bred in Britain more than 2,000 years ago, at the time of the Roman invasion, and it had a reputation for fierceness in medieval times. Similar fighting dogs were used in battle, and in various blood sports, including bear baiting. By 1945, however, Mastiffs were nearly extinct in Britain and only survived due to imports of American bloodlines.

Appearance This breed is significantly bigger and heavier than the Bull Mastiff. It has a characteristically dignified appearance, with deep flanks that emphasize its strong physique. Mastiffs have a double coat, dense and short underneath and coarser on top. The face should be covered with a black mask that extends up around the eyes, and the neck is broad and muscular.

Personality The Mastiff's temperament has changed considerably through the centuries, and these dogs are much friendlier today than in the past. Even so, they are still capable of displaying strong territorial instincts and do not take readily to strangers.

Health and care Mastiffs often show signs of discomfort in hot weather, panting and drooling heavily. They should be kept cool and should not be exercised during the hottest part of the day. The skin folds on the head sometimes develop localized infections, which will require topical treatment. Due to the dog's great weight, pressure sores in the form of hard, hairless pads may develop on the elbows where the dog lies down. These tend not cause the dog any pain but are unsightly.

As an owner Mastiffs have prodigious appetites, and they should not be allowed to put on weight. A careful diet and plenty of exercise are essential. Grooming is straightforward, although more brushing may be needed in early summer when the undercoat is shed.

Also consider The Mastiff's smaller relative, the Bullmastiff (see pages 222–223), may be an option, as are other mastiff breeds from various European countries, such as the Pyrenean Mastiff, which has a slightly longer coat. Another breed that may appeal is the Dogue de Bordeaux (see page 98) – dogue means 'mastiff' – which has been bred from French mastiff stock.

Tech Spec

Features

A *Head:* Broad and flat between the ears, with powerful cheeks, a clear stop and a short, broad muzzle

B *Eyes:* Well-spaced, medium-sized and dark brown

C *Ears:* Small and V-shaped with rounded tips, lying against the cheeks at rest

D *Chest:* Rounded, wide and deep, reaching the elbow

E *Tail:* Set high and tapered to the level of the hocks; not carried above the back

F *Bite:* Scissors bite preferred; moderately undershot is acceptable

G *Height at shoulder:* Dogs at least 76cm (30 in) or more; bitches 70cm (27½ in) or more

H *Weight:* 79–86kg (175–190 lb)

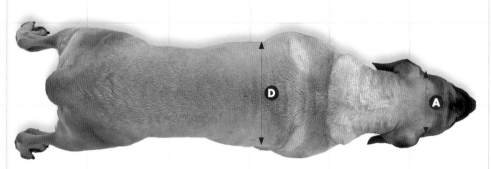

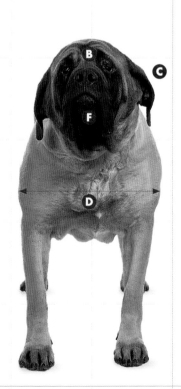

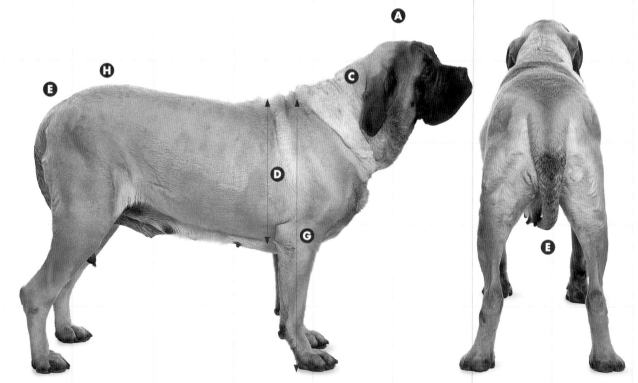

Overview

Recognition
North America, Britain and
FCI member countries

Life expectancy
10–12 years

Colour
Tawny, mahogany, grey
(known in this breed as
blue), and black; tan
brindling is allowed, as are
prescribed white markings
on the underparts

Grooming

Feeding

Child friendliness

Exercise
This dog needs plenty
of exercise

This huge, lumbering breed has been likened to a hippopotamus in the form of a dog. The Neapolitan Mastiff is not a dog for the faint-hearted – it is immensely strong, which will make it overpowering in a home with young children; its sheer size means that it should only be kept in spacious surroundings, and it has an appetite to match its physique.

Origin This is one of the oldest surviving breeds in the world. It was reputedly a favourite of Alexander the Great, who is said to have obtained the ancestral stock from a king in northern India. The dog was then taken to Rome and used as a fighting breed over many years. The modern Neapolitan Mastiff owes its origins to the artist Piero Scanziani, who oversaw its development and saw the breed accepted by the Italian Kennel Club. In recent years it has become popular internationally.

Appearance A massive, wrinkled, rounded head, with a dewlap extending from the lower jaw down to the middle of the neck, is the most striking aspect of this breed. The neck is powerful and the body is strong and muscular. The fur is dense, short and unusually fine. It feels hard to the touch and has a good sheen. White markings are acceptable on the underparts.

Personality Today's Neapolitan Mastiff is far less aggressive than its predecessors, but it will be protective of its home surroundings. Despite their fearsome appearance, these dogs are usually calm, friendly and placid, and they respond well to training.

Health and care The skin folds on the face can become infected, and they will need to be carefully treated to prevent the problem recurring. Infection is more likely if the skin around the mouth is allowed to trap deposits of food, so clean this area as part of your regular grooming routine. Grooming is straightforward, and regular brushing will help to emphasize the coat's distinctive sheen. Non-breeding males are usually neutered to reduce any latent aggressive tendencies.

As an owner Neapolitan Mastiffs drool heavily, especially around food or in hot weather. Owners become used to carrying cloths or paper towels around to wipe the dog's face and prevent it from depositing pools of saliva on carpets or soft furnishings. These massive dogs are also susceptible to the heat, so avoid exercising them when the sun is at its hottest.

Also consider The other mastiff breeds are alternative possibilities, although none is perhaps as imposing. The Mastiff (*see pages 234–235*) and the Tibetan Mastiff, which has equal size and presence but a longer coat, are possible choices. The latter is another dog reputed to have been admired by Alexander the Great.

Tech Spec

Features

A *Head:* Large, with the top of the skull being wide and flat, a well-defined stop and a muzzle whose breadth matches its length

B *Eyes:* Set deep, with drooping lids

C *Ears:* Medium-sized and triangular; held against the cheeks

D *Chest:* Powerful, broad and deep

E *Tail:* Broad at its base and tapered along its length; can be raised just above the horizontal

F *Bite:* Scissors or level bite, with a slight undershot bite being permitted

G *Height at shoulder:* Dogs 66–79cm (26–31 in); bitches 61–73.5cm (24–29 in)

H *Weight:* Dogs 68kg (150 lb); bitches 50kg (110 lb)

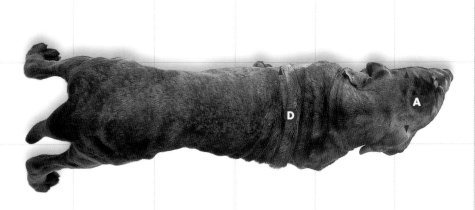

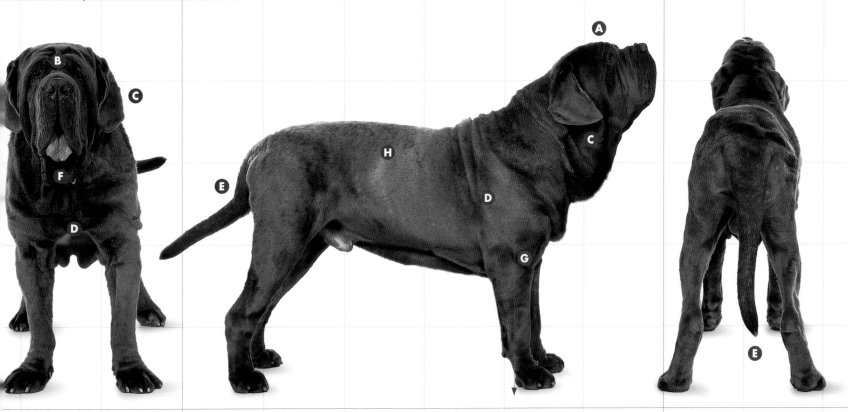

Newfoundland

Overview

Recognition
North America, Britain and
FCI member countries

Life expectancy
10–12 years

Colour
Brown, grey, black
or black and white

Grooming

Feeding

Child friendliness

Exercise
A long daily walk is
essential

Its calm, gentle temperament, with a total absence of aggression, means that the Newfoundland is one of the most suitable choices as a companion from among the working breeds. If you have the space to accommodate it, this dog makes an ideal family pet. However, as with other large breeds, these are expensive dogs to keep, due to their hearty appetites.

Origin The Newfoundland's precise origins are unclear, but we know that it is descended partly from breeds brought to its homeland from Europe. The Pyrenean Mountain Dog probably played a role, and it may have been mated with native Inuit dogs. The new breed emerged during the late 18th century, and it was initially used to pull carts. When the Newfoundland's exceptional swimming abilities became clear, however, it began to be used to work with fishermen. It was strong enough – and intelligent enough – to rescue a drowning man, although its primary job was to help pull in the nets.

Appearance The Newfoundland is a powerful breed with a heavy, water-resistant double coat. The dense undercoat becomes thinner during the summer months. The toes are webbed, aiding its swimming ability. The black-and-white form is known as the Landseer, in commemoration of Queen Victoria's favourite dog artist, Edwin Landseer, and is sometimes also recognized as a separate breed, although it is identical in all respects other than its colouring.

Personality A calm and loyal companion, this dog has long been portrayed – with justification – as a protector of children. The Newfoundland's innate intelligence and relaxed nature mean that these dogs usually adapt well to different situations.

Health and care Puppies should be regularly checked up to the age of 6 months for subaortic stenosis, a condition that leads to a narrowing of the aorta. Affected dogs become breathless after exercise, and may even faint. If undetected, the condition can lead to sudden death, but once diagnosed it may be possible to correct the problem surgically.

As an owner The gentle nature of the Newfoundland is not an excuse for inadequate training. Any dog, especially a large one, is a potential liability if is not properly trained from the beginning. This is a breed that is instinctively keen to please, so the job is usually straightforward.

Also consider The various Swiss Mountain dogs may be alternative possibilities. The Bernese (*see pages 216–217*) most closely approximates to the Newfoundland in type of coat and their temperaments are similar. The Leonberger, a massive working breed from Germany, may be another option.

Tech Spec

Features

A *Head:* Large, with a broad skull, well-developed cheeks and a broad, deep muzzle

B *Eyes:* Dark brown

C *Ears:* Triangular-shaped and small, with rounded tips

D *Chest:* Deep and full, with brisket reaching the elbows

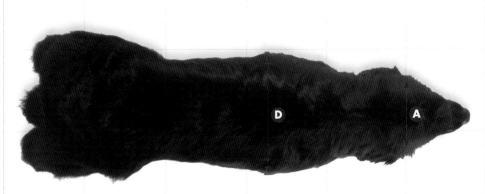

E *Tail:* Broad and powerful, attaching to the croup (in the pelvic area)

F *Bite:* Scissors or level bite

G *Height at shoulder:* Dogs 71cm (28 in); bitches 66cm (26 in)

H *Weight:* Dogs 59–68kg (130–150 lb); bitches 45.5–54.5kg (100–120 lb)

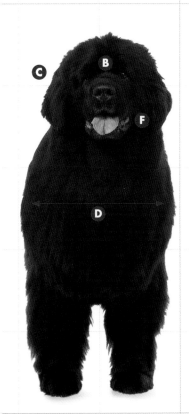

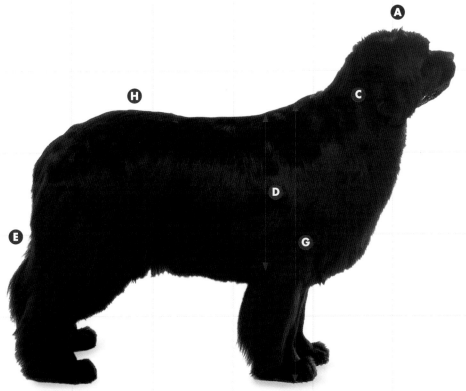

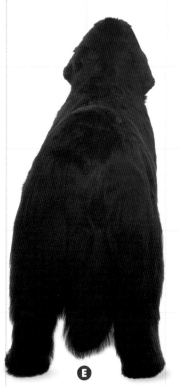

Overview

Recognition
North America, Britain and
FCI member countries

Life expectancy
10–12 years

Colour
Black with rust markings

Grooming

Feeding

Child friendliness

Exercise
Good periods of daily
exercise are needed

The Rottweiler has become deservedly popular in recent years, due in part to its intelligent and responsive nature. These are powerful dogs, however, and need to be properly controlled at all times. This breed displays strong territorial instincts and often will not take well to strangers on your premises, so it needs to be introduced carefully to new people.

Origin Named after the town of Rottweil in southwest Germany, the Rottweiler is thought to have been developed by crossbreeding between ancient mastiff stock and sheepdogs native to the region. The breed was originally responsible for herding cattle to market, returning with the money raised from their sale in a special collar around its neck. The role of the Rottweiler subsequently changed to that of a general-purpose guard dog, and today the breed is popular both in the show ring and as a pet.

Appearance The Rottweiler is muscular and well built, with dogs having a distinctly more masculine appearance than bitches. The breed has a short, straight, flat coat, which is predominantly black, with distinctive rust markings. These should be present over each eye, on the cheeks and the sides of the muzzle, on each side of the chest and on the lower part of the front legs, as well as covering much of the lower hind legs.

Personality Strong-minded and confident, the Rottweiler will instinctively seek to defend its territory, especially if challenged. These dogs respond positively to training, displaying great devotion to those they know well.

Health and care Rottweilers can develop entropion, a condition in which the eyelids turn inwards, rubbing on the eyeball and causing irritation. It is likely to need surgical correction. This is a breed that is also at particular risk of developing diabetes mellitus. Symptoms include weight loss, accompanied by constant hunger and thirst. Diabetes can be confirmed by urine and blood tests, and can usually be controlled by regular insulin injections and a supervised diet.

As an owner The Rottweiler has an instinctively dominant nature and firm training from puppyhood is essential, particularly because these are immensely strong dogs. This is a breed that will benefit from puppy-training classes. A responsive Rottweiler will then be an excellent companion dog. It has minimal grooming needs.

Also consider The Dobermann (see pages 224–225) is a leaner dog than the Rottweiler, but is similar both in colouring and temperament. Another possibility would be the French breed known as the Beauceron (see page 250). If you are looking for a smaller dog that shares the Rottweiler's distinctive colouring, the black-and-tan form of the German Pinscher (see page 250) may appeal.

Tech Spec

Features

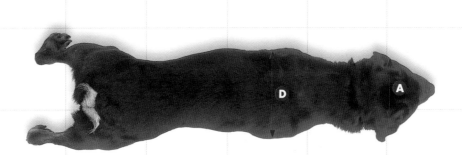

(A) *Head:* Medium-length, broad between the ears, and with a well-developed stop and a powerful muzzle

(B) *Eyes:* Almond-shaped, set deep and dark brown

(C) *Ears:* Triangular and medium-sized; hang forwards

(D) *Chest:* Deep, broad and muscular

(E) *Tail:* Set creates an impression of lengthening the topline; can be carried above the horizontal

(F) *Bite:* Scissors bite

(G) *Height at shoulder:* Dogs 61–68.5cm (24–27 in); bitches 56–63.5cm (22–25 in)

(H) *Weight:* 41–50kg (90–110 lb)

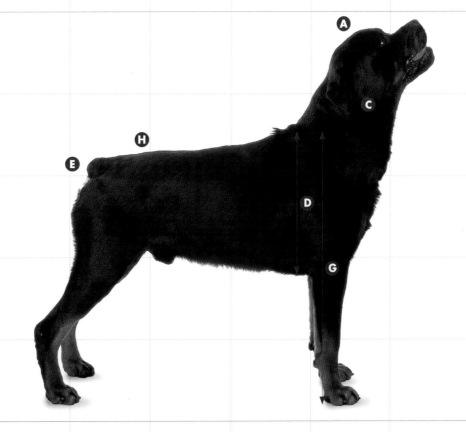

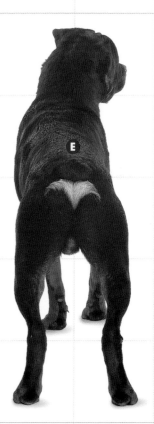

St. Bernard

Overview

Recognition
North America, Britain and
FCI member countries

Life expectancy
9–11 years

Colour
White and red
combinations, including
brindle, with red colouring
varying in depth

Grooming

Feeding

Child friendliness

Exercise
Young dogs must not be
overworked, but this is a
breed that needs regular
exercise

The St Bernard is named after Bernard de Mentho, founder of the Bernardine Hospice in the Swiss Alps, where the breed was developed. Its devotion to people is well known and, unsurprisingly, St Bernards make trustworthy and affectionate companions. These gentle dogs get along well with children, but they are not particularly effective as guard dogs.

Origin The St Bernard is descended from the Alpine mastiffs, bred in the region from Roman times. Although smaller, this original stock was similar in overall appearance to the breed of today. Crossbreeding in the 18th century, probably with Great Danes and Bloodhounds, increased the St Bernard's size and developed its scenting skills. St Bernards gained a reputation for locating and rescuing stranded travellers, especially in the heavy snows of winter. They are still used for this purpose and have been credited with saving over 2,000 lives.

Appearance A powerful head with a massive skull shows the input of this breed's mastiff ancestors. Both longhaired and shorthaired forms exist – the longhaired variety has a slightly wavy coat of medium length, and both types have dense fur that provides good protection against the cold. There should be a white spot on the nape, a blaze between the eyes, a white noseband, and white on the chest, extending down to the feet and out to the tip of the tail.

Personality Well disposed towards people, the St Bernard is determined and, unsurprisingly in view of its working ancestry, possesses a keen sense of smell. These dogs may often show an independent streak, having been bred to take the initiative in searches.

Health and care This is a breed that has more than its share of inherited health problems, possibly due to the small gene pool from which it was developed. The St Bernard can develop various blood-clotting disorders, and can also have problems that affect the structure of the eyes and eyelids. Older dogs are vulnerable to cancerous bone tumours in the legs, which are known as osteosarcomas. Lameness is an early sign, and rapid diagnosis is essential to prevent the cancer spreading to the lungs. Ask your breeder about the health of their breeding stock and the incidence of these specific conditions before acquiring a puppy.

As an owner St Bernards can be clumsy around the house – in particular their broad, sweeping tails are a hazard, sweeping objects off any low surface. This is a breed that needs plenty of space to be comfortable. Like other square-muzzled mastiff breeds, it is not necessarily a breed for those with immaculate homes – it also has a tendency to drool.

Also consider The Pyrenean Mountain Dog (*see pages 230–231*), which evolved in a similar landscape, and is similar in appearance, may be an alternative choice, as is the slightly larger Pyrenean Mastiff. Both breeds have the same type of coat as the St Bernard. In terms of temperament, the Bernese Mountain Dog (*see pages 216–217*) represents another option.

Tech Spec

Features

A *Head:* Massive and wide with high cheek bones; the short muzzle does not taper along its length

B *Eyes:* Medium-sized, directed forwards and dark brown

C *Ears:* Set high, held away from the head at their base, but dropped down alongside the head

D *Chest:* Deep, but not extending down to the elbows

E *Tail:* Broad and long, hanging straight down at rest; otherwise, carried upward

F *Bite:* Scissors bite preferred but level bite acceptable

G *Height at shoulder:* Dogs 70cm (27½ in) or more; bitches 64.75cm (25½ in) or more

H *Weight:* 50–91kg (110–200 lb)

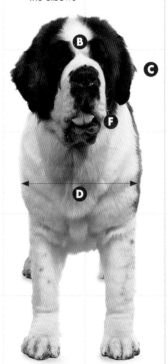

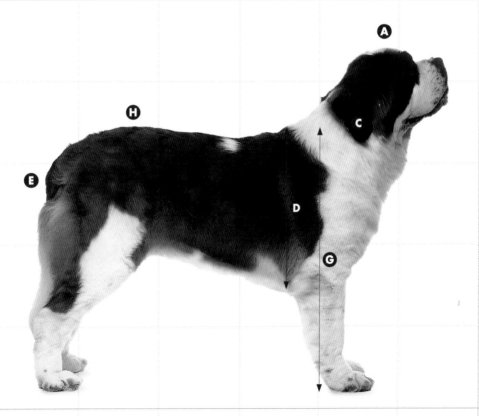

Samoyed

Overview

Recognition
North America, Britain and
FCI member countries

Life expectancy
10–12 years

Colour
Pure white, cream, biscuit,
or white and biscuit

Grooming

Feeding

Child friendliness

Exercise
Plenty of exercise is needed

This breed may look decorative, but under their luxuriant coats Samoyeds are tough working dogs, originating from one of the most inhospitable regions in the world. When alert, the corners of the mouth turn up, making the dog look as though it is smiling. The Samoyed thrives on attention, and it will soon become bored if it is left alone for long periods.

Origin This breed is named after the Samoyede tribe of northern Siberia, who bred these dogs primarily as reindeer herders, but also for pulling sleds. The dog's thick fur was also made into clothing. The first Samoyeds seen in the West were brought back to England by fur traders in the late 19th century, and they caused a sensation. Modern bloodlines are based on just 12 of these dogs, one of which had accompanied an expedition to the Antarctic, before being sent first to Australia and then on to England.

Appearance Pure white is the colour most commonly associated with the Samoyed, but other varieties are accepted. There is a distinctive ruff around the neck, which is more pronounced in males, and will be more profuse through the winter months. Samoyeds have 'hare' feet – that is, long and narrow – which enable them to walk over snow without sinking down into it. Their toes are thickly furred to protect against frostbite.

Personality Intelligent and active, the Samoyed displays great stamina. The breed is naturally friendly and gregarious, but it can also be wayward, particularly if it is bored. The independent streak in its nature can make training difficult.

Health and care Samoyeds are strong dogs, but some congenital circulatory problems have been recorded in the breed. Some family breed lines are also predisposed to diabetes, and a dog diagnosed with this condition will need regular insulin injections. Ask your breeder about any instances of these problems in their breeding stock.

As an owner It is important to prevent Samoyeds from becoming overweight, because obesity is a significant predisposing factor in diabetes. Daily grooming of the thick coat is essential, because the Samoyed sheds heavily. This is an excellent choice if you are looking for a show dog, because the breed is not usually overawed in the show ring and most have an upbeat personality that performs well.

Also consider Some of the other spitz breeds, especially those that have been bred primarily as working companions rather than as sled dogs, may be options. These include the Norwegian Buhund (*see pages 36–37*) and the Finnish Spitz (*see page 99*). The Norwegian Elkhound (*see pages 64–65*) represents another possibility. In contrast to breeds developed primarily as sled dogs, such as the Alaskan Malamute, these dogs tend to work better on an individual basis with people.

Tech Spec

Features

A *Head:* Broad and wedge-shaped, in the form of an equilateral triangle with a medium-length, tapering muzzle

B *Eyes:* Well-spaced, almond-shaped and ideally dark

C *Ears:* Triangular, thick and rounded at their tips; well-spaced and held erect

D *Chest:* Deep, reaching down to the elbows

E *Tail:* Long, with plenty of fur; carried over the back or side and sometimes lowered at rest

F *Bite:* Scissors bite

G *Height at shoulder:* Dogs 53–59.75cm (21–23½ in); bitches 48–53cm (19–21 in)

H *Weight:* 22.5–29.5kg (50–65 lb)

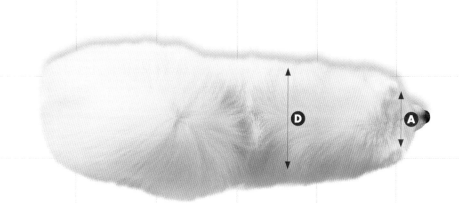

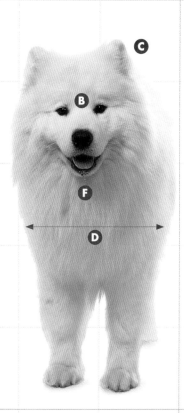

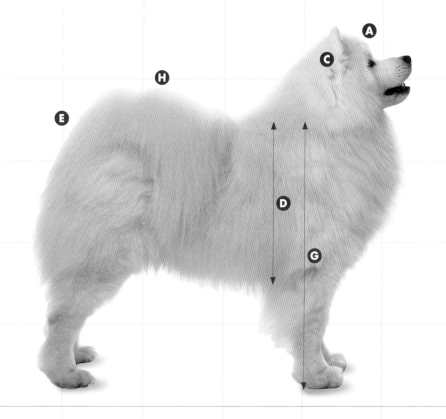

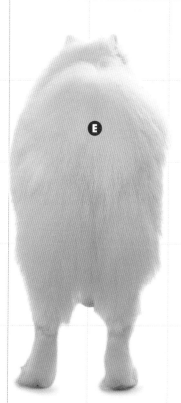

Siberian Husky

Recognition
North America, Britain and
FCI member countries

Life expectancy
10–12 years

Colour
Any colour acceptable

Grooming

Feeding

Child friendliness

Exercise
This dog needs plenty
of regular exercise

This is perhaps the best known of the various sled dog breeds. It is also known as the Arctic Husky. In spite of their wolflike appearance, Siberian Huskies are friendly and outgoing, and will be exuberant companions. If you want to participate in sledging, an active racing scene has been developed for them by Husky owners, and events are organized in some areas even in the absence of snow.

Origin The Siberian Husky was originally developed by the Chukchi people and originated from northeast Asia. The breed was introduced to North America for the first time in the early 20th century, taking part in the All-Alaska Sweepstakes Race in 1909. In 1925 these dogs attracted public attention when a relay of them managed to get crucial diphtheria medicine through to the city of Nome, which was snowbound and cut off from any other means of transport.

Appearance The Siberian Husky is a well-built breed, with long legs and a coat of medium length, which does not obscure the breed's muscular profile. The outer coat is straight and weather-resistant and is supported by the dense undercoat. Its shaded colouring is highly individual and Siberian Huskies often have striking blue eyes.

Personality Determined and enthusiastic, the Siberian Husky forms a strong bond with its handler. This is not a breed that makes a good guard dog, because it is usually open and friendly towards strangers, although older dogs may sometimes be more reserved.

Health and care Siberian Huskies are usually healthy and fit, but they can develop the genetic weakness known as Von Willebrand's disease. This is an abnormality of the body's blood-clotting mechanism. Bitches in season may bleed more profusely during oestrus, and any injury that causes bleeding will result in increased blood loss. Blood blisters known as haematomas may also develop beneath the skin following trauma. This is likely to be more of a problem in some bloodlines than others. Medication may be needed, especially for more active dogs.

As an owner In common with other sled breeds, the Siberian Husky has plenty of stamina, and it will need a correspondingly large amount of exercise. If you enjoy long country walks, this breed is a good choice as a pet. Unusually among sled dogs, which tend to fight, Siberian Huskies generally get on well together, so this is also a good breed to choose if you want more than one dog.

Also consider The Eskimo Dog or Husky, which is of Canadian origin, may be an alternative. Just like the Siberian Husky, it must be well trained to discourage wandering when off the leash. Another possibility is the Norwegian Elkhound (*see pages 64–65*).

Tech Spec

Features

A *Head:* Slightly rounded top to the skull, with a well-defined stop and a medium-length muzzle, tapered towards the nose

B *Eyes:* Almond-shaped, set slightly obliquely; brown, blue, or one of each colour

C *Ears:* Triangular and slightly rounded tips; set high and erect

D *Chest:* Deep and powerful, but not especially wide

E *Tail:* Plenty of fur and set just below the topline; carried up, but trailing at rest

F *Bite:* Scissors bite

G *Height at shoulder:* Dogs 53–59.75cm (21–23½ in); bitches 51–56cm (20–22 in)

H *Weight:* Dogs 20.5–27kg (45–60 lb); bitches 16–22.5kg (35–50 lb)

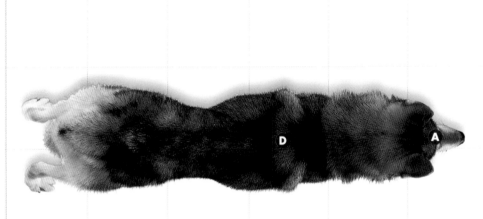

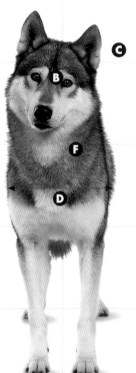

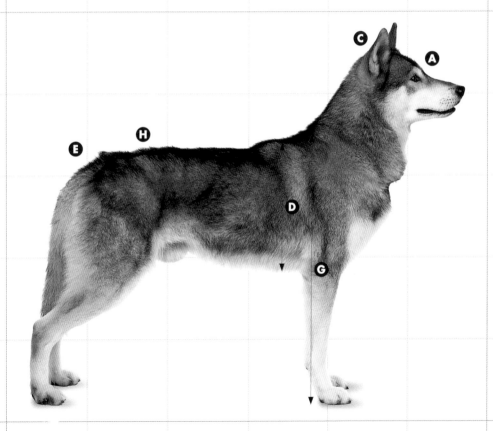

Overview

Recognition
North America, Britain and
FCI member countries

Life expectancy
11–13 years

Colour
Pepper and salt (greys
ranging from a silvery
shade to iron grey) or
solid black

Grooming

Feeding

Child friendliness

Exercise
A daily run off the leash
is important

The Standard is the ancestral form of both the Giant and Miniature breeds. It was originally known as the Wirehaired Pinscher. These dogs make ideal family pets – lively and social with those whom they know well – and thrive in the company of children. They are also an easily manageable size.

Origin Schnauzers have a long ancestry dating back more than 600 years. They appear in early portraits by a number of artists, including Rembrandt. This breed was originally developed as a farm ratter, but it gradually evolved into a versatile farm dog, carrying out other tasks, including herding stock and pulling carts. The breed's current name derives from that given to a pet dog entered at a show in 1879 – the word *schnauzer* literally means 'whiskered snout'.

Appearance These Schnauzers are rough-coated. Some are an unusual mixed grey colour known as pepper and salt, which can vary significantly in depth between individuals. The coat should be dense, with a tight, wiry texture, and the outer coat is raised away from the body. The hair on the back measures up to 5cm (2 in) in length. The back has a sloping line from the shoulders down to the hindquarters.

Personality Bold and dependable, the Schnauzer is a quick learner, thanks to its natural intelligence. It forms a strong bond with everyone in its immediate circle, and a Schnauzer puppy will soon become an enthusiastic member of the family.

Health and care Puppies may occasionally develop an absence of drainage holes in the tear glands, meaning that tear fluid cannot drain normally out of the eyes and overflows down the face. The problem can be corrected with surgery.

As an owner Coat care is important. The hair needs to be plucked because Schnauzers do not shed. Be prepared for a lively dog that is keen to be constantly involved in family life, participating in whatever is happening and enthusiastic about games.

Also consider The other forms – the Miniature (*see pages 152–153*), and the Giant (*see pages 226–227*) – may be possibilities if you like the Schnauzer's, looks but would prefer a smaller or a larger dog. Some terrier breeds, such as the Airedale (*see pages 136–137*) and the Welsh Terrier (*see pages 166–167*), are other options, although they may not be so well disposed towards children.

Tech Spec

Features

(A) *Head:* Rectangular and powerful, with a flat skull and a slight stop; the muzzle corresponds in length and width

(B) *Eyes:* Oval, dark brown and medium-sized

(C) *Ears:* V-shaped, set high; and carried so the inner edges lie close to the cheeks

(D) *Chest:* Medium-width; oval in cross section

(E) *Tail:* Set high and carried erect

(F) *Bite:* Scissors bite

(G) *Height at shoulder:* Dogs 47–49.5cm (18½–19½ in); bitches 44.5–47cm (17½–18½ in)

(H) *Weight:* Dogs 16–20.5kg (35–45 lb); bitches 13.5–18kg (30–40 lb)

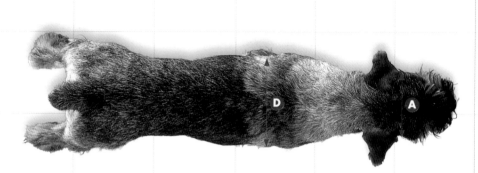

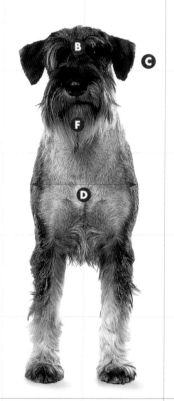

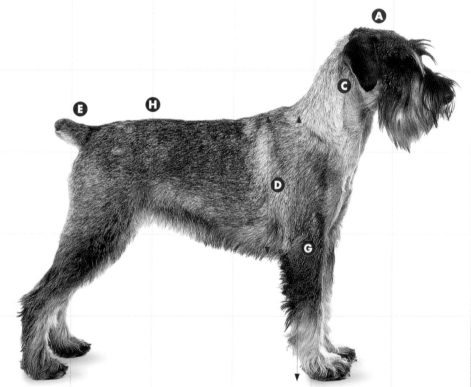

Pet Spec
Anatolian Shepherd Dog

Pet Spec
Beauceron

Pet Spec
German Pinscher

This ancient Turkish breed was unknown outside its homeland until 1967, when an American serviceman took a breeding pair back to North America. Three years later, in 1970, they produced a litter. The resulting strain was not representative of the pure strains found in Turkey, which are known as Akbash, Kangal and Kars, depending on their area of origin The current tendency is for all four different types to be recognized separately.

Appearance Large and powerfully built, the Anatolian is variable in appearance, and all coat colours are acceptable. Coat length also differs between individuals, ranging from 1 to 2.5–10cm (4 in), reflecting the dog's mixed origins. As with many larger breeds, male Anatolians are slightly taller than bitches. The ears are set well back on the head and must curl over at the tips. The long tail extends down to the hocks.

Breed care and health The Anatolian is a breed that is slow to mature, and these dogs will not be fully grown until they are at least 2 years old. Avoid overexercising them while they are still developing. They sometimes display double dew claws on their hind feet. Wall eyes (eyes of different colours from one another) or blue eyes are not acceptable by the breed standard.

As an owner These are strong and determined dogs that need firm training. The Anatolian is not instinctively friendly and is usually suspicious of strangers. This breed needs space, and it's not suited to living in a flat.

Also consider There are a number of other similar flock guardians from East Europe and Asia. Choices include the three close relatives of the Anatolian Shepherd Dog, of which the Akbash Dog is probably the best known outside its homeland, and is characterized by its whitish fur. Another similar breed is the Caucasian Sheepdog, bred in a wider range of colours, which originated in the area between Turkey and Iraq.

Height 68.5–81cm (27–32 in)
Weight 36–68kg (80–150 lb)
Exercise These dogs display great stamina, and need plenty of exercise

This French sheepdog is named after the plains surrounding Paris, where its ancestors started working more than 500 years ago. In its homeland, it is also known as the Berger de Beauce. The breed saw active service in both World Wars, carrying ammunition belts to frontline troops, among other tasks. Today, the Beauceron is still a working dog and is often trained by police.

Appearance A shorthaired breed, with ears that naturally hang down over the sides of the head, the Beauceron has a muscular build with a deep-chested appearance. It is typically black and tan, although there is a rare Harlequin variety, too, which has areas of grey in the coat. The breed standard calls for double dew claws on each of its hind legs.

Breed care and health This is a breed that should only be considered if you are prepared to invest sufficient time in training your dog adequately. The strong-willed, somewhat aggressive element in the Beauceron's nature needs to be controlled.

As an owner This breed can develop a remarkably close understanding with its owner. The Beauceron also has strong territorial instincts and is an alert guard dog, reinforcing the need for these dogs to be properly trained.

Also consider The short-coated German Shepherd Dog (see pages 34–35) is a possibility to consider, although it is not bred in the same colours as the Beauceron. If you like the sleek black-and-tan appearance in particular, a Dobermann (see pages 224–225) may appeal to you. If you prefer a shaggy-coated dog, then the Briard (see page 44) is another option – one that probably descends from the same ancestral stock as the Beauceron.

Height 61–70cm (24–27½ in)
Weight 30–38.5kg (66–85 lb)
Exercise These active dogs need plenty of exercise

As its name suggests, this breed is of German origin It was created in the late 19th century and, in turn, was used in the development of what is now the more popular Dobermann. There have been times, particularly during the late 1940s, when the German Pinscher faced extinction, and it is still rare. The breed was originally created to catch rats, but it makes a good companion dog, too.

Appearance A sleek, short, glossy coat and a well-muscled appearance typify this breed. The German Pinscher tends to be reddish in colour, but there are fawn variants, and black- or blue-and-tan combinations. It has a square profile, with a powerful neck and a tight-fitting skin The head is broad, with a blunt nose and jawline.

Breed care and health This dog sometimes develops a sensitive skin, manifested by constant nibbling and scratching at the body. Seek veterinary advice for the condition – it can be a reflection of a food intolerance or allergy.

As an owner This breed is an instinctive barker, so it makes a good watchdog – but it may not always know when to stop. Lively by nature, the German Pinscher has an independent streak and is boisterous, so is better suited to a home with older children.

Also consider The larger Dobermann (see pages 224–225) is an obvious candidate; conversely, if you want a scaled-down version of the breed, consider the Miniature Pinscher (see pages 194–195). About half the size of the German Pinscher, this is another lively dog. In true terrier style it may not always agree with other dogs. The word 'pinscher' is derived from the French word pincer and gives a clue to its character – it means 'to nip'.

Height 43–50cm (17–20 in)
Weight 11–16kg (24–35 lb)
Exercise A daily run, with an opportunity to explore, will be necessary for this lively dog

Pet Spec
Komondor

The Komondor is the largest of Hungary's native breeds, where it has served as a flock guardian for centuries. It is believed that its ancestors were brought from the steppes lying further east. It is now being used as a working dog in some parts of North America, protecting flocks from coyotes. Its distinctive colouring allows it to merge in with the sheep. The plural of its name is Komondorok.

Appearance The Komondor is white, with a distinctive corded coat that extends over its entire body and hangs down over its eyes. With a dense, woolly undercoat, this offers protection from the cold, and it also serves to guard these dogs against wolves and other predators. Puppies have soft coats, and the adult 'dreadlocks' take up to two years to develop fully.

Breed care and health This has proved to be a healthy breed. The skin colour under the coat is grey, and the nose should be black. The coat itself needs little care, and its natural, somewhat unkempt appearance is considered a key feature of the breed.

As an owner Komondorok are bold, fearless working dogs. They are loyal and active by nature, and they are equipped with a formidable canine intelligence. Cooperation needs to be carefully taught as part of their training routine.

Also consider A breed with a similar corded coat, but smaller in size, is the Hungarian Puli (*see page 45*). This breed actually herded the sheep in Hungary, working alongside the Komondor, which acted as the flock guardian.

Height 64.75–76cm (25½–30 in)
Weight 36–61kg (80–135 lb)
Exercise Long walks are essential for this breed

Pet Spec
Kuvasz

Another Hungarian breed corresponding in size and colouring to the Komondor is the Kuvasz. Its ancestors were first brought into the country in the 13th century by Turkish shepherds. It fulfilled a similar role to that of the Komondor, helping to protect flocks against predators, such as wolves and bears. Its name derives from the Turkish word *kavas*, which means 'armed guard'. The plural form is Kuvaszok.

Appearance The thick white coat is double layered, with the fine dense undercoat providing good insulation, offset against the coarser guard hairs above. The hair on the head is smooth and short, while that on the body is coarser, although still short, and slightly wavy. The hair on the tail is much longer, measuring up to 15cm (6 in) long. The proportions of the head are considered important, with the V-shaped ears set well back. The eyes are dark brown and the nose is black.

Breed care and health This is a healthy breed that displays plenty of stamina. In the past, these dogs were reputedly even bigger than they are today. They possess a keen sense of smell, which has led to them being used for hunting, where they are capable of tackling large game.

As an owner You must be prepared to meet the considerable exercise needs of this breed. The Kuvasz requires plenty of grooming, especially in the spring, when it sheds much of the thick coat. It is a loyal dog but does not take readily to strangers.

Also consider The Tatra Mountain Sheepdog from Poland, where it is known as the Owczarek Podhalanski, is like the Kuvasz but taller. Another possibly to consider is the similar Slovakian Shepherd Dog, also known as the Slovensky Kuvac. Both these breeds are white, with coats of similar length to that of the Kuvasz, and both have well-plumed tails covered in longer hair.

Height 66–76cm (26–30 in)
Weight 32–52kg (70–115 lb)
Exercise These dogs need plenty of opportunity to exercise at their own pace

Pet Spec
Portuguese Water Dog

Unlike other European breeds of water dog, this breed was not originally a retriever but was a true working companion for fishermen on the Algarve coast of Portugal. These dogs looked out for shoals of fish from the side of the boat, and then jumped overboard and literally herded them into the nets. The Portuguese Water Dog was also trained to bark loudly in foggy weather, alerting nearby vessels to their boat's presence.

Appearance The breed exists in two coat types – one a compact, curly coat, the other a longer coat with a wavy texture. Traditionally, the hindquarters were clipped, helping the dog to swim more easily. When alert, this dog curls its tail up over its back, distinguishing it from other water dogs. This breed can be black, brown or white in colour, or bicoloured.

Breed care and health This breed was facing extinction by the 1960s, with its numbers reduced to fewer than 50 individuals, so today's Portuguese Water dogs are descended from a small gene pool. Nonetheless, no significant health problems are recognized.

As an owner Portuguese Water Dogs retain a close affiliation with water and they can swim and dive well. Their native name, Cao de Agua, means 'dog of water', so do not be surprised if your dog is keen to swim in any available water, from pond to ocean.

Also consider With two different coat options available there is a natural choice within the breed. Other possibilities you may want to consider include both the Irish Water Spaniel (*see page 134*) and the Standard Poodle (*see pages 92–93*). There is also the much rarer Spanish Water Dog, which is thought to be related to the Portuguese breed and is a similar size, although it has a heavily corded coat.

Height 43–58.5cm (17–23 in)
Weight 16–27kg (35–60 lb)
Exercise Lively by nature, this breed displays plenty of stamina

Resources

FURTHER READING

The Atlas of Dog Breeds of the World by Bonnie Wilcox & Chris Walkowicz (TFH Publications, 1989).

The Canadian Kennel Club Book of Dogs by The Canadian Kennel Club (Stoddard Publishing, 1988).

Canine Lexicon by Andrew De Prisco & James B. Johnson (TFH Publications, 1993).

The Complete Book of Australian Dogs by Angela Sanderson (The Currawong Press, 1981).

The Complete Dog Book by The American Kennel Club (Ballantine Books, 2006).

The Complete Dog Book by Peter Larkin & Mike Stockman (Lorenz Books, 1997).

Dictionary of Canine Terms by Frank Jackson (Crowood Press, 1995).

The Dog: The Complete Guide to Dogs & Their World by David Alderton (Macdonald, 1984).

Dogs: The Ultimate Dictionary of Over 1000 Dog Breeds by Desmond Morris (Ebury Press, 2001).

Gun Dog Breeds. A Guide to Spaniels, Retrievers and Sporting Dogs by Charles Fergus (Lyons & Burford, 1992).

Herding Dogs: Their Origins and Development in Britain by I. Combe (Faber & Faber, 1987).

Hounds of the World by David Alderton (Swan Hill Press, 2000).

The Kennel Club's Illustrated Breed Standards by The Kennel Club (Ebury Press, 1998).

Legacy of the Dog: The Ultimate Illustrated Guide to over 200 Breeds by Testsu Yamazaki (Chronicle Books, 1995).

The New Terrier Handbook by Kerry Kern (Barron's, 1988).

Smithsonian Handbooks: Dogs by David Alderton (Dorling Kindersley, 2002).

Toy Dogs by Harry Glover (David & Charles, 1977).

KENNEL CLUBS

American Kennel Club, 260 Madison Avenue, New York, NY 10016, USA.
www.akc.org

Australian National Kennel Council, PO Box 285, Red Hill South, Victoria 3937, Australia.
www.ankc.aust.com

Canadian Kennel Club, 89 Skyway Avenue, Suite 100, Etobicoke, Ontario M9W 6R4, Canada.
www.ckc.ca

Continental Kennel Club, PO Box 1628, Walker, LA 70785, USA.
www.continentalkennelclub.com

Irish Kennel Club, Fottrell House, Harold's Cross Bridge, Dublin 6W, Republic of Ireland.
www.ikc.ie

The Kennel Club, 1–5 Clarges Street, London W1Y 8AB, UK.
www.the-kennel-club.org.uk

National Kennel Club, 255 Indian Ridge Road, PO Box 331, Blaine, Tennessee 37709, USA.
www.nationalkennelclub.com

New Zealand Kennel Club, Prosser Street, Private Bag 50903, Porirua 6220, New Zealand.
www.nzkc.org.nz

United Kennel Club, 100 East Kilgore Road, Kalamazoo, MI 49002, USA.
www.ukcdogs.com

Universal Kennel Club International, PO Box 574, Nanuet, NY 10954, USA.
www.universalkennel.com

World Kennel Club®, PO Box 60771, Oklahoma City, OK 73146, USA.
www.worldkennelclub.com

World Wide Kennel Club, PO Box 62, Mount Vernon, NY 10552, USA.
www.worldwidekennel.qpg.com

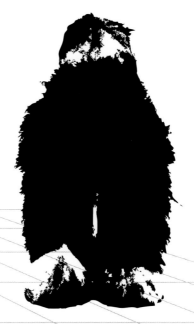

Index

A

Affenpinscher 176, 210
Afghan Hound 46–47
Ainu 90
Airedale Terrier 136–137
Akbash Dog 250
Akita Inu *see* Japanese
  Akita Inu
Alaskan Malamute 214–215
Alsatian *see* German
  Shepherd Dog
American Cocker Spaniel
  100–101
American Fox Terrier 192,
  210
Anatolian Shepherd Dog
  250
Appenzell Mountain Dog
  216
Arkansas Giant Bulldog 74
Australian Cattle Dog 18–19
Australian Shepherd 20–21
Australian Silky Terrier *see*
  Silky Terrier
Australian Terrier 138–139
Azawakh 68, 71

B

Basenji 48–49
Basset Artesian-Normand 50
Basset Fauve de Bretagne 70
Basset Hound 50–51
Beagle 52–53
Bearded Collie 22–23
Beauceron 250
Bedlington Terrier 172
Belgian Laekenois 24
Belgian Malinois 24

Belgian Shepherd Dog 44
Bergamasco Sheepdog 38
Berger de Picard 44
Bernese Mountain Dog
  216–217
Bichon Frise 174–175
Black and Tan Setter *see*
  Gordon Setter
Black Elkhound 64
Bloodhound 54–55
Bolognese 174, 190
Border Collie 26–27
Border Terrier 140–141
Borzoi 56–57
Boston Terrier 72–73
Bouvier des Ardennes 28
Bouvier des Flandres 28–29
Boxer 220–221
Brabançon 176
Briard 44
Brittany 102–103
Bruno Laufhund 54
Brushwood Dog *see*
  Japanese Shiba Inu
Bull Terrier 150–151
Bulldog 74–75
Bullmastiff 222–223

C

Cairn Terrier 142–143
Canaan Dog 44

Cardigan Welsh Corgi
  30–31
Caucasian Sheepdog 250
Cavalier King Charles
  Spaniel 178–179
Chesapeake Bay Retriever
  104–105
Chihuahua 180–181
Chinese Crested 182–183
Chow Chow 78–79
Circassian Wolfhound 56
Cirneco dell'Etna 71
Clumber Spaniel 134
Cocker Spaniel *see*
  English *and* American
  Cocker Spaniel
Collie 32–33
Coton de Tulear 184–185
Curly Coated Retriever 134
Czesky Fousek 98, 116
Czesky Terrier 98

D

Dachshund 58–59
Dalmatian 80–81
Dandie Dinmont Terrier
  144–145
Deerhound 71
Dobermann 224–225
Dogue de Bordeaux 98
Drever 58
Dunker 52
Dutch Partridge Dog 102

E

English Cocker Spaniel
  106–107
English Setter 108–109
English Springer Spaniel
  110–111
Entelbuch Mountain Dog
  216
Épagneul Français *see*
  French Spaniel
Épagneul Picard 108, 132
Eskimo Dog 246

F

Field Spaniel 100, 106
Finnish Spitz 99
Flat Coated Retriever
  112–113
Fox Terrier *see* Smooth Fox
  Terrier; Wire Fox Terrier

French Bulldog 82–83
French Spaniel 110

G

German Longhaired Pointer
  114
German Pinscher 250
German Shepherd Dog
  34–35
German Shorthaired Pointer
  114–115
German Spitz 200
German Toy Spitz 200
German Wirehaired Pointer
  116–117
Giant German Spitz 84,
  200
Giant Schnauzer 226–227
Glen of Imaal Terrier 146–
  147
Golden Retriever 118–119
Gordon Setter 120–121
Grand Basset Griffon
  Vendéen 70
Great Dane 228–229
Great Pyrenees *see* Pyrenean
  Mountain Dog
Greater Swiss Mountain
  Dog 216

Greyhound 60–61
Griffon Bruxellois 176–177
Griffon Nivernais 70

H

Hamiltonstovare 52
Havanese 174, 190
Hovawart 232–233
Hungarian Greyhound 60
Hungarian Puli 45
Hungarian Vizsla 128–129

I

Ibizan Hound 70
Icelandic Sheepdog 36
Indian hound 46
Irish Setter 122–123
Irish Terrier 172
Irish Water Spaniel 134
Irish Wheaten Terrier *see* Soft
  Coated Wheaten Terrier
Irish Wolfhound 62–63
Italian Greyhound 186–187

J

Jack Russell Terrier 156
Japanese Chin 188–189
Japanese Akita Inu 212–
  213

Japanese Shiba Inu 90–91

K
Kai Dog 88
Keeshond 84–85
Kerry Blue Terrier 148–149
King Charles Spaniel 210
Klein Spitz 200
Komondor 251
Korthals Griffon 135
Kuvasz 251
Kyi Leo 86

L
Labrador Retriever 124–125
Lakeland Terrier 172
Lancashire Heeler 30, 45
Leonberger 238
Lhasa Apso 86–87
Löwchen 99
Lurcher 71

M
Magyar Agar *see* Hungarian
    Greyhound
Malinois 44
Maltese 190–191
Manchester Terrier 192
Maremma Sheepdog 230

Mastiff 234–235
Mini Aussie 20
Miniature Australian
    Shepherd *see* Mini Aussie
Miniature Bull Terrier 150–
    151
Miniature Pinscher 194–195
Miniature Poodle 92
Miniature Schnauzer 152–
    153
Munsterlander 120

N
Neapolitan Mastiff 236–237
New Guinea Singing Dog
    44
Newfoundland 238–239
Niederlaufhund 54
Norfolk Terrier 173
Norrbottenspets 99
North American Shepherd
    see Mini Aussie
Norwegian Buhund 36–37
Norwegian Elkhound 64–65
Norwich Terrier 154–155
Nova Scotia Duck Tolling
    Retriever 135

O
Old English Mastiff *see*
    Mastiff
Old English Sheepdog

38–39
Olde English Bulldog 98
Otterhound 70

P
Papillon 196–197
Parson Russell Terrier
    156–157
Pekingese 198–199
Pembroke Welsh Corgi
    40–41
Perdiguero Portugueso *see*
    Portuguese Pointer
Peruvian Hairless Dog 182
Petit Basset Griffon Vendéen
    70
Petit Brabançon 210
Phalene 196, 210
Pharaoh Hound 70
Picardy Shepherd 44
Picardy Spaniel *see*
    Épagneul Picard
Plummer Terrier 156
Pointer 126–127
Polish Lowland Sheepdog
    45
Pomeranian 200–201
Portuguese Pointer 134
Portuguese Water Dog 251
Pug 202–203
Puli *see* Hungarian Puli

Pumi 45
Pyrenean Mastiff 234
Pyrenean Mountain Dog
    230–231

R
Red and White Irish Setter
    122
Red Setter *see* Irish Setter
Rhodesian Ridgeback 66–67
Rottweiler 240–241
Rough Collie 32
Russian Black Terrier 218–
    219

S
St. Bernard 242–243
St. Hubert Jura Laufhund 54
Saluki 71
Samoyed 244–245
Schipperke 88–89
Schnauzer 248–249
Scottish Terrier 158–159
Sealyham Terrier 173
Shar-Pei 76–77
Shetland Sheepdog 42–43
Shih Tzu 204–205
Shower of Hail Setter 122
Siberian Husky 246–247

Siberian Laika 44
Sicilian Greyhound 70, 71
Silky Terrier 206–207
Skye Terrier 173
Sloughi 68, 71
Slovakian Shepherd Dog
    251
Slovensky Kuvac 251
Smooth Collie 32
Smooth Fox Terrier 160–161
Soft Coated Wheaten Terrier
    162–163
Spanish Water Dog 251
Spinone Italiano 135
Stabyhound 102
Staffordshire Bull Terrier
    164–165
Standard Mexican Hairless
    99
Standard Pinscher 194
Standard Poodle 92–93

Stumpy-tailed Cattle Dog 18
Sussex Spaniel 135
Swedish Vallhund 45

T
Tatra Mountain Sheepdog
    230, 251
Tepeizcuintli 99
Tervuren 24–25
Tibetan Mastiff 236
Tibetan Spaniel 94–95
Tibetan Terrier 96–97
Toy American Eskimo 211
Toy Fox Terrier 211

V
Vizsla *see* Hungarian Vizsla

W
Weimaraner 130–131
Welsh Springer Spaniel
    132–133
Welsh Terrier 166–167
West Highland White Terrier
    168–169
Whippet 68–69
Wire Fox Terrier 170–171
Wirehaired Pointing
    Griffon 135

Y
Yorkshire Terrier 208–209

Acknowledgements

With thanks to the owners for permission to photograph the following:

Herding

p. 19 Morrow Blue Eucalyptus At Gilsand; p. 21 Versache Sauve Des Chemins Cathares *IMP FR*; p. 23 *CH* Moonhill's Forever Classic; p. 25 *CH/FCI INT/NED/BELG CH* Fullani Flekkefjord; p. 27 Bonvivant Moonrush; p. 29 *ShCH* Tefryn Mackinley At Beltane; p. 31 CH Quiche's Douglas At Kanix *IMP CAN*; p. 33 Blondie's Read My Lips For Bymil; p. 35 Darahill Hufflepuff At Sablemyst; p. 37 Linsdown Georgia With Strco ; p. 39 Beauvallon Philanderer *JW*; p. 41 *CH* Bymil Sherry Twist; p. 43 Peerieglen Pearl *JW*.

Hounds

p. 47 Karak Lord of The Isles; p. 49 Embeau Rive Gauche At Jethard; p. 51 Switherland Double Delight At Feorlig; p. 53 Trigger At Sunrise; p. 55 Chigwri Uncanny; p. 57 Strelkos Sillmarion; p. 59 *CH* Drakesleat Otto Bahn; p. 61 *CH* Boughton Benvoluto; p. 63 Borka Sequel; p. 65 *NED/BELG CH* Ravenstone Bersin Krisen; p. 67 *CH* Mirengo's Muko Mako; p. 69 Lotsmoor Wild Passion.

Non-sporting

p. 73 Wynele Mz Dee Meana; p. 75 *CH* Nobozz Drunk and Disorderley; p. 77 Mabina Made At Inzadi; p. 79 Chopan Miss Chandelle; p. 81 Elaridge Quincie *JW*; p. 83 *CH* Mid Shipman Of Vardene; p. 85 Rossvale Latin Lover; p. 87 *CH* Avonbourne Mandzari At Chobrnag *JW ShCM*; p. 89 *CH* Vanitonia Well Did You Evah; p. 91 *CH* Nocte Boris Karloff; p. 93 Naka No Benihana Go Kazusa Nakanosow *IMP*; p. 95 Kensing Henry Higgins *JW ShCM*; p. 97 Kokonor Always Ina Pickle To Ludgate.

Sporting:

p. 101 *ShCH* Goldenmist Pepamint Patti *JW*; p. 103 *ShCH* Brittyhill Sorrel; p. 105 Arnac Bay Pride; p. 107 Falconers Cotillon Of Ware; p. 109 Bournhouse Paper Parade For Oaktrish; p. 111 Feorlig Chrystal Clear *JW*; p. 113 Branchalwood Aylanmhor For Burpham *JW ShCM*; p. 115 *ShCH* Jennaline Ello Ello Ello; p. 117 *CH* Bareve Bandari *JW*; p. 119 *ShCH* Goldenquest Ambassador *JW*; p. 121 ShCH Abelard Scotch Poacher By Brobruick; p. 123 *ShCH* Carnbargus Congratulation *JW*; p. 125 CH Carpenny Anchorman; p. 127 *ShCH* Lokmadi Nick The Brief; p. 129 Nicael Oak At Helmlake; p. 131 Stormdancer Apple Turnover To To To Castanho; p. 133 *CH* Highclare Energizer

Terriers

p. 137 *ENG & AM CH* Joval Jumpin Jack Flash At Jokyl; p. 139 Jenina Jay Jay; p. 141 *CH* Gameaway Kiwi *JW*; p. 143 Fourheatons Grandopera Libertine; p. 145 Inglecourt Magical Annie; p. 147 Inzievar Silver Gilt; p. 149 Emeldir Princess Astrid At Glenwellieka; p. 151 *CH* Lunabrook Hot Shot *ShCH*; p. 153 Canteba R-Ne Schwarzenegger; p. 155 Jaeva Jingle Bell Rock With Zippor; p. 157 Moonreapers Vandal; p. 159 Berrybrezze Illumination; p. 161 Belfox Belstar; p. 163 *CH* Snowmeadow Jellybean Jilly *JW ShCH*; p. 165 Araìdh Ditto; p. 167 *CH* Saradon Dressed To Impress; p. 169 *CH* Krisma Jammy Dodger; p. 171 Ashleyheath Pot of Gold

Toys

p. 175 *CH* Warmingham Looks To Thrill At Ashoka; p. 177 Beauview Hot Gossip; p. 179 *CH* Miletree Nijinski *JW*; p. 181 Natimuk Keenaughts Bobby Dazzler; p. 183 Vanitonia Blue Murder; p. 185 Cotonneux Athos; p. 187 Sangria Fabiola; p. 189 Benatone Love Me Tender Abbyat; p. 191 Sophyla Sable; p. 193 *CH* Bellpins Wear The Fox Hat At Dimogen; p. 195 Ringlands Golden Dollar; p. 197 *CH* Delwins Paddy O'Reilly; p. 199 Lireva's The Future's In Focus; p. 201 Lokmadi Kabuki *JW ShCM*; p. 203 Bakalo Shayna Punim At Shanita; p. 205 Marshdae Bobbi-Bobbi With Mazeena; p. 207 Chelanis In Cahoots; p. 209 Phalbrienz Lady Lavender

Working

p. 213 *CH* Redwitch Heaven Can Wait; p. 215 Chayo Blue Thunder; p. 217 Chiorny Lider Of Potterspride; p. 219 Osemans Percyverance At Sargebilko; p. 221 *CH* Tartarian Gold Dust; p. 223 *CH* Coxellot Buttons And Beaux By Flintstock; p. 225 Helmlake Tara Time *JW ShCM*; p. 227 Valter The Master of Baronsloch; p. 229 Helmlake Titan; p. 231 *IR CH* Darmarnor Bertie Bear *JW ShCM*; p. 233 Pines Mercedes; p. 235 Cenninpedr Ferch Bert At Fearnaught; p. 237 Rayvonley Lion; p. 239 *CH* Mountcook Tiger Lily *IMP*; p. 241 Schutzer Valentino; p. 243 *CH* Poolsway I've Got Spirit; p. 245 *CH* Roybridge Ruff Diamond *JW ShCM*; p. 247 Benninghof Cody; p. 249 *CH* Forstal's Kaliznik

Key to abbreviations

CH= Champion, which may be prefixed by the country, e.g., *AM CH*=American Champion; *ShCH*=Show Champion; *ShCM*=Show Certificate of Merit; *JW*=Junior Warrant; *IMP*=Imported, often followed by country, e.g., *AM*=USA, *BELG*=Belgium, *CAN*=Canada, *FR*=France, *NED*=Netherlands

Marc Henrie wishes to thank the following for their invaluable contribution to this book: Debbie Deucher, Sally Kimber, Dorothy McIntyre, Terry Thorn and Peter Young of the Kennel Club; Karina Le Mare and Glyn Payne of Wey Farm.

Pictures

The publishers would like to thank the following for permission to use their images:
Courtesy American Kennel Club: page 210 right. Corbis: Neal Preston page 2; Chris Collins pages 6–7; Phil Banko page 9 right; LWA-Sharie Kennedy/zefa page 9 middle; Herbert Spichtinger/zefa page 9 bottom; Yann Arthus-Bertrand page 44 left, page 45 left, centre, page 98 right, page 99 centre right, page 134 left, right, page135 left, centre, page172 right, page173 centre, right, page 210 left, centre, page 250 left, page 251 centre; Robert Dowling page 98 left. Getty Images/Sharon Montrose/The Image Bank: page 8; GK Hart/Vikki Hart/The Image Bank page 9 left; Tracy Morgan/Dorling Kindersley page 211 centre. Marc Henrie: page 44 centre, page 45 right, page 70, page 71, page 98 centre, page 99 left, page 134 centre, page 172 left, centre, page 173 left, page 211 left, right, page 251 left, right. The Kennel Club: page 44 right, page 135 right, page 250 centre, right.